World War II:
Roots and Causes

PROBLEMS IN
EUROPEAN CIVILIZATION

Under the editorial direction of
John Ratté
Amherst College

World War II: Roots and Causes

Edited and with an introduction by

Keith Eubank
Queens College

D. C. HEATH AND COMPANY
Lexington, Massachusetts   Toronto   London

CONTENTS

IV FROM MUNICH TO MOSCOW

V A VERDICT

INTRODUCTION

World War II changed recent history not only by altering the balance of power in the world, but also by ending European overseas empires, which led eventually to the founding of new independent nations. The war left the world with two major power centers: the United States and the Soviet Union, who each now possess nuclear power sufficient to destroy all of civilization. The war was a catastrophe that brought death to millions of innocent people. What, then, led to this war?

The readings in this collection form a case study of the ideas, the events, and the people involved in the origins of World War II. Through these readings it is hoped that the student will be introduced to some of the problems and issues that have concerned historians about the roots and causes of World War II.

This topic is intriguing because after an earlier world war, 1914–1918, governments were unable to avoid an even more ghastly war. It would seem that after one world bloodbath, statesmen and politicians ought to have been wise enough to have prevented another conflict from overwhelming the world. Why did they not see the mounting threat and take action when it would not, perhaps, have been so costly? Why did the unthinkable become reality and the democracies have to face the very war they had hoped to avoid?

War was finally thrust on the democracies because of the German invasion of Poland, ordered by Adolf Hitler. The Austrian-born chancellor had come to power in Germany because he was able to exploit the crisis created in Germany by the Great Depression. By taking advantage of this economic catastrophe, it was possible for Hitler to organize his own political movement, National Socialism, and to build the largest and strongest political party in Germany. His party gave him the necessary leverage to achieve power in January 1933. Once in power, Hitler destroyed all political opposition and at the same time created one of the most authoritarian governments in modern history.

In his rise to power, Hitler had also exploited the popular dissatisfaction stemming from the German defeat in World War I and the disgrace arising from the terms imposed on Germany by the Treaty of Versailles. To reverse the verdict of 1919 and to break the bonds imposed on Germany by the treaty became Hitler's aim. Once this had been achieved, Hitler would then be able to restore Germany to predominance in European affairs. But Hitler's ultimate intention was to dominate Europe. It was this drive to dominate Europe that finally led to war in September of 1939.

The war cannot be separated from Hitler, his ideas, and his plans. For it was he who issued the order for German soldiers to invade Poland and to begin a European war that would escalate into a great global conflict. His responsibility for issuing this order is acknowledged even by German historians. But at this point questions begin to arise.

Why did Hitler make this decision? What forces led him to end the twenty-year peace? What were the ideas and the philosophy that shaped his decision for war? Was the war the product of a carefully thought-out plan, developed over the years by Hitler? Or was the war the result of events and decisions he could not control and which set off a chain reaction resulting in the outbreak of war? There is some evidence that war might have resulted from errors when signals were misread.

To what degree was the policy of appeasement responsible for causing the war? The policy was respectable in the 1920s and 1930s when it was eagerly pursued by British politicians. It did not have the notoriety it would acquire after the Western powers failed to prevent Hitler's aggressive actions. Appeasement came to mean outright surrender to the aggressor's demands, but that was not the original meaning. Appeasement then referred to a policy of attempting to satisfy—by negotiations—German complaints over the Treaty of Versailles, which would lead to detente and a general relaxation of tension in Europe once Germany became satisfied with her position there.

Those who practiced appeasement had to contend with a handicap: conditions in post-1919 Europe were made to order for Hitler. After the collapse of the Romanov, Hohenzollern, and Habsburg Empires, new nations appeared—weak, jealous, and divided. The situation would tempt a stronger power to pick them off, one by one, until that power (in this case Germany) was dominant. Such was the political arrangement between the wars, setting the stage for Hitler's aggression, examined by Arnold Toynbee in the first selection of this book. Hitler did not create the political structure of Europe; others did it for him. They offered him an opportunity to utilize Germany's position in Europe; it was an opportunity Hitler would not forego.

To understand why Hitler exploited the opportunity in this situation, it is necessary to examine his ideas, aims, and plans. These are considered in a selection from his posthumously published *Hitler's Secret Book* (1958), written about 1928. It presents some of his ideas on foreign policy five years before he took office. These ideas were dictated when he was still struggling to rebuild his party after the debacle caused by the failure of the Munich Beer Hall Putsch and his subsequent imprisonment.

Among historians there have been differences of opinion over what Hitler really intended. The task of discovering his intentions has been complicated because, except for his speeches and two books, he did not leave quantities of memoranda and letters setting them forth. Among the explanations of Hitler and his policies, the most controversial is found in A. J. P. Taylor's *Origins of the Second World War.* The book created a storm of criticism when it was published, because Taylor seemed to imply that Hitler was really no worse than his contemporaries and that the outbreak of the war was not the result of a premeditated effort on Hitler's part. Taylor's book was controversial because it appeared to whitewash Hitler while blaming others for the outbreak of the war.

In contrast to Taylor, Norman Rich, in a selection from his *Hitler's War Aims,* found a continuity extending through Hitler's thinking that amounted to an ideology of expansionism. German security could be guaranteed only by expanding into Eastern Europe. War could not be avoided, not even a two-front war, since France could be expected to attack Germany once her armies were committed against Bolshevik Russia. Gerhard Weinberg, in a selection from his *Foreign Policy of Hitler's Germany: Diplomatic Revolution in Europe, 1933–36,* analyzes Hitler's ideas on foreign policy, developed before he had attained power and which were to influence his conduct of foreign policy from 1933 through 1939. Both Rich and Weinberg argue that even before 1939 Hitler was thinking seriously about a war against other nations, and that he deliberately chose a war policy. It was neither a mistake nor a policy thrust upon Hitler by others.

Hitler's plans required that Germany restore her military sovereignty by controlling the development and the size of the armed forces. The Treaty of Versailles specifically limited the exercise of German military sovereignty. Despite the treaty limitations on German military forces, the generals and the admirals, with the blessing of the Weimar Republic, secretly carried on a program of rearmament. This program was suddenly jeopardized by proposals presented to the Geneva Disarmament Conference by Britain and France in 1933. Hitler chose to challenge them, even at the risk of war, by ordering the German delegation to leave the Disarmament Conference and to withdraw Germany from the League of Nations in October 1933. Esmonde Robertson, in a selection from *Hitler's Pre-War Policy and Military Plans, 1933–1939,* examines Hitler's action at Geneva, which was the first successful step in restoring German military sovereignty. Eighteen months later, Hitler regained full military sovereignty for Germany by announcing the existence of the German Air Force (*Luftwaffe*), the resumption of military conscription, and plans for an army of thirty-six divisions. By this action Hitler completely annulled Part V of the Treaty of Versailles, which had limited the German armed forces.

Hitler's next action—the remilitarization of the Rhineland—not only violated another provision of the Treaty of Versailles (as well as the Treaty of Locarno), but it altered the European balance of power. Jean-Baptiste Duroselle, in his essay, "France and the Crisis of March 1936," considers the French policy in this crisis. Critics of the French government's policy have argued that if the Western governments had retaliated against the remilitarization with force, the German military units would have been withdrawn and perhaps Hitler would have been overthrown; the drift to war would have been halted and World War II averted. The French leaders, however, chose not to retaliate because they feared, and perhaps rightly so, that retaliation would have meant a general European war that neither they nor the nation desired.

Another reason for the failure to retaliate with force was the determination of the British government to practice a policy of appeasement. No prewar policy has been so bitterly denounced as appeasement has; no statesmen have been condemned as harshly as those who advocated this policy, because it seemed to lead to war. In a selection from his *The Origins of World War II,* Keith Eubank surveys the practice of appeasement in the 1920s and the 1930s when it was regarded as a sensible policy that would benefit the world.

In the summer of 1936 the Spanish Civil War erupted. Western nations were frightened when Germany and Italy began to aid the rebel armies, because the conflict seemed to be a dress-rehearsal for a future European war. Appeasement appeared more necessary than ever if Paris and London were to avoid the fate of Madrid and Barcelona.

Meanwhile, in Germany Hitler was pushing for greater rearmament in order to have the means to overawe other nations and, if necessary, launch a lightning attack (*Blitzkrieg*) on smaller, neighboring states. Hitler found, however, that the demands made by the military services on the German economy were overwhelming. The leaders of the armed services were soon quarreling over who would get what from the limited output, but Hitler did not dare put Germany on a wartime economy because he feared domestic political repercussions. To restore harmony among his generals and admirals, Hitler summoned them to a conference on November 5, 1937 in which he discussed his goals as well as specific cases in which military action might be necessary. The only surviving record of this conference, the "Hossbach Memorandum," is the next selection. Because this document was used at the Nuremberg trials as evidence that Hitler had planned a war of aggression, it has since been a source of historical controversy. At this conference, Hitler seemed to imply that he considered Czechoslovakia more dangerous to German security than Austria, but when the German armies made their first move, it was into Austria.

A chapter from Christopher Thorne's *The Approach of War* traces the history of the *Anschluss* (union) of Germany with Austria, a small neighboring state suffering from the Depression, and containing many citizens who were attracted to Nazism. The Austrian chancellor, Kurt von Schuschnigg, as Thorne shows, was no match for Hitler, for after his armies occupied Austria he annexed it to the Third Reich.

As soon as Austria had been annexed, Hitler turned toward

Czechoslovakia. No crisis during the prewar years aroused more controversy than that involving the Sudeten Germans and their demand for self-determination. Hitler had seized on this issue as the wedge to split apart Czechoslovakia, a state that contained a variety of minorities who were all formerly part of the defunct Habsburg Empire. If the Sudetens were granted their demands, which amounted to autonomy, other minorities would insist on equal treatment. Czechoslovakia would then become a collection of weak, autonomous states unable to withstand German domination. The British and the French, dreading a war over an issue in which they believed justice was on the side of the Sudetens, pushed the Czechs to make concessions to the Sudeten Germans, who were now led by their own Nazis. To increase the pressure, Hitler ordered the mobilization of the German armed forces.

When negotiations between the Sudeten Germans and the Czechoslovak government collapsed in September of 1938, Neville Chamberlain, the British prime minister, hoping to reach an understanding with Hitler and avoid war, attempted personal negotiations with Hitler.

When the Sudeten Nazis increased their demands, insisting they become a part of Nazi Germany, Hitler called for the ceding of Sudetenland to Germany and an occupation by his troops. Although the British and French governments accepted the idea of occupation and cession, their negotiations with Hitler reached an impasse over the timing of the occupation. At the four-power Munich Conference of September 29–30, 1938, the impasse was resolved. Laurence Thompson, in a selection from *The Greatest Treason,* describes the drama of this "summit conference" when four men—Hitler, Mussolini, Chamberlain, and Edouard Daladier, the French premier—settled the fate of Czechoslovakia and the Sudetenland.

Appeasers considered the Munich Conference one of their finest hours, because the Sudeten question had been resolved without bloodshed, and because after the conference, Chamberlain and Hitler in another personal meeting had signed an agreement pledging to settle future questions through consultation. But critics of the Munich settlement condemned Britain and France for failing to call Hitler's bluff and making him fight for Czechoslovakia. They argued that it would have been better to have gone to war with Hitler in 1938 than in 1939. In a selection from *Munich,* Keith Eubank analyzes the questions: Why did Britain and France draw back from a war with Hitler in 1938? Why did they concede instead of fight?

Although Hitler had acquired the Sudetenland without war, he was dissatisfied and even regretted the Munich Agreement. He preferred to destroy Czechoslovakia even though the action would dismay everyone who had supported the policy of appeasement. Within less than a month after the signing of the Munich Agreement, Hitler ordered his generals to prepare to liquidate the remainder of the Czechoslovak state. In a selection from his *On Borrowed Time,* Leonard Mosley recounts Hitler's plotting and scheming to liquidate Czechoslovakia. Mosley's account is important because it reveals so vividly Hitler's eagerness to tear up the Munich Agreement and his willingness to sabotage the appeasers' efforts to achieve a detente. Was there now no alternative to appeasement except war? What nation would be Hitler's next target?

In London, the government, shaken by the events of March 15, groped for a new policy. Suddenly, in what appeared to be a complete reversal of British policy, Chamberlain on March 31 pledged that the government would guarantee Polish independence. The momentous change in British policy was little short of revolutionary, because never before had His Majesty's Government guaranteed the independence of a nation in Eastern Europe. It is the odd chain of events, rumors, and threats that led to the guarantee of Poland that Roger Parkinson describes in a chapter from *Peace in our Time.* As Parkinson shows so well, the British Cabinet made an historic decision on the basis of false reports and scraps of information.

To Hitler, the guarantee was a challenge he accepted; he ordered preparations for an attack on Poland. However, he was gambling that Britain as well as France (who had also guaranteed Poland's autonomy) would not take the guarantee seriously, and that they would desert Poland as they had deserted Czechoslovakia. In order to strengthen their promise, the British and French governments asked Stalin to join in the guarantee. While London and Paris asked for Stalin's help, his representatives dropped broad hints in Berlin that a Nazi–Soviet agreement was quite possible. To increase the odds in his favor, Hitler finally accepted the terms offered by Stalin in an agreement that surprised the world and shocked the other Communist parties. In *Expansion and Coexistence: The History of Soviet Foreign Policy, 1917–1967,* Adam B. Ulam traces the negotiations between Britain, France, and Russia, as well as those between Germany and Russia, which resulted in the Nazi–Soviet Non-Aggression Pact. For their failure to accept Stalin's terms, the British and French governments were much criticized. But as Ulam argues, had they agreed to all of the Soviet terms, Stalin's representatives would only have presented new ones. Only a threat *not* to protect Poland unless Soviet Russia came to her defense would have produced a tripartite alliance against Hitler.

In the last days before the outbreak of war, there were negotiations between Britain and Germany in which Chamberlain tried to avert a showdown. Hitler would only settle for the immediate return to Germany of both Danzig and an extraterritorial strip across the Polish Corridor, which separated East Prussia from the rest of Germany. When Poland rejected Hitler's conditions, he had no alternative other than to go to war on September 1, 1939. The Chamberlain government, trapped by the public pledge and pressured by an angry Parliament, went to war on September 3, followed later in the day by France.

In a concluding essay, Allan Bullock surveys Hitler's role in the origins of World War II. Bullock finds Hitler's policy to be consistent and opportunist but not tied to a fixed timetable. Based on the available evidence, Bullock concludes that it was not because of any mistake or misunderstanding that Hitler ordered his armies to invade Poland. Instead, Hitler deliberately chose to risk the fate of Germany on the battlefield.

These materials are relevant to the question that was often asked after 1939. Should force have been used to stop Hitler's aggressions before 1939 in the hope of avoiding World War II? By submitting to blackmail, were not the Western powers only tempting Hitler to demand more? If the Western powers had forced a showdown with Hitler earlier, would not the price have been reduced?

But at the time it seemed more prudent and humane to make every effort, to pay any price, to seek every course of action in order to avoid a war that would cost the lives of millions of men, women, and children. Stopping Hitler by war did not seem worth the price until he settled the question by initiating the war himself. Would the price of a war before 1939 have been cheaper? We shall never know.

I THE SETTING

Arnold J. Toynbee
HITLER AND THE MAP OF EUROPE

Although he is better known for his most unique work, A Study of History, *Arnold J. Toynbee's broad knowledge of history and international affairs is evident in the many volumes he wrote for the* Survey of International Affairs *(1958), from which the selection below is taken. Toynbee was a member of the British delegation at the Paris Peace Conference in 1919 and again in 1946, and he has been director of studies in the Royal Institute of International Affairs. In this selection, Toynbee analyzes the frontiers drawn by the victors during the peace settlement of 1919–1921, when they tried to provide for self-determination for subject peoples and at the same time to restrict Germany. But instead of insuring peace for Europe, the peacemakers set the stage for World War II.*

The makers of the European territorial settlement of 1919–21, like their predecessors in 1814–15, were trying to achieve two distinct aims at once; and they, too, did not realize—though this was easy for an historian to see after the event—that their measures for achieving one of these aims were going to militate against the achievement of the other aim. In both peace settlements one of the aims had been to prevent a strong aggressor Power, which had just been foiled with the utmost difficulty by the combined exertions of all its threatened neighbors, from repeating its late attempt to dominate the world. The other aim had been to redraw the political map of Europe—on which the old landmarks had been obliterated by the recent aggressor's temporary conquests—on a consistent plan, governed by a principle. On the first occasion the recent aggressor had been France; on the second, it was Germany. On the first occasion the principle which the statesmen of the victorious Powers had sought to apply had been "legitimacy"; on the second it was "self-determination." "Legitimacy" had meant the right of a dynasty to be reinstated in the rule over territories equivalent to, if not exactly identical with, those over which it had ruled before the wars of 1792–1815. "Self-determination" meant the right of a nationality to constitute a sovereign independent state including all, or most, of its own nationals and no more than a minimum of people of other nationali-

From *Survey of International Affairs, 1939–1946: The Eve of War, 1939*, edited by Arnold and Veronica M. Toynbee and published by the Oxford University Press under the auspices of The Royal Institute of International Affairs. Footnotes omitted.

ties. On both occasions the governing principle was applied in good faith in the sincere belief that the principle was just and right in itself and that for this reason it would make for stability and peace.

Thus, on both occasions, the two aims appeared, at the time, to be not only compatible but complementary. But on both occasions the sequel showed that the principle to which the architects of the peace settlement had committed themselves was not capable of bearing the stresses and strains to which it was to be exposed in the course of the next chapter of history. In both cases, again, the collapse of the governing principle brought disaster upon the Powers that had put their trust in this principle, because its bankruptcy opened up an unexpected opportunity for aggressors. The increasing unpopularity of the principle of "legitimacy" in the course of the fifty-five years following the settlement of 1814–15 gave an opportunity to Prussia and Sardinia to the undoing of Austria. The unsatisfactory working of the principle of "self-determination" in the course of the eighteen years following the settlement of 1919–21 gave an opportunity to the Third German Reich and Fascist Italy to the undoing of France. The principle of national self-determination, which had been applied in Eastern Europe in 1919–21, was successfully undermined there in the 1930s by the novel "totalitarian" ideologies, as, between 1848 and 1871, the principle of dynastic legitimacy had been successfully undermined in Italy and Germany by the ideology of national self-determination; and in these new circumstances, which the makers of the foregoing peace settlement had not foreseen, the map which they had drawn played into the hands of a new aggressor on each occasion. In giving the Rhineland to Prussia and giving Genoa to Sardinia in order to build up these two Powers into bulwarks for the Habsburg Monarchy against possible future aggression on the part of France, Metternich turned out to have paved the way for Bismarck and Cavour to achieve national unification for the German and Italian peoples at the Habsburg Monarchy's expense. In giving sovereign independence to a number of small nations, lying between Germany and Italy on the west and Russia on the east, which had previously been under the rule of the Habsburg, Hohenzollern, and Romanov Empires, the makers of the peace settlement of 1919–21 turned out to have paved the way for Hitler to make himself master of nearly the whole of Western as well as Eastern continental Europe for a period which, short though it was, gave him time to do immeasurable evil.

Though the principle of national self-determination was to give Hitler an opportunity for aggression which the makers of the territorial settlement of 1919–21 had not, and perhaps could not have, foreseen, it would hardly have been possible for them to have made the settlement on any other basis, even if they had seen farther into the future than they did. A territorial settlement must be based on some generally recognized and widely approved principle if it is to be something better than a mere pact between thieves, such as the pact between Hitler and Stalin in 1939, and the pacts between the Romanov, Hohenzollern, and Habsburg Powers in 1772, 1793, and 1795, for the partition of Poland. The makers of the peace settlement of 1919–21, like their predecessors in 1814–15, were men of principle, though, like those predecessors and, indeed, most other statesmen, they failed to live up to their principles with complete integrity where the principles conflicted with their countries' selfish interests; and in 1919–21 the principle of self-determination was the inevitable basis for several reasons. The dissatisfaction of those nationalities in the Habsburg Monarchy which had been left, or placed, in a subordinate position by the *Ausgleich* of 1867 had been one of the underlying causes of the war that had just been fought. The nationalism of the Serbs—a nation that had been divided between the Habsburg Monarchy and the adjoining independent Kingdom of Serbia—had been the spark that had exploded the European powder magazine; and the event that had made Britain's intervention in the war inevitable had been the German invasion of Belgium—a country whose people had asserted their right to self-determination in 1830 and whose neutrality, as a sovereign independent national state, had been guaranteed by all the Great Powers of Europe in 1839. Thus, in 1919, prudence and justice alike seemed to call for the satisfaction of hitherto unsatisfied national aspirations; and, when the principle of national self-determination was applied in Eastern Europe, it necessarily revolutionized the political map there.

In 1815 the political map of Eastern Europe had been a simple one. The whole of this great region, from the southern extremity of Greece to the northern extremity of Finland, had been included in the domains of four Great Powers: the Ottoman, Habsburg, Romanov, and the Hohenzollern Monarchies. Since the fourth partition of Poland and fourth partition of the Venetian dominions in 1814–15 those four monarchies had had common frontiers all along the line, without any interstices occupied by small states. In 1815 Montenegro was the only independent small state in the whole of this vast area. After that the previously simple political map of Eastern Europe soon began to be broken up into a mosaic of new small states through the progressive liberation of the subject nationalities of the Ottoman Empire in Southeastern Europe. By 1913 the whole of the former domain of the Ottoman Empire west and north of Adrianople had been "balkanized." But it was not till 1918 that this process of "balkanization" suddenly spread, beyond the bounds of what had once been "Turkey-in-Europe," over the whole of the former Habsburg Monarchy and, north of it, over the eastern fringes of the former Hohenzollern Empire and the western fringes of the former Romanov Empire as far north as Finland inclusive. This sudden immense northward expansion of the area occupied by small and weak successor states of large and powerful empires changed the political structure of Europe by creating a large political vacuum in an area in which, for more than a hundred years past, the Great Powers had been mortised together, with no smaller states in between them. And this change of structure opened up a new opportunity for aggression by Germany if she were to come under the rule of an adventurer who could see this opportunity and turn it to account.

A first glance at the interwar political map of Europe showed that Germany had lost severely by the territorial settlement of 1919–21. Germany too, like Russia and the now defunct Habsburg Monarchy, had been compelled to contribute to the pool of territory out of which the new East European successor states had been created. At a second glance, however, it could be seen that Germany had a chance of gaining by the new dispensation in the long run because it opened up for her a possibility of being the ultimate heir of her two former big neighbors' territorial contributions to the successor states, as well as of her own comparatively small contribution.

This possibility was open to Germany because her losses in the peace settlement of 1919–21 had not deprived her of the two main foundations of her political and military power: her industrial potential and her central position. Her industrial potential would enable her to hold her new small eastern neighbors militarily at her mercy if ever France and Great Britain were to abandon or lose the guarantees which they had taken for themselves against Germany in the military provisions of the Versailles Peace Treaty. Except for Czechoslovakia the new states in Eastern Europe were backward in their industrial development; and Germany's central position would enable her to insulate them from their natural allies, France and Great Britain, if and when a rearmed Germany managed to regain the military command of the Rhineland. Germany did achieve this on 7 March 1936, without being resisted by the West European Powers, and, from that time onward, she once again enjoyed the full advantage of being both the central Power and the strongest industrial Power in the European system.

This system had been in operation since the political union of the Spanish Monarchy with the Burgundian and Habsburg dominions in the person of Charles V in 1516. From that date down to the time of writing in 1955 there had always been in Europe a central Power threatening, at intervals, to break out in all directions and to bring the whole Western world under its domination, and a ring of outer Powers trying to cooperate with one another for the common purpose of "containing" the central aggressor and so preserving their own independence. The roles had remained constant, though the actors had changed. The role of central Power had been played by France from the close of the fifteenth century down to the close of the Napoleonic Wars; from 1871 to 1945 it was played by Germany; since 1945 it was being played by the Soviet Union. The role of leader of the ring of outer Powers had been played in turn by the Habsburg Monarchy, Holland, Britain, and the United States. While the "containing" Powers usually enjoyed a superiority over the central Power in their aggregate resources, these could not be brought to bear without a concerted effort that was difficult to achieve. The central Power, on its side, had the political advantage of unity and the military advantage of holding the interior lines.

In this fluctuating balance of forces, the geographical distribution of the small states was a factor that might be of decisive weight. It was an advantage for the central Power to have a zone of weak states interposed between her and the ring of outer Powers that were trying to "contain" her. This advantage had been enjoyed by France on her eastern frontier from the time of the establishment of the modern European balance of power at the turn of the fifteenth and sixteenth centuries down to the territorial settlement of 1814–15 that had led on to the political unification of Italy and of Germany in the years 1859–71. For more than three centuries ending with the annexation of the Rhineland to Prussia in 1814–15, France had been insulated by a zone of petty states from both Brandenburg-Prussia and the Habsburg Monarchy. This political vacuum immediately to the east of France had been one of the circumstances favoring French aggression from 1494 to 1813. The subsequent entrenchment of Prussia in the Rhineland was one of the causes of the French disaster in 1870. As a result of the Franco-Prussian War of 1870–71 the role of central Power had passed from France to Germany; but from 1871 to 1918 the political structure of Eastern Europe had withheld from Germany the advantage that her predecessor France had formerly enjoyed. During those years Germany's immediate eastern neighbors had still been the two Great Powers, Russia and Austria-Hungary; and these two, between them, had blocked the path for Germany's expansion eastwards, extending, as they did, right across the breadth of Europe, from the Baltic Sea to the Adriatic.

This insurmountable obstacle to Germany's expansion eastwards was suddenly removed in 1918 at the moment of Germany's defeat and by the operation of the very forces that had defeated her. As a result of the territorial settlement of 1919–21, Germany found herself now flanked, on the east, by a zone of small and weak states of the kind that France had had for her eastern neighbors down to 1813. Hitler could merely perceive this favorable situation without being able to exploit it, so long as the West European Powers occupied the Rhineland and the bridgeheads to the east of the Rhine and, thereafter, so long as it was still open to them to reoccupy these German territories without a risk of effective German resistance. As soon as Hitler had occupied the Rhineland with his own military forces, he was able to make full use of Germany's potential advantage of having small and weak states for her neighbors in Eastern Europe as well as in Scandinavia and in the Low Countries.

The East European successor states were weak for several reasons. All of them were weak materially—in terms of area, population, and industrial development—by comparison with even the weakest of the European Great Powers, and *a fortiori* by comparison with Germany. Those of them that had been on the losing side in the First World War were also weak because in most of the disputes during the peace settlement, over territory and other material assets between them and their neighbors on the winning side, the decision had gone against the defeated states.

The Principal Allied and Associated Powers had not deliberately set out to penalize their ex-opponents and to favor their ex-allies. In redrawing the political map of Europe, they had genuinely tried to apply the principle of national self-determination impartially. But in Eastern Europe in 1919 the nationalities were not distributed, as they were in Western Europe, like the patches in a patchwork quilt, with sharply defined boundaries between one patch and another. They were intermingled like the cubes in a mosaic or like the threads in a piece of shot silk. It was impossible here to draw clear-cut frontiers demarcating the limits of national domains without leaving large minorities on the wrong side of the line; and, in these numerous East European cases in which justice could not be done to one nationality without doing injustice to another, the Principal Allied Powers had been inclined to find in favor of their friends. For instance, they had transferred from Hungary to Rumania the territories in eastern Hungary in which the Rumanian element in the population was in a majority, at the inevitable cost of also transferring the less numerous, but still considerable, Magyar population occupying an isolated enclave, entirely surrounded by a Rumanian population, in the southeast corner of Transylvania. The Principal Allied Powers had also been reluctant, and perhaps powerless as well, to restrain their friends when these had taken the law into their own hands. The Poles, for example, had done this in forcibly annexing Eastern Galicia, against the will of the Ukrainian majority of its population, and the White Russian district of Vilna against the will of Lithuania, and in imposing the Riga Treaty frontier on the Soviet Union at a moment when the Soviet Government were not in a position to bring their vastly superior latent strength into play. As a result of the cumulative effect of such adverse settlements of contentious territorial issues, the ex-vanquished small countries in Eastern Europe were left physically weak but, like Germany and Russia, unreconciled and therefore on the lookout for the first opportunity of securing a revision of the settlement in their favor.

On the other side, the ex-victor countries in Eastern Europe were weakened morally and politically by their forcible acquisition of territories inhabited by alien minorities that were their unwilling and

resentful subjects. Every such minority that they had insisted on including within their swollen postwar frontiers brought upon the ex-
victor countries the nemesis of finding themselves between two fires.
They had to fear concerted hostile action between the resentful minority within their frontiers and the resentful ex-vanquished state to
which the minority wished to return and which, on its side, wished
to recover its lost nationals. This menace would have been serious
for an ex-victor state that had had only one discontented subject
minority and one discontented neighbor state to deal with. But most
of the East European ex-victor states had been prodigal in making
enemies. Yugoslavia, for example, had made an enemy of Hungary
by annexing a Magyar population on the left bank of the Danube,
after having made an enemy of Bulgaria, before the First World War,
by annexing Northern Macedonia. Rumania, after having annexed the
Southern Dobruja from Bulgaria at the same date, had gone on to
annex Transylvania and more besides from Hungary, and to make
an enemy of the Soviet Union by annexing Bessarabia. Czechoslovakia had annexed a Magyar population along the southern border
of Slovakia as well as a German population round the fringes of
Bohemia and Moravia. Czechoslovakia had been undone when Hitler
had turned the principle of national self-determination against her
by taking up the cause of the Sudeten Germans and coming to the
rescue of Czechoslovakia's Magyar subjects as well. Czechoslovakia
and Rumania, who each held territory claimed by a Great Power, as
well as territory claimed by two small East European countries, were
evidently in a more dangerous position than Yugoslavia, who held
territory desired by two small East European countries only. Czechoslovakia had been liquidated during the half year ending on 15 March
1939. But Czechoslovakia's position had not been so dangerous as
Poland's was; for, of the three claimants against Poland—namely,
Germany, the Soviet Union, and Lithuania—two were Great Powers
whom Poland had been able to despoil simultaneously owing to a
conjunction of historical circumstances which was as transitory as
it had been extraordinary. During the interwar years the successor
states that had been created or enlarged at the expense of the Habsburg, Romanov, and Hohenzollern Empires had been known in Germany by the sinister nickname of *Saisonsstaaten,* meaning states
born to die within the brief span of one season, in contrast to states
with a perennial expectation of life. In the flock of East European

interwar *Saisonsstaaten,* Poland was the representative of the type which displayed the typical characteristics in the most extreme form and with the greatest effects on the fortunes of the rest of the world.

In March 1939 Poland stood possessed of frontiers which were unacceptable to both Germany and the Soviet Union and which either of these two neighboring Great Powers was bound to insist on redrawing, at the first opportunity, in the sectors where its own interests were concerned. In other respects, however, the conflicts of interest between Poland and these two neighbors of hers were not on all fours.

The conflict between Poland and Germany was irremediable; for, unless the ex-Prussian territories of Posnania (alias Posen) and Pomorze (alias Polish Pomerania or "the Polish Corridor") were embraced within Poland's frontiers, there could be no political reunion of the Polish people under the Polish flag, and, unless the likewise ex-Prussian territory of Danzig were separated politically from the Reich, there could be no effective access for a reunited Poland to the sea. Therefore Poland could not, and in the event did not, compromise with Germany on any of these grave issues, while, from the German nationalist standpoint, a permanent compromise on any of them with Poland was equally out of the question. Ever since the First Partition of Poland in 1772 had for the first time established territorial continuity between the German nucleus of Ost-Elbisch Prussia around Berlin and its outlying German enclave in East Prussia, it had been the ambition of successive German imperialists, from Frederick the Great through Bismarck to Hitler, to make the intervening territory not merely Prussian in its color on the political map, but also German instead of Polish in its population. In other words, Germany could never be induced to renounce her aspiration to consolidate the German *Volkstum*'s national domain at the cost to Poland of denationalizing half her heartland, while, conversely, Poland could never be induced to renounce her aspiration of securing her national unity and her access to the sea at the cost to Germany of serving East Prussia politically as well as ethnographically from the main body of the Reich.

While the Polish-German territorial dispute was thus an impasse, the Polish-Russian territorial dispute was not inherently intractable. Between the southern tip of the Lithuanian national domain on the Niemen and the eastern tip of the Slovak national domain in the

Carpathians, it was possible to draw an approximate ethnographic boundary between a predominantly Polish-inhabited area to the west of the line and a predominantly White Russian and Ukraine-inhabited area to the east of it. If this ethnographic boundary were to be adopted as the political frontier between Poland and the Soviet Union—as it had been followed in the so-called Curzon Line worked out by the British Government during the peace settlement after the First World War—this would create no impossible situation for either party. A few pockets of Ukrainian population would be placed under Polish rule, and a few outlying enclaves of Polish population would be placed under Soviet rule; the largest losers would be Polish land-lords owning estates inhabited by an Ukrainian and a White Russian peasantry. But these prospective losses on either side were compa-rable with each other in magnitude and were not intolerable in them-selves for either party.

These circumstances showed clearly the policy which a resurgent Poland ought to have pursued in the peace settlement after the First World War. A Polish Bismarck (if such an incarnate contradiction in terms were conceivable) would have set himself unhesitatingly in 1919–20 to exact from a temporarily defeated Germany the territorial terms which the actual Polish statesmen of the day did in fact suc-ceed in exacting from her on this favorable occasion, at the unavoid-able price of earning for Poland Germany's implacable enmity. But he would have taken the utmost care to avoid earning for her simul-taneously the implacable enmity of a temporarily defeated Russia. He would consequently have refrained from seizing the same favor-able occasion for taking from Russia predominantly Ukrainian and White Russian territories with which Poland could dispense without any deadly detriment to her national well-being, but which Russia, for her part, could not be expected permanently to renounce.

Unfortunately, the historical Polish statesmen who had in fact determined their country's destinies in the fateful years 1919–21 had lacked the two cardinal Bismarckian virtues of moderation and fore-sight. Disregarding the protests and warnings of the British Govern-ment (whose good offices they had been ready to accept a few weeks earlier, when Polish fortunes in the Russo-Polish war of 1920 had been at their lowest ebb) the Poles had exploited politically a capri-cious turn in the tide of the fortunes of war in order to force upon the Soviet Union a Polish-Soviet frontier—drawn some 150 miles east of the ethnographic Curzon Line, and bringing about 4.5 million Ukrainians and 1.5 million White Russians under Polish rule—which was bound, for so long as it lasted, to make confidence and cooperation between the two countries impossible. Since the revival of both the Soviet Union and Germany could only be a matter of time, Poland, in the act of forcing the Riga frontier upon the Soviet Union, had condemned herself to be a *Saisonsstaat*. She had, in fact, insisted on signing an advance copy of her own death-warrant.

The interwar frontiers of Poland were a standing incitement to Germany and Russia to make common cause for partitioning Poland for the fifth time, as the Fourth Partition of Poland in 1814–15 had impelled Prussia-Germany and Russia to keep the peace with one another for a hundred years for the sake of their common interest in preventing Poland from making her reappearance on the political map. The signature of the Russo-German Treaty of Rapallo on 16 April 1922 had been an early indication that a fellow-feeling between two Great Powers that had both been mulcted of territory at a moment of temporary weakness might prevail over the antipathy arising from a difference in ideology; and a residue or revival of this fellow-feeling—both against interwar Poland and against the West European Powers to whom interwar Poland owed her existence—may have been one of the psychological factors that made the Russo-German Agreement of 23–24 August 1939 practicable. No doubt, neither party to this agreement saw in it more than a temporary makeshift; for Hitler, unlike any previous ruler of Prussia-Germany, had territorial ambitions which went far beyond the limited aim of securing a share in a partition of Poland. Hitler's ultimate goal was to conquer for Germany a vast *Lebensraum* at Russia's expense in the Ukraine and the Urals, and Stalin and his colleagues in the Kremlin were well aware of this. Yet, at a juncture at which, in spite of this ultimately "irrepressible" conflict between the Soviet Union and the Third Reich, a temporary accommodation was convenient for both parties, their common interest in repartitioning Poland—though a minor point of agreement when measured by the scale of the latent issue between them over the Ukraine—may have been part of the inducement that led them to do their temporary deal with one another.

If the existence of Poland, within her interwar frontiers, was an inducement to Russia to come to terms with Germany provisionally in the summer of 1939, the existence of an insulating zone of small states around Germany was a serious obstacle to the establishment of any effective anti-German coalition between the two West European Powers and the Soviet Union, and was therefore a valuable political asset for Germany, since an Anglo-Franco-Russian coalition was the only potential combination of European Powers that would be strong enough to cause Hitler serious anxiety. The advantage to Germany was very great, because, if the West European Powers shrank from the cost of attacking Germany across her short common frontier with France after this had been strengthened by the improvisation of the Siegfried Line, they could not help any country east of Germany whom Germany might attack, except by themselves attacking Germany across the Low Countries. Conversely, Russia could not help any country whom Germany might attack, except by herself attacking Germany across Poland and Rumania. This geopolitical situation made the possibility of cooperation between the West European Powers and the Soviet Union dependent upon the attitude of the small states lying between them and Germany and upon the three outer Great Powers' own attitude towards these small intervening states if they proved, as they did prove, unwilling to make arrangements with all three Great Powers, for common defense against Germany, in advance of a German attack on any of the parties.

II THE HITLER ENIGMA

Adolf Hitler
A POLICY FOR GERMANY

Adolf Hitler's second book, although dictated in 1928, was not discovered until 1958 by Professor Gerhard Weinberg among the mass of captured German documents stored in Alexandria, Virginia. The book had not been published in Germany because Hitler's first book, Mein Kampf, *had not been a financial success for the publisher, and he was unwilling to lose more money. Moreover, the original reason for writing the book no longer existed. Hitler wrote the book to explain his position on the question of the South Tyrol, an area awarded to Italy by the Treaty of St. Germain, which had become a heated political issue. After the controversy over the South Tyrol subsided, Hitler was unwilling to endure the drudgery of revising the manuscript. In this book, Hitler argued against the spirit of reconciliation that seemed to be developing between France and Germany after the signing of the Treaty of Locarno in 1925. He called on Germany to ignore the League of Nations and to prepare to seize* Lebensraum *(living space) in Communist Russia.*

What is Germany's present situation and what are the prospects for her future and what kind of a future will this be?

The collapse which the German people suffered in 1918 lies, as I want once more to establish here, not in the overthrow of its military organization, or in the loss of its weapons, but rather in its inner decay which was revealed at that time and which today increasingly appears. This inner decay lies just as much in respect to the worsening of its racial value as in the loss of all those virtues which condition the greatness of a people, guarantee its existence and promote its future.

Blood value, the idea of personality and the instinct for self-preservation slowly threatened to be lost to the German people. Internationalism triumphs in its stead and destroys our folk-value, democracy spreads by stifling the idea of personality and in the end an evil pacifistic liquid manure poisons the mentality favoring bold self-preservation. We see the effects of this vice of mankind appear in the whole life of our people. Not only does it make itself noticeable in the field of political concerns, no, but also in that of economy,

From *Hitler's Secret Book,* translated by Salvatore Attanasio (New York, 1961), pp. 78–79, 85, 128–129, 132–135, 140–145, 208–210. Reprinted by permission of Grove Press, Inc. Copyright © 1961 by Grove Press, Inc.

and not least in that of our cultural life, so that if it is not brought to a halt once and for all our people will be excluded from the number of nations with a future.

The great domestic task of the future lies in the elimination of these general symptoms of the decay of our people. This is the mission of the National Socialist movement. A new nation must arise from this work which overcomes even the worst evils of the present, the cleavage between the classes, for which the bourgeoisie and Marxism are equally guilty.

The aim of this reform work of a domestic political kind must finally be the regaining of our people's strength for the prosecution of its struggle for existence and thereby the strength to represent its vital interests abroad.

Our foreign policy is also presented by this with a task that it must fulfill. For the more domestic policy must furnish the folkish instrument of strength to foreign policy, the more must also foreign policy, through the actions and measures it adopts, promote and support the formation of this instrument.

If the foreign policy task of the old bourgeois-national state had primarily been that of the further unification in Europe of those belonging to the German nation in order then to work up to a higher territorial policy viewed in folkish terms, then the foreign policy task of the postwar period must at the outset be one that promotes the forging of the internal instrument of power. . . .

Hence today the first task of German domestic policy ought to be that of giving the German people a military organization suitable to its national strength. Since the forms of the present *Reichswehr* could never suffice for this goal and, conversely, are determined by foreign policy motives, it is the task of German foreign policy to bring about all the possibilities that could permit the reorganization of a German national army. For that must be the immovable aim of any political leadership in Germany, so that one day the mercenary army will again be replaced by a truly German national army.

For just as the purely technical-military qualities of the present are superior, so must the general qualities of the German *Reichswehr* deteriorate in their development in the future. The former without doubt is to be credited to General von Seeckt and to the *Reichswehr's* Officers' Corps altogether. Thus the German *Reichswehr* could really be the army framework for the future German national army. Just as in general the task of the *Reichswehr* itself must be, by the educational stress placed on the national fighting task, to train the mass of [later] officers and sergeants for the later national army.

No true national-thinking German can dispute that this aim must be held immovably in sight. Even less can he dispute that its execution is possible only if the nation's foreign policy leaders assure the general necessary prerequisites.

Thus the first task of German foreign policy is primarily the creation of conditions which make possible the resurrection of a German army. For only then will our people's vital needs be able to find their practical representation. . . .

* * *

Hence from whatever side we consider the possibilities of foreign policy, for Germany one case must in principle be excluded: we will never be able to proceed against the forces now mobilized in Europe by relying only on our military means. Thus any combination which brings Germany into conflict with France, England, Poland and Czechoslovakia, etc., without beforehand giving her the possibility of a thorough preparation, is therefore void.

This fundamental perception is important because there are still among us in Germany, even today, well-meaning national-minded men who in all earnestness believe that we must enter into an association with Russia.

Even if considered only from a purely military point of view such an idea is unviable or catastrophic for Germany.

Just as before the year 1914, today also we can assume as unconditionally established for always that in any conflict involving Germany, regardless on what grounds, regardless for what reasons, France will always be our adversary. Whatever European combinations may emerge in the future, France will always take part in them in a manner hostile to Germany. This lies in the traditionally anchored intention of French foreign policy. It is false to believe that the outcome of the war has changed anything on this score. On the contrary the World War did not bring about for France the complete fulfillment of the war aim she had in mind. For this aim was by no means only the regaining of Alsace-Lorraine, but on the contrary Alsace-Lorraine itself represents only a small step in the direction of the goal of French foreign policy. That the possession of Alsace-Lorraine in no way abolished the tendencies of French policy, aggressively directed against Germany, is most strikingly proved by the fact that at the very time France possessed Alsace-Lorraine, the tendency of French foreign policy directed against Germany was, nevertheless, already in existence. The year 1870 showed more clearly than the year 1914 what France ultimately intended. At that time no need was felt to veil the aggressive character of French foreign policy. In the year 1914, perhaps wisened by experiences, perhaps also influenced by England, the French considered it more correct to profess general ideals of humanity on the one hand and to limit their aim to Alsace-Lorraine on the other. These tactical considerations, however, did not in the least signify an inner deflection from the former goals of French policy, but only a concealment of the same. Afterward, as before, the leading idea of French foreign policy was the conquest of the Rhine borders whereby the mutilation of Germany into individual states, linked as loosely as possible to each other, was viewed as the best defense of this border. That this safeguarding of France in Europe, achieved thereby, was to serve the fulfillment of greater world political aims does not alter the fact that for Germany these French continental-political intentions are a question of life and death.

As a matter of fact, indeed, France also had never taken part in a coalition in which German interests in any way would have been promoted. In the last three hundred years Germany had been attacked by France twenty-nine times all told up to 1870. A fact which on the eve of the battle of Sedan moved Bismarck to oppose the French general Wimpffen most sharply when the latter tried to achieve a mitigation of the terms of surrender. It was Bismarck at that time who, in response to the declaration that France would not forget a German concession but would remember it gratefully forever in the future, immediately stood up and confronted the French negotiator with the hard, naked facts of history. Bismarck stressed, in this sense, that France had attacked Germany so often in the last three hundred years, regardless of the prevailing form of government, that for all the future he was convinced that regardless how the capitulation was formulated, France would immediately attack Germany anew as soon as she felt strong enough for it either through her own strength or through the strength of allies.

Thereby Bismarck had more correctly appraised French mentality than our present political leaders of Germany. He could do this because he, who himself had a policy aim in view, could also have an inner understanding of the policy goals others set themselves. For Bismarck the intention of French foreign policy was clearly established. It is incomprehensible to our present-day leaders, however, because they are lacking in every clear political idea. . . .

French foreign policy has always received its inner impulse from this mixture of vanity and megalomania. Who in Germany wants to wait and hope that the more France is estranged from rational clear thinking, in consequence of her general Negrification, she will yet one day undertake a change in her disposition and intentions toward Germany?

No, regardless of how the next development in Europe proceeds, France, by utilizing momentary German weaknesses and all the diplomatic and military possibilities at her disposal, will always seek to inflict harm on us and to split our people so that she can ultimately bring it to a complete disintegration.

Hence for Germany any coalition which does not signify a binding of France is by itself impermissible.

The belief in a German-Russian understanding is in itself fantastic as long as a regime rules in Russia which is permeated by only one aim: to carry over the Bolshevist poisoning to Germany. It is natural, therefore, for Communist elements to agitate for a German-Russian alliance. They thereby hope, rightfully, to be able to lead Germany herself to Bolshevism. It is incomprehensible, however, if national Germans believe that it is possible to achieve an understanding with a state whose greatest interest is the destruction of this very national Germany. Obviously, should such an alliance finally come into being today its result would be the complete rule of Jewry in Germany exactly as in Russia. Likewise incomprehensible is the opinion that one can wage a war against the capitalist West European world with this Russia. For in the first place present-day Russia is anything but an anticapitalist state. It is, to be sure, a country that has destroyed its own national economy but, nevertheless, only in order to give international finance capital the possibility of an absolute control. If this were not so how could it be, secondly, that the very capitalist world in Germany takes a position in favor of such an alliance? It is after all the Jewish press organs of the most outspoken stock-exchange interests who espouse the cause of a

German-Russian alliance in Germany. Does one really believe that the *Berliner Tagblatt* or the *Frankfurter Zeitung* and all their illus-trated papers speak more or less overtly for Bolshevik Russia be-cause the latter is an anticapitalist state? In political matters it is always a curse when the wish becomes father to the thought.

To be sure, it is conceivable that in Russia itself an internal change within the Bolshevik world may ensue to the extent that the Jewish element, perhaps, could be crowded out by a more or less Russian national element. Then the possibility might not be excluded that present-day Bolshevik Russia, in reality Jewish-capitalistic, would be driven toward [to a] national-anticapitalist tendencies. In this case, to which many things seem to point, it would be conceiv-able, to be sure, that West European capitalism would seriously take a position against Russia. But then an alliance of Germany with this Russia would also be complete insanity. For the idea that such an alliance could somehow be held secret is as unjustified as the hope to arm ourselves for the conflict through military preparations that are made quietly.

Then there would only be two real possibilities: either this alliance would be viewed by the Western European world, poising itself against Russia, as a danger, or not. If yes, then I don't know who can seriously believe that there will be time for us to arm ourselves in a manner suitable at least to prevent a collapse in the first twenty-four hours. Or do people really believe in earnest that France will wait until we have built our air defense and our tank defense? Or do they believe that this can happen secretly in a country in which treason is no longer considered shameless, but a courageous deed worthy of emulation? No, if Germany really wants to enter into an alliance with Russia against Western Europe then Germany will again become a historic battlefield tomorrow. On top of this it requires an entirely uncommon fantasy to fancy that Russia could somehow come to Germany's help, in what way I know not. The only success of such an action would be that Russia could thereby still escape a catastrophe for a certain time, as it would first break over Germany. But a popular inducement for such a struggle against Germany could hardly exist, especially in the Western states. Just imagine Germany allied with a real anticapitalist Russia and then picture how this democratic world Jewish press would mobilize all the instincts of the other nations against Germany. How especially in France complete harmony would immediately be established between French national chauvinism and the Jewish stock-exchange press. For let one not confuse such a process with the struggle of White Russian generals against the Bolshevism of an earlier time. In the years [19]19 and [19]20 national White Russia fought against the Jewish stock-exchange revolution, in truth international-capitalist red revolution in the highest sense. Today, however, anticapitalist Bolshevism, become national, would stand in a struggle against world Jewry. Whoever understands the importance of press propaganda, and its infinite possibilities for inciting nations and besotting people, can imagine to what orgies of hate and passion against Germany the European Western nations would be whipped. For then Germany would no longer be allied with the Russia of a great, noteworthy, ethical, bold idea, but with the despoilers of the culture of mankind.

Above all there could be no better chance for the French government to master its own inner difficulties than to undertake a fully danger-free struggle against Germany in such a case. French national chauvinism could be all the more satisfied since then, under the protection of a new world coalition, it could come much closer to the fulfillment of the ultimate war aim. For regardless of the nature of the alliance between Germany and Russia, militarily, Germany alone would have to sustain the most terrible blows. Wholly apart from the fact that Russia does not border directly on Germany and, consequently, must itself first overrun the Polish state—even in the case of a subjugation of Poland by Russia which as such is quite improbable—in the best of circumstances such Russian help could essentially arrive on German territory only when Germany no longer existed. But the idea of a landing of Russian divisions anywhere in Germany is completely excluded as long as England and France have complete control of the Baltic Sea. Moreover, the landing of Russian troops in Germany would fail because of countless technical deficiencies.

Thus should a German-Russian alliance some day have to undergo the test of reality, and there is no such thing as an alliance without the idea of war, Germany would be exposed to the concentrated attacks of all West Europe without being able to provide for her own defense in a serious way.

But now there remains the question of just what meaning a

German-Russian alliance should have in general. Only the one of preserving Russia from destruction and sacrificing Germany for that? Regardless of how this alliance would turn out in the end, Germany could not arrive at setting a decisive foreign policy goal. For thereby nothing would be changed regarding the fundamental vita/ question, indeed regarding the vital needs, of our people. On the contrary Germany, thereby, would be more than ever cut off from the only rational territorial policy in order to pad out her future with the scuffle over unimportant border adjustments. For the question of space for our people cannot be solved either in the west or in the south of Europe.

The hope in a German-Russian alliance, which haunts the minds of even many German national politicians, however, is more than questionable for still another reason.

In general, it seems self-evident in national circles that we cannot very well ally ourselves with a Jewish-Bolshevist Russia since the result, according to all probability, would be a Bolshevization of Germany. Obviously, we do not want this. But we base ourselves on the hope that one day the Jewish character—and thereby the most fundamentally international capitalistic character of Bolshevism in Russia —might disappear in order to make place for a national communism, anticapitalist on a world scale. Then this Russia, permeated once more by national tendencies, might very well come up for consideration in terms of an alliance with Germany.

This is a very great error. It rests on an extraordinary ignorance of the psyche of the Slavic folk-soul. This should not amaze anybody if we reflect on how little knowledge even politically minded Germany had of the spiritual conditions of her erstwhile allies. Otherwise we would never have fallen so low. If, therefore, today the national politicians in favor of friendship with Russia try to motivate their policy by reference to Bismarck's analogous attitudes, they disregard a whole multitude of important factors which at that time, but not today, spoke in favor of Russian friendship. . . .

In view of Germany's hopeless military situation the following must be borne in mind in the formulation of future German foreign policy.

1. Germany cannot bring about a change in her present situation by herself, so far as this must ensue by means of military power.

2. Germany cannot hope that a change of her situation will emerge through measures taken by the League of Nations, as long the determining representatives of this institution are at the same time the parties interested in Germany's destruction.

3. Germany cannot hope to change her present situation through a combination of powers which brings her into conflict with the French system of alliances surrounding Germany, without first acquiring the possibility of eliminating her sheer military powerlessness so that in case the commitments [of an application] of the alliance go into effect she may be able to come forward immediately with the prospect of military success.

4. Germany cannot hope to find such a combination of powers as long as her ultimate foreign policy aim does not seem clearly established, and, at the same time does not contradict the interests of those states which can be considered in terms of an alliance with Germany—indeed even appear serviceable to them.

5. Germany cannot hope that these states can be found outside the League of Nations. On the contrary her only hope must consist in her eventual success in extricating individual states from the coalition of victor states and building a new group of interested parties with new aims which cannot be realized through the League of Nations because of its whole nature.

6. Germany may only hope to achieve success in this way if she finally renounces her former vacillating see-saw policy and fundamentally decides upon a single direction, and at the same time assumes and bears all the consequences.

7. Germany should never hope to make world history through alliances with nations whose military value seems sufficiently characterized by the fact of their former defeats, or whose general racial importance is inferior. For the struggle for the regaining of German freedom will thereby again raise German history to the level of world history.

8. Germany should never forget for a moment that regardless how, and along what ways, she thinks to change her fate, France will be her enemy, and that France from the outset can count on any combination of powers that turns against Germany.

We cannot examine Germany's foreign policy possibilities without first possessing clarity on what we want in Germany itself, that is on how Germany itself thinks to shape her future. Further, we must then try to determine clearly the foreign policy goals of those powers in Europe which, as members of the coalition of victors, are important as world powers.

I have already dealt with Germany's various foreign policy possibilities in this book. Nevertheless I shall once more briefly present the possible foreign policy goals so that they may yield a basis for the critical examination of the relations of these individual foreign policy aims to those of other European states.

1. Germany can renounce setting a foreign policy goal altogether. This means that in reality she can decide for anything and need be committed to nothing at all.

Thus in the future she will continue the policy of the last thirty years, but under other conditions. If now the world consisted just of states with a similar political aimlessness, Germany could at least endure this even though it could hardly be justified. But this is not at all the case. Thus just as in ordinary life a man with a fixed life-goal that he tries to achieve at all events will always be superior to others who live aimlessly, exactly likewise is it in the life of nations. But, above all, this is far from saying that a state without a political goal is in the position to avoid dangers which such a goal may bring in its train. For just as it seems exempt from an active function, in consequence of its own political aimlessness, in its very passiveness it can also just as easily become the victim of the political aims of others. For the action of a state is not only determined by its own will, but also by that of others, with the sole difference that in one case it itself can determine the law of action, whereas in the other case the latter is forced upon it. Not to want a war because of a peaceful sentiment, is far from saying that it can also be avoided. And to avoid a war at any price is far from signifying saving life in the face of death.

Germany's situation in Europe today is such that she is far from allowing herself to hope that she may go forward to a condition of contemplative peace with her own political aimlessness. No such possibility exists for a nation located in the heart of Europe. Either Germany itself tries actively to take part in the shaping of life, or she will be a passive object of the life-shaping activity of other nations. All the sagacity hitherto supposedly able to extricate nations from historical dangers through declarations of a general disinterest has, up to now, always shown itself to be an error as cowardly as it is stupid. Whoever will not be a hammer in history, will be an anvil. In all its development up to now our German people has had a choice only between these two possibilities. When it itself wanted to make history, and accordingly joyfully and boldly staked all, then it was still the hammer. When it believed that it could renounce the obligations of the struggle for existence it remained, up to now, the anvil on which others fought out their struggle for existence, or it itself served the alien world as nutriment.

Hence, if Germany wants to live she must take the defense of this life upon herself, and even here the best parry is a thrust. Indeed Germany may not hope at all that she can still do something for shaping her own life, if she does not make a strong effort to set a clear foreign policy aim which seems suitable for bringing the German struggle for existence into an intelligent relation to the interests of other nations.

If we do not do this, however, aimlessness on a large scale will cause planlessness in particulars. This planlessness will gradually turn us into a second Poland in Europe. In the very proportion that we let our own forces become weaker, thanks to our general political defeatism, and the only activity of our life is spent in a mere domestic policy, we will sink to being a puppet of historical events whose motive forces spring from the struggle for existence and for their interests waged by other nations.

Moreover, nations which are not able to take clear decisions over their own future and accordingly would like best of all not to participate in the game of world development, will be viewed by all the other players as a spoil-sport and equally hated. Indeed, it can even happen that, on the contrary, the planlessness of individual political actions, grounded in the general foreign policy aimlessness, is regarded as a very shrewd impenetrable game and responded to accordingly. It was this which befell us as a misfortune in the pre-war period. The more impenetrable, because they were incomprehensible, were the political decisions of the German governments of that time, the more suspicious they seemed. And all the more, therefore, were especially dangerous ideas suspected behind the most stupid step.

Thus if today Germany no longer makes an effort to arrive at a clear political goal, in practice she renounces all possibilities of a revision of her present fate, without in the least being able to avoid future dangers.

2. Germany desires to effect the sustenance of the German people by peaceful economic means, as up to now. Accordingly even in the future she will participate most decisively in world industry, export and trade. Thus she will again want a great merchant fleet, she will want coaling stations and bases in other parts of the world and finally she wants not only international sales markets, but also her own sources of raw material if possible in the form of colonies. In the future such a development will necessarily have to be protected especially by maritime means of power.

This whole political goal for the future is a utopia, unless England is seen as defeated beforehand. It establishes anew all the causes which in 1914 resulted in the World War. Any attempt by Germany to renew her past along this way must end with England's mortal enmity, alongside which France may be reckoned as a most certain partner from the outset.

From a folkish standpoint setting this foreign policy aim is calamitous, and it is madness from the point of view of power politics.

3. Germany establishes the restoration of the borders of the year 1914 as her foreign policy aim.

This goal is insufficient from a national standpoint, unsatisfactory from a military point of view, impossible from a folkish standpoint with its eye on the future, and mad from the viewpoint of its consequences. Thereby even in the future Germany would have the whole coalition of former victors against her in a compact front. In view of our present military position, which with a continuation of the present situation will worsen from year to year, just how we are to restore the old borders is the impenetrable secret of our national-bourgeois and patriotic government politicians.

4. Germany decides to go over to [her future aim] a clear, far-seeing territorial policy. Thereby she abandons all attempts at world-industry and world-trade and instead concentrates all her strength in order, through the allotment of sufficient living space for the next hundred years to our people, also to prescribe a path of life. Since this territory can be only in the East, the obligation to be a naval power also recedes into the background. Germany tries anew

to champion her interests through the formation of a decisive power on land.

This aim is equally in keeping with the highest national as well as folkish requirements. It likewise presupposes great military power means for its execution, but does not necessarily bring Germany into conflict with all European great powers. As surely as France here will remain Germany's enemy, just as little does the nature of such a political aim contain a reason for England, and especially for Italy, to maintain the enmity of the World War. . . .

Thus if we submit Germany's foreign policy possibilities to a closer examination only two states remain in Europe as possible valuable allies for the future: Italy and England. Italy's relation to England itself is already a good one today and, for reasons which I have discussed in another passage, will hardly be clouded in the immediate future. This, too, has nothing to do with mutual sympathies but rests, on the Italian side above all, on a rational appraisal of the actual power relations. Thus an aversion to a boundless and unlimited French hegemony in Europe is common to both states. For Italy because her most vital European interests are threatened, for England because an overpowerful France in Europe can inflict a new threat on England's present-day naval and world supremacy which in itself is no longer completely unquestionable.

That already today probably Spain and Hungary are also to be reckoned as belonging to this community of interests, even if only tacitly, lies grounded in Spain's aversion to French colonial activity in North Africa as well as in Hungary's hostility to Yugoslavia, which is at the same time supported by France.

If Germany would succeed in taking part in a new state coalition in Europe, which either must lead to a shift of emphasis in the League of Nations itself or allow decisive power factors altogether outside the League of Nations to develop, then the first domestic political prerequisite for a later active foreign policy would be realizable. The weaponlessness imposed on us by the Versailles treaty and thus our practical defenselessness could come to an end, albeit slowly. This is possible only if the coalition of victors itself quarrels over this question but never, however, in an alliance with Russia, let alone in a union with other so-called oppressed nations, against the front of the coalition of the former victor states that encircle us.

Then in the far future it may be possible to think of a new association of nations, consisting of individual states with a high national value, which could then stand up to the threatening overwhelming of the world by the American Union. For it seems to me that the existence of English world rule inflicts less hardships on present-day nations than the emergence of an American world rule.

Pan-Europe cannot be summoned to the solution of this problem, but only a Europe with free and independent national states whose areas of interest are divergent and precisely delimited.

Only then can the time ripen for Germany, secured by a France pushed back within her own boundaries and supported by her army born anew, to lead the way toward the elimination of her territorial need. Once our people, however, will have grasped this great geopolitical aim in the East the consequence will not only be clarity regarding German foreign policy but also stability, at least for a humanly predictable time, will make it possible to avoid political insanities like those which ultimately entangled our people in the World War. And then we will also have ultimately overcome the period of this petty daily clamor and of the completely sterile economic and border policy.

Germany then, also domestically, will have to take steps toward the strongest concentration of her means of power. She will have to realize that armies and navies are set up and organized not along romantic lines but according to practical requirements. Then she will automatically select as our greatest task the formation of a superior strong land army since our future as a matter of fact does not lie on the water, but in Europe rather.

Only if we will have completely perceived the meaning of this proposition and put an end to our people's territorial need, in the East and on the largest scale, along the lines of this perception will German economy also cease to be a factor of world unrest which brings a thousand dangers down upon us. It will then at least serve the satisfaction of our domestic needs in their major aspects. A people which no longer needs to shunt off its rising rural generations into the big cities as factory workers, but which instead can settle them as free peasants on their own soil, will open up a domestic sales market to German industry which can gradually remove and exempt it from the frenzied struggle and scramble for the so-called place in the sun in the rest of the world.

It is the foreign policy task of the National Socialist movement to prepare and ultimately to carry out this development. It must also place foreign policy in the service of the reorganization of our folkdom on the basis of its philosophical range of ideas. Even here it must anchor the principle that we do not fight for systems but for a living people, that is for flesh and blood, which must be preserved and whose daily bread must not be lacking so that in consequence of its physical health it can also be healthy spiritually.

A. J. P. Taylor
A REVISIONIST VIEW

A. J. P. Taylor, whose books are contentious and lively, was a fellow of Magdalen College, Oxford, and is the curator of the Beaverbrook Library. His books, including The Struggle for Mastery in Europe, 1848–1914; English History, 1914–1945; The Course of German History; *and* Sarajevo to Potsdam *are provocative, well-written, and display a wide range of knowledge. The* Origins of the Second World War *was praised and condemned even on television. Taylor's critics argued that he was apologizing for Hitler, but he replied that he was only attempting to explain Hitler's success. In this book, as in his other works, Taylor stresses the human blunders as being more important in history than preconceived plans. He downplays premeditation on the part of Hitler in starting the war.*

Hitler . . . changed most things in Germany. He destroyed political freedom and the rule of law; he transformed German economics and finance; he quarrelled with the Churches; he abolished the separate states and made Germany for the first time a united country. In one sphere alone he changed nothing. His foreign policy was that of his predecessors, of the professional diplomats at the foreign ministry, and indeed of virtually all Germans. Hitler, too, wanted to free Germany from the restrictions of the peace treaty; to restore a great German army; and then to make Germany the greatest power in

From *The Origins of the Second World War,* by A. J. P. Taylor (London, 1961), pp. 68–72, 102–104, 131–135. Copyright © 1961 by A. J. P. Taylor. Reprinted by permission of Hamish Hamilton, Ltd., London, and Atheneum Publishers, New York. Footnotes omitted.

Europe from her natural weight. There were occasional differences in emphasis. Perhaps Hitler would have concentrated less on Austria and Czechoslovakia if he had not been born a subject of the Habsburg Monarchy; perhaps his Austrian origin made him less hostile originally to the Poles. But the general pattern was unchanged.

This is not the accepted view. Writers of great authority have seen in Hitler a system-maker, deliberately preparing from the first a great war which would destroy existing civilization and make him master of the world. In my opinion, statesmen are too absorbed by events to follow a preconceived plan. They take one step, and the next follows from it. The systems are created by historians, as happened with Napoleon; and the systems attributed to Hitler are really those of Hugh Trevor-Roper, Elizabeth Wiskemann, and Alan Bullock. There is some ground for these speculations. Hitler was himself an amateur historian, or rather a generalizer on history; and he created systems in his spare time. These systems were daydreams. Chaplin grasped this, with an artist's genuis, when he showed the Great Dictator transforming the world into a toy balloon and kicking it to the ceiling with the point of his toe. Hitler always saw himself, in these daydreams, as master of the world. But the world which he dreamt to master and the way he would do it changed with changing circumstances. *Mein Kampf* was written in 1925, under the impact of the French occupation of the Ruhr. Hitler dreamt then of destroying French supremacy in Europe; and the method was to be alliance with Italy and Great Britain. His *Table Talk* was delivered far in occupied territory, during the campaign against Soviet Russia; and then Hitler dreamt of some fantastic Empire which would rationalize his career of conquest. His final legacy was delivered from the Bunker, when he was on the point of suicide; it is not surprising that he transformed this into a doctrine of universal destruction. Academic ingenuity has discovered in these pronouncements the disciple of Nietzsche, the geopolitician, or the emulator of Attila. I hear in them only the generalizations of a powerful, but uninstructed, intellect; dogmas which echo the conversation of any Austrian café or German beer-house.

There was one element of system in Hitler's foreign policy, though it was not new. His outlook was "continental," as Stresemann's had been before him. Hitler did not attempt to revive the "World Policy" which Germany had pursued before 1914; he made no plans for a great battle-fleet; he did not parade a grievance over the lost colonies, except as a device for embarrassing the British; he was not even interested in the Middle East—hence his blindness to the great opportunity in 1940 after the defeat of France. One could attribute this outlook to Hitler's Austrian origin, far from the ocean; or believe that he learned it from some geopolitician in Munich. But essentially it reflected the circumstances of the time. Germany had been defeated by the Western Powers in November 1918; and had herself defeated Russia the preceding January. Hitler, like Stresemann, did not challenge the Western settlement. He did not wish to destroy the British Empire, nor even to deprive the French of Alsace and Lorraine. In return, he wanted the Allies to accept the verdict of January 1918; to abandon the artificial undoing of this verdict after November 1918; and to acknowledge that Germany had been victorious in the East. This was not a preposterous program. Many Englishmen, to say nothing of Milner and Smuts, agreed with it even in 1918; many more did so later; and most Frenchmen were coming around to the same outlook. The national states of Eastern Europe enjoyed little popularity; Soviet Russia still less. When Hitler aspired to restore the settlement of Brest-Litovsk, he could pose also as the champion of European civilization against Bolshevism and the Red peril. Maybe his ambitions were genuinely limited to the East; maybe conquest there would have been only the preliminary to conquest in Western Europe or on a world scale. No one can tell. Only events could have given the answer; and by a strange twist of circumstances they never did. Against all expectations, Hitler found himself at war with the Western Powers before he had conquered the East. Nevertheless, Eastern expansion was the primary purpose of his policy, if not the only one. . . .

In principle and doctrine, Hitler was no more wicked and unscrupulous than many other contemporary statesmen. In wicked acts he outdid them all. The policy of Western statesmen also rested ultimately on force—French policy on the army, British policy on sea-power. But these statesmen hoped that it would not be necessary to use this force. Hitler intended to use his force, or would at any rate threaten to use it. If Western morality seemed superior, this was largely because it was the morality of the status quo; Hitler's was the immorality of revision. There was a curious, though only superficial, contradiction in Hitler between aims and methods. His aim was change, the overthrow of the existing European order; his method was patience. Despite his bluster and violent talk, he was a master in the game of waiting. He never made a frontal attack on a prepared position—at least never until his judgment had been corrupted by easy victories. Like Joshua before the walls of Jericho, he preferred to wait until the forces opposing him had been sapped by their own confusions and themselves forced success upon him. He had already applied this method to gain power in Germany. He did not "seize" power. He waited for it to be thrust upon him by the men who had previously tried to keep him out. In January 1933 Papen and Hindenburg were imploring him to become Chancellor; and he graciously consented. So it was to be in foreign affairs. Hitler did not make precise demands. He announced that he was dissatisfied; and then waited for the concessions to pour into his lap, merely holding out his hand for more. Hitler did not know any foreign countries at first hand. He rarely listened to his foreign minister, and never read the reports of his ambassadors. He judged foreign statesmen by intuition. He was convinced that he had taken the measure of all *bourgeois* politicians, German and foreign alike, and that their nerve would crumble before his did. This conviction was near enough to the truth to bring Europe within sight of disaster.

Perhaps this waiting was not at first conscious or deliberate. The greatest masters of statecraft are those who do not know what they are doing. In his first years of power, Hitler did not concern himself much with foreign affairs. He spent most of his time at Berchtesgaden, remote from events, dreaming in his old feckless way. When he turned to practical life, his greatest concern was to keep his own absolute control over the National Socialist party. He watched, and himself promoted, the rivalry between the principal Nazi leaders. Then came the maintenance of Nazi control over the German state and the German people; after that, rearmament and economic expansion. Hitler loved details of machinery—tanks, airplanes, guns. He was fascinated by road building, and even more by architectural schemes. Foreign affairs came at the bottom of the list. In any case, there was little he could do until Germany was rearmed. Events imposed upon him the waiting which he preferred. He could safely leave foreign policy to the old professionals of the foreign office. After all, their aims were the same as his; they, too, were concerned to sap the settlement of

Versailles. They needed only an occasional spur to action, the sporadic and daring initiative which suddenly brought things to a head.

This pattern was soon shown in the discussions over disarmament. Allied statesmen were under no illusions as to Hitler's intentions. They were given precise and accurate information by their representatives at Berlin—information which Sir John Simon found "terrifying." For that matter they could read the truth in any newspaper, despite the steady expulsion from Germany of British and American correspondents. There is no greater mistake than to suppose that Hitler did not give foreign statesmen plenty of warning. On the contrary he gave them only too much. . . .

*   *   *

The German reoccupation of the Rhineland marked the end of the devices for security which had been set up after the First World War. The League of Nations was a shadow; Germany could rearm, free from all treaty restrictions; the guarantees of Locarno were no more. Wilsonian idealism and French realism had both failed. Europe returned to the system, or lack of system, which had existed before 1914. Every sovereign state, great or small, again had to rely on armed strength, diplomacy, and alliances for its security. The former victors had no advantage; the defeated, no handicap. "International anarchy" was restored. Many people, including some historians, believe that this in itself is enough to explain the Second World War. And so, in a sense, it is. So long as states admit no restriction of their sovereignty, wars will occur between them—some wars by design, more by miscalculation. The defect of this explanation is that, since it explains everything, it also explains nothing. If "international anarchy" invariably caused war, then the states of Europe should never have known peace since the close of the Middle Ages. In fact there have also been long periods of peace; and before 1914 international anarchy gave Europe its longest peace since the end of the Roman Empire.

Wars are much like road accidents. They have a general cause and particular causes at the same time. Every road accident is caused, in the last resort, by the invention of the internal combustion engine and by men's desire to get from one place to another. In this sense, the "cure" for road accidents is to forbid motorcars. But a motorist, charged with dangerous driving, would be ill-advised if he pleaded the existence of motorcars as his sole defense. The police and the courts do not weigh profound causes. They seek a specific cause for each accident—error on the part of the driver; excessive speed; drunkenness; faulty brakes; bad road surface. So it is with wars. "International anarchy" makes war possible; it does not make war certain. After 1918 more than one writer made his name by demonstrating the profound causes of the First World War; and, though the demonstrations were often correct, they thus diverted attention from the question why that particular war happened at that particular time. Both enquiries make sense on different levels. They are complementary; they do not exclude each other. The Second World War, too, had profound causes; but it also grew out of specific events, and these events are worth detailed examination.

Men talked more about the profound causes of war before 1939 than they had done previously; and in this way these causes counted for more. It became a commonplace after 1919 that future wars could be avoided only if the League of Nations succeeded. Now the League had failed; and men were quick to say that henceforth war was inevitable. Many even felt that it was wicked to try to prevent war by the old-style instruments of alliances and diplomacy. Men said also that Fascism "inevitably" produced war; and there was no denying this, if one believed the pronouncements of the two Fascist leaders themselves. Hitler and Mussolini glorified war and the warlike virtues. They used the threat of war to promote their aims. But this was not new. Statesmen had always done it. The rhetoric of the dictators was no worse than the "saber-rattling" of the old monarchs; nor, for that matter, than what English public-schoolboys were taught in Victorian days. Yet there had been long periods of peace then despite the fiery talk. Even the Fascist dictators would not have gone to war unless they had seen a chance of winning; and the cause of war was therefore as much the blunders of others as the wickedness of the dictators themselves. Hitler probably intended a great war of conquest against Soviet Russia so far as he had any conscious design; it is unlikely that he intended the actual war against Great Britain and France which broke out in 1939. He was as much dismayed on 3 September 1939 as Bethmann had been on 4 August 1914. Mussolini, despite all his boasting, strove desperately to keep out of war, more desperately even than the despised last leaders of the third French republic; and he went to war only when he thought that it was already won. Germans and Italians applauded their leaders; but war was not popular among them, as it had been in 1914. Then cheering crowds everywhere greeted the outbreak of war. There was intense gloom in Germany during the Czech crisis of 1938; and only helpless resignation the following year when war broke out. The war of 1939, far from being welcome, was less wanted by nearly everybody than almost any war in history. . . .

*   *   *

The watershed between the two world wars extended over precisely two years. Postwar ended when Germany reoccupied the Rhineland on 7 March 1936; prewar began when she annexed Austria on 13 March 1938. From that moment, change and upheaval went on almost without interruption until the representatives of the Powers, victorious in the Second World War, met at Potsdam in July 1945. Who first raised the storm and launched the march of events? The accepted answer is clear: it was Hitler. The moment of his doing so is also accepted: it was on 5 November 1937. We have a record of the statements which he made that day. It is called "the Hossbach memorandum," after the man who made it. This record is supposed to reveal Hitler's plans. Much play was made with it at Nuremberg; and the editors of the *Documents on German Foreign Policy* say that "it provides a summary of German foreign policy in 1937–38." It is therefore worth looking at in detail. Perhaps we shall find in it the explanation of the Second World War; or perhaps we shall find only the source of a legend.

That afternoon Hitler called a conference at the Chancellery. It was attended by Blomberg, the minister of war; Neurath, the foreign minister; Fritsch, commander-in-chief of the army; Raeder, commander-in-chief of the navy; and Goering, commander-in-chief of the air force. Hitler did most of the talking. He began with a general disquisition on Germany's need for *Lebensraum.* He did not specify where this was to be found—probably in Europe, though he also discussed colonial gains. But gains there must be. "Germany had to reckon with two hate-inspired antagonists, Britain and France. . . . Germany's problem could only be solved by means of force and this was never without attendant risk." When and how was there to be this resort to force? Hitler discussed three "cases." The first "case" was "period 1943–1945." After that the situation could only change for the worse; 1943 must be the moment for action. Case 2 was civil war in France;. if that happened, "the time for action against the Czechs had come." Case 3 was war between France and Italy. This might well occur in 1938; then "our objective must be to overthrow Czechoslovakia and Austria simultaneously." None of these "cases" came true; clearly therefore they do not provide the blueprint for German policy. Nor did Hitler dwell on them. He went on to demonstrate that Germany would gain her aims without a great war; "force" apparently meant to him the threat of war, not necessarily war itself. The Western Powers would be too hampered and too timid to intervene. "Britain almost certainly, and probably France as well, had written off the Czechs and were reconciled to the fact that this question of Germany would be cleared up in due course." No other Power would intervene. "Poland—with Russia in her rear—will have little inclination to engage in war against a victorious Germany." Russia would be held in check by Japan.

Hitler's exposition was in large part daydreaming, unrelated to what followed in real life. Even if seriously meant, it was not a call to action, at any rate not to the action of a great war; it was a demonstration that a great war would not be necessary. Despite the preliminary talk about 1943–1945, its solid core was the examination of the chances for peaceful triumphs in 1938, when France would be preoccupied elsewhere. Hitler's listeners remained doubtful. The generals insisted that the French army would be superior to the German even if engaged against Italy as well. Neurath doubted whether a Mediterranean conflict between France and Italy were imminent. Hitler waved these doubts aside: "he was convinced of Britain's non-participation, and therefore he did not believe in the probability of belligerent action by France against Germany." There is only one safe conclusion to be drawn from this rambling disquisition: Hitler was gambling on some twist of fortune which would present him with success in foreign affairs, just as a miracle had made him Chancellor in 1933. There was here no concrete plan, no directive for German policy in 1937 and 1938. Or if there were a directive, it was to wait upon events.

Why then did Hitler hold this conference? This question was not asked at Nuremberg; it has not been asked by historians. Yet surely it is an elementary part of historical discipline to ask of a document not only what is in it, but why it came into existence. The conference of 5 November 1937 was a curious gathering. Only Goering was a Nazi. The others were old-style Conservatives who had remained in office to keep Hitler under control; all of them except Raeder were to be dismissed from their posts within three months. Hitler knew that all except Goering were his opponents; and he did not trust Goering much. Why did he reveal his inmost thoughts to men whom he distrusted and whom he was shortly to discharge? This question has an easy answer: he did not reveal his inmost thoughts. There was no crisis in foreign policy to provoke a broad discussion or sweeping decisions. The conference was a maneuver in domestic affairs. Here a storm was brewing. The financial genius of Schacht had made rearmament and full employment possible; but now Schacht was jibbing at further expansion of the armament program. Hitler feared Schacht and could not answer his financial arguments. He knew only that they were wrong: the Nazi regime could not relax its momentum. Hitler aimed to isolate Schacht from the other Conservatives; and he had therefore to win them for a program of increased armaments. His geopolitical exposition had no other purpose. The Hossbach memorandum itself provides evidence of this. Its last paragraph reads: "The second part of the conference was concerned with questions of armament." This, no doubt, was why it had been called.

The participants themselves drew this conclusion. After Hitler had left, Raeder complained that the German navy would be in no strength to face war for years ahead. Blomberg and Goering pulled him into a corner, where they explained that the sole object of the conference was to prod Fritsch into demanding a larger arms program. Neurath made no comment at the time. He is said to have grasped the full import of Hitler's wickedness some days later, and then to have suffered "several severe heart-attacks." These attacks were first revealed in 1945 when Neurath was being tried as a war criminal; he showed no sign of ill-health in 1937 or for years afterwards. Fritsch prepared a memorandum, insisting that the German army must not be exposed to the risk of war against France, and took this to Hitler on 9 November. Hitler replied that there was no real risk and that, in any case, Fritsch would do better to speed up rearmament instead of dabbling in political questions. Despite this rebuke, Hitler's maneuver had succeeded: henceforward Fritsch, Blomberg, and Raeder had no sympathy with Schacht's financial scruples. Otherwise, none of the men who attended the meeting on

5 November gave it another thought until Goering found the record produced against him at Nuremberg as evidence of his war guilt. From that moment it has haunted the corridors of historical research. It is the basis for the view that there is nothing to be discovered about the origins of the Second World War. Hitler, it is claimed, decided on war, and planned it in detail on 5 November 1937. Yet the Hossbach memorandum contains no plans of the kind, and would never have been supposed to do so, unless it had been displayed at Nuremberg. The memorandum tells us, what we knew already, that Hitler (like every other German statesman) intended Germany to become the dominant Power in Europe. It also tells us that he speculated how this might happen. His speculations were mistaken. They bear hardly any relation to the actual outbreak of war in 1939. A racing tipster who only reached Hitler's level of accuracy would not do well for his clients.

The speculations were irrelevant as well as mistaken. Hitler did not make plans—for world conquest or for anything else. He assumed that others would provide opportunities, and that he would seize them. The opportunities which he envisaged on 5 November 1937 were not provided. Others were. We must therefore look elsewhere for the man who provided an opportunity which Hitler could take and who thus gave the first push towards war. Neville Chamberlain is an obvious candidate for this position. From the moment that he became prime minister in May 1937, he was determined to start something. Of course he resolved on action in order to prevent war, not to bring it on; but he did not believe that war could be prevented by doing nothing. He detested Baldwin's sceptical, easy-going policy of drift. He had no faith in the hesitant idealism associated with the League of Nations which Eden half-heartedly put forward. Chamberlain took the lead in pressing for increases in British armaments. At the same time, he resented the waste of money involved, and believed it to be unnecessary. The arms race, he was convinced, sprang from misunderstandings between the Powers, not from deep-seated rivalries or from the sinister design of one Power to dominate the world. He believed, too, that the dissatisfied Powers—and Germany in particular—had legitimate grievances and that these grievances should be met. He accepted, to some extent, the Marxist view, held by many people who were not Marxists, that German discontent had economic causes, such as lack of access to foreign markets. He accepted more fully the "liberal" opinion that Germans were the victims of national injustice; and he had no difficulty in recognizing where this injustice lay. There were six million Germans in Austria, to whom national reunification was still forbidden by the peace treaties of 1919; three million Germans in Czechoslovakia, whose wishes had never been consulted; three hundred and fifty thousand people in Danzig who were notoriously German. It was the universal experience of recent times that national discontent could not be challenged or silenced —Chamberlain himself had had to acknowledge this unwillingly in regard to Ireland and India. It was the general belief, though less sustained by experience, that nations became contented and pacific, once their claims were met.

Here was a program for the pacification of Europe. It was devised by Chamberlain, not thrust upon him by Hitler. These ideas were in the air, shared by almost every Englishman who thought about international affairs. . . .

Norman Rich
THE IDEOLOGY OF EXPANSION

Norman Rich, professor of history at Brown University, is a specialist in German history and a former editor of the German Foreign Ministry documents captured at the end of World War II. This selection is taken from the first volume of his study, Hitler's War Aims. *In this two-volume work, Rich studies Hitler's program for expansion, the machinery he used, the course he followed, and the policies pursued in the countries he dominated. Hitler's scheming and plotting, Rich discovered, were affected by the knowledge that time was not on Germany's side.*

Not the least of Hitler's crimes against the German people was his exploitation and perversion of some of Germany's most cherished values, notably the German veneration for a broadly conceived (and generally somewhat vague) ideal of humanist culture. Yet it was with undoubted sincerity that Hitler, the frustrated artist, paid homage to the German ideal of *Kultur* and made it the foundation of his entire ideological system. It was his conviction that only through culture was the beauty and dignity of a higher humanity, the only justification for the existence of mankind, to be attained. To clear away the obstructions to true culture was the aim of the Nazi revolution; to build on the healthy foundations of the past the goal of the Nazi renaissance.

But if Hitler was sincere about his admiration for culture (however perverse his own conception of culture may have been), there is also no doubt that he self-consciously exploited the cultural ideal to provide his followers with a moral impulse more edifying than a mere drive for political power, and a value to reinforce the emotional qualities of nationalism. In culture Hitler thought he had found a spiritual counterpoise to supernatural religions; and, even more important, an ideal he believed could overtrump the crass materialism of Marxism.

Indeed, the ideal of culture might have been even more effective than that of a classless society in transcending the narrow ideological boundaries of nationalism had not Hitler strait-jacketed his own principle the moment he advanced it. For in a concomitant proposition he maintained that only members of the Aryan race were endowed with the creative ability to produce great culture. The preposterous nature of this claim, instead of rendering the entire Nazi movement ridiculous, actually contributed to its strength, for it made Nazism something more than a political movement; it made the acceptance of National Socialism an act of faith—but a faith open only to Germans. For this reason, although the Nazi faith might concentrate tremendous moral energy in one group of people, the racial bomb would never explode with a chain reaction. By limiting the cultural ideal to the Aryans, Hitler had merely loosed upon the world another German particularist religion.

The assumption that the past and future of human civilization depended exclusively on the Aryans, that therefore they alone among the peoples of the earth deserved to live and prosper—this was the basis on which rested the entire superstructure of Hitler's ideological program, his concept of the role of party and state, his plans for the future of the German people. Race, far from being a mere propagandistic slogan, was the very rock on which the Nazi church was built.

Hitler never appears to have had any doubts about the literal truth of his racial theories, nor did his more fanatic followers. With greater objectivity Alfred Rosenberg, the self-appointed high priest of the Nazi movement, saw the difficulty educated people might have in accepting the racial doctrine, and he attempted to give it intellectual plausibility by calling it a myth—*the* myth of the twentieth century. But the racial myth, he hastened to add, embodied the essence of truth, and in an excess of analogical zeal he declared that the mysteries of the blood had overwhelmed and supplanted the old sacraments. Rosenberg actually acclaimed the particularist character of National Socialism and rejected universality as the intellectual concept of a decadent society. This can hardly have been Hitler's intention. There can be no doubt that for him the Germanic race, supporting as it did the entire complex of his values, was, from a spiritual standpoint, in itself universal. Herein exactly lay the implication of his ideas. Because the Germans were the only true creators of culture, because they were universal in a cultural sense, it followed that they had the moral right to be universal in a territorial sense as well; in other words, that they had a moral right to world territorial dominion.

Hitler did not dwell at length on the morality of German territorial expansion. After his many years of patriotic brooding on the subject, this was something he by now took for granted. What concerned him most at the time he wrote *Mein Kampf,* and in all his subsequent analyses of the problem, was the desperate immediacy of the Germans' territorial requirements.

As Hitler surveyed the international scene, the position of the Germans seemed grim. Across the channel lay England, jealous of any potential rival on the Continent and perennial opponent of any effort on the part of the Germans to improve their position. But if England desired no increase in German power, France desired no German power at all. The French attitude toward Germany was founded on the motive of self-preservation. Only through the obliteration of Germany could France maintain its world importance. French policy would always be one of waiting to engage in the final destruction of the Germans.

Great as was the danger from France, however, Hitler believed that the truly vital threat to the existence of the Germans lay in the east, where a vast expanse of territory provided the breeding grounds for an inexhaustible supply of a particularly brutal species of humanity. These lesser breeds, separated from Europe by no natural barriers, had been held at bay over the centuries only by the bravery of the Germans, whose racial qualities had enabled them so far to withstand a numerically superior foe. But the peoples of the east, although inferior racially and lacking creative ability, could and did imitate German technology and organization. With their unlimited numbers, equipped with German-invented weapons and using German military techniques, it was only a question of time before these eastern masses would overrun the insignificant area to which the Germans were restricted. The exigencies of Germanic security could only be met by the possession of more land. Hitler examined the alternatives to territorial expansion and rejected each as he considered it.

The Germans could, Hitler reasoned, follow the French example and restrict the percentage of population increase by a wider use of birth control. But once propagation was limited, the natural struggle for existence which selected those who were most worthy to survive would give way to an effort to keep alive every human being that was born. The number of people would certainly be restricted, but the value of each individual would also be lowered. A people that defied nature in this way would some day be forced to give up its place to a stronger generation. To restrict the natural growth of the German population would mean nothing less than to rob the German people of their future.

Hitler next disposed of the possibility of solving the problem by the intensification of domestic production. Through industry and trade food could be purchased to support a growing population, but the First World War had proven to Hitler that an imported food supply was hardly a source of security to a nation. Real economic security could only be achieved by ensuring a people its daily bread within the sphere of its domestic economy. There was, however, a limit to the possibility of increasing agricultural productivity. In Germany higher living standards had already consumed the increased yield resulting from better farming methods, and the constant use of artificial fertilizers was beginning to burn out the soil. A further growth of German agricultural production, therefore, seemed out of the question.

Hitler was a thoroughgoing Malthusian in his fear of the time when it would no longer be possible to adapt the fertility of the soil to the increasing population. In the distant future, nature would have to solve this problem in her own way, but Hitler believed that in his own era only those nations would be in distress which lacked the will to secure for themselves the soil they required of the world. Should the Germans out of mistaken humanitarianism restrict their own expansion and thereby be forced to limit their population, they would be overwhelmed in the future by the sheer weight of numbers of inferior races who had space to reproduce without limit.

Hitler's decisive argument in favor of territorial expansion, however, was the disastrous effect of territorial deficiency on the German military position. It was not only a question of inadequate manpower. Hitler's study of military history had convinced him that a nation's strategic security was in direct proportion to its territorial dimensions. Military victories over nations restricted to narrow boundaries were always more easily achieved and more complete than over nations inhabiting a large land mass. As Germany was situated at the time Hitler wrote *Mein Kampf,* a coalition of hostile powers could not only defeat Germany. They could destroy it for good.

What was involved here, Hitler said, was not the fate of some insignificant Negro tribe; the German mother of all life was in danger. The threat embraced not simply a people, but world civilization. Greater territory alone could give the Germans adequate security for the present; only more land could guarantee their future. Since the rest of the world could not become German, the Germans would have to spread more widely over the rest of the world. This was not simply a moral right; it was a moral duty.

Hitler next addressed himself to the question of where the most practicable territorial acquisitions could be made at the lowest possible cost. Although a demand for colonies was embodied in the official Nazi party program, Hitler himself was convinced that overseas colonies could meet but few of Germany's requirements. The problem was not one of conquering and exploiting people, but of acquiring agriculturally useful space. The majority of so-called colonial territories were hardly fit for large-scale European settlement. Nor would overseas colonies provide the national security Hitler demanded of an expansionist policy. The Netherlands and Portugal were cases in point, and even Britain was no longer proof to the contrary. In admiring the strength of the British Empire, Hitler said, one was prone to forget its dependence on the Anglo-Saxon world as such. Not Britain's colonial empire but its fortunate linguistic and cultural communion with the United States was the real strength of its position. So for Britain, too, security ultimately resided in the resources of a continental power. Germany, which could not depend on American support, must seek its security elsewhere. Overseas colonies were for Hitler no more than a diplomatic and propagandistic weapon. He definitely rejected them as a solution to German needs. The struggle that would in any case be involved in the acquisition of territory could be carried out most suitably, not in faraway lands across the sea, but in the home continent itself. Through the conquest of contiguous territory the natural reproduction of the race, its bread, and its strategic security would all be assured.

Hitler then specifically named his intended victim. If one wanted land and soil on the European continent, the conquests of real value for the future could be achieved by and large only at Russia's expense. There was no question but that there had to be a final reckoning with France, but the defeat of France would be a hollow victory if German policy were restricted thereto. The elimination of the French threat would have and would retain significance only if it provided the rear cover for an enlargement of the German domain in Eastern Europe. National Socialism, therefore, consciously abandoned the foreign policy of the Second Reich. Germany was to cease its fruitless pursuit of a colonial policy and, above all, its drive to the south and west. The Third Reich intended to resume the Germanic expansionist program where it had stopped six hundred years ago, and to press once again over the routes of the medieval crusading orders into the lands of the east.

Hitler believed that fate itself had given the Germans an advantage at this point. In the surrender of Russia to Bolshevism, the Russian people had been robbed of that intelligentsia which heretofore had produced and guaranteed Russia's stability as a state. The Russian Empire was not an achievement of the Slavs, but rather a wonderful example of the state-building capacity of the Germans as leaders of an inferior race. According to the precepts of Hitler's theology, inferior nations with German organizers had more than once expanded into powerful state structures and endured as long as the nucleus of the constructive race maintained itself. As a result of the Bolshevik Revolution, however, the Germanic governing stratum of Russia had been destroyed and replaced by that ferment of decomposition, the Jews. Russia was ripe for Germany's plucking.

Hitler envisioned a German future based primarily on independent German landowners. The lands which in the past had been profitably Germanized were those which the ancient Germans had acquired by the sword and settled with German peasants. The mission of the National Socialist movement was to give the German nation such political insight as to see its future goal fulfilled, not in the intoxicating impressions of a new Alexandrian campaign, but in the consolidation of military victories by the industrious labor of the German peasant. The Germans would thereby gain not only national security but social security. A nation in communion with the soil would no longer be subject to the restlessness that besets industrial societies and would automatically be freed from many of the social evils of the industrial age. Industry and trade would be forced out of their unwholesome positions of leadership in the national economy into the framework of a more balanced national life. Cities were to be decentralized and made the servants rather than the focal points of society. A people living close to nature and the real fountains of life, a people divorced from the artificial cultural flowering of city pavements, would form a stable society, rich in its appreciation of the real values of life, a sound foundation for true cultural creativity. Never should Germany feel itself secure until it was able to give each citizen his own bit of earth. To possess his own land and to till his own soil was the most sacred right of man.

Hitler had no intention of repeating the mistakes of the ancient Germans whose conquests of land had included conquests of people. The incorporation of non-Germans had in the past resulted in the cleavage in the soul as well as in the body politic of the nation which had been so disastrous in German history, and which had so long prevented the Germans from assuming their natural position of leadership in the world. To establish a sound foundation for German security, the acquisition of soil would have to be accompanied by the purification, by which Hitler meant the Germanization, of the population. In the many areas where Germanization would be impossible, the indigenous population was to be made useful, or removed. In this way alone could expansion be effected without diluting and thereby defeating the conquerors. It was only necessary to recall the suicidal example of the Spaniards, whose intermarriage with inferior native peoples had resulted in racial degradation and national decay. The British, although largely avoiding the error of intermarriage, were also pursuing a mistaken policy, for ultimately they would find it impossible to hold together an empire of three hundred million with a population of forty-five million.

Neither Spain nor Britain should be the models of German expansion, but the Nordics of North America, who had ruthlessly pushed aside an inferior race to win for themselves soil and territory for the future. To undertake this essential task, sometimes difficult, always cruel—this was Hitler's version of the White Man's Burden.

Hitler warned that the fulfillment of his program would require work and sacrifice on an unprecedented scale. The needs of the German race could only be met by pouring into their fulfillment the undivided devotion and entire energy of the German people. The entire authority of the state, too, would have to be dedicated to this end. All policies would have to be based on the consideration of the future security of the German race. To guarantee this security, and with it the future of world civilization, any and all means were justified. One had to make clear to oneself that this goal could only be achieved through fighting, and quietly to face the passage at arms.

There would be war. The attacker would have to overcome the proprietor. Professors and other intellectuals might talk of peaceful economic conquest, but such folly could emanate only from the wishful thinking of those unacquainted with life. Only naive idealists could believe that through friendly and civilized behavior a people might gather the fruits of its ability and endeavor in peaceful competition. Where had economic interests not clashed as brutally as political interests? There were those who pointed to Britain as an example of the success of peaceful economic penetration, but it was precisely in Britain that this theory was most strikingly refuted. No nation had more savagely prepared its economic conquests with the sword, and none had defended those conquests more ruthlessly.

Although Hitler looked to the east as the land of the German future, he realized that in all probability he would not be allowed a free hand there. The moment Germany was deeply involved in campaigns in the east, France would almost certainly seize the opportunity to fall on Germany's flank. The result would be a two-front war, which would be all the more dangerous because the French, by penetrating German land or air defenses in the Ruhr, could deal a mortal blow to the German war economy. To enable Germany to neutralize or eliminate the French threat, Hitler advocated alliances with Italy and Britain. For this purpose he was prepared to concede Italy hegemony in the Mediterranean and give up all German claims to the South Tyrol, and to abandon or drastically curtail Germany's colonial, naval, and economic rivalry with Britain. Hitler actually concluded an alliance with Italy and, as late as his attack on Russia in 1941, he clung to the hope that the British, recognizing how much to their own advantage was the destruction of Russia and international Bolshevism, might yet be persuaded to concede Germany supremacy on the Continent in return for a German guarantee of the British Empire and other favors.

By the later 1930s, however, Hitler had begun to take into account the possibility that his efforts to woo Britain might fail, and that a major drive to extend German dominion in the east would be opposed by Britain as well as France. In that event the danger to the

Ruhr would be even greater and it would be all the more necessary to knock out the threat in the west before launching his drive in the east.

Hitler foresaw the possibility of a near future totally consecrated to the needs of war. During that period the abnormal demands of military necessity might exclude cultural tasks altogether, but the sacrifice would be justified. The cultural opportunities of a nation were almost always linked to its political freedom and independence. After the concentration of all endeavor in military affairs had won the required freedom, there would follow a period of compensation in which the hitherto neglected fountains of culture would flow as never before. Out of the Persian Wars had emerged the Golden Age of Pericles, and out of the tortured era of the Punic Wars the Roman state, too, began to dedicate itself to the service of a higher culture. So it would be with Germany.

The conquest of Russia was to be the first step. What would be required by Germans at a later date would have to be left to subsequent generations. The development of great worldwide national bodies was naturally a slow process. But of one thing Hitler was certain, and he concluded *Mein Kampf* with the thought: "A state which, in the epoch of race poisoning, dedicates itself to the cherishing of its best racial elements, must some day be master of the world."

When the Aryan race should at last have spread over the entire world, one might then think of an era of peace as an ideal. But it would be a peace supported not by the palm branches of tearful pacifists, but founded on the victorious sword of a people of overlords who had put the world into the service of a higher culture.

Gerhard L. Weinberg
HITLER'S WORLD

German-born Gerhard L. Weinberg, professor of history at the University of North Carolina, is the author of Germany and the Soviet Union, 1939–1941. *His career has centered on the study of Hitler's Germany, particularly its foreign policy. In* The Foreign Policy of Hitler's Germany: Diplomatic Revolution in Europe, 1933–1936, *Weinberg traces the diplomatic revolution that began in 1933 and ended in 1936 with Germany the dominant power in Europe. By that time a general European war was once more a terrible possibility.*

When Adolf Hitler became chancellor of Germany at the age of forty-three in 1933, he had held no previous position of authority in government. He had neither read intensively nor traveled extensively. He knew no foreign language. Yet he had a clearly formulated set of ideas on major issues of foreign policy, and these ideas were intimately interwoven with his concepts of domestic affairs. It is essential for an understanding of world history since 1933 that these ideas be examined in some detail, for a great part of the impact of Hitler on Germany—and of Germany on the world—lies precisely in the fact that by exertion of his will and the response it elicited inside Germany, Hitler was to be able to impress his ideas on events rather than allow events and realities to reshape his ideas. It is true that the effort failed in the end. Realities that did not conform to Hitler's visions proved stronger even than his fanatic will and the mighty energies and resources the German people harnessed to it. But the great burst of activity in Germany in the 1930s that soon spilled over Europe and affected the whole globe was no random excitement, no accidental explosion.

There have been those who argue that Hitler was a pure opportunist, a manipulator of power, without guideposts. The shifts in the pattern of his alliances—now with the center of world communism, now with one of the sources of the so-called Yellow Peril—have suggested to some that plan, pattern, and ideological considerations of

From Gerhard L. Weinberg, *The Foreign Policy of Hitler's Germany: Diplomatic Revolution in Europe, 1933–1936* (Chicago, 1970), pp. 1–8, 12–24. Copyright © 1970 by the University of Chicago. Reprinted by permission of the University of Chicago Press. Footnotes omitted.

continuing influence must have been absent from the National Socialist scene. Recent efforts to rehabilitate Hitler's diplomatic reputa-
tion tend to be based on such a view. Alan J. P. Taylor has attempted
to convert Hitler into an eighteenth-century diplomat, striving for revision of the most recent treaty in the same way Maria Theresa attempted to recover Silesia for Austria from the Prussia of Frederick
the Great. David Hoggan and Philip Fabry present Hitler in somewhat
similar terms, only they show him victimized by unscrupulous opponents, Lord Halifax in one case, Josef Stalin in the other.

The available evidence, however, shows that Hitler had some very
definite, fixed ideas on foreign policy before he came to power.
This evidence comes primarily from his speeches and writings, a
not unnatural source in the case of a man who devoted his full time
to political agitation and who did not hesitate to include in his published views ideas he knew to be unpopular alongside others likely
to elicit frenetic applause. The evidence also indicates that during
the years from 1933 to 1939 Hitler kept these ideas very much in
mind in the actual conduct of affairs, though he tended to reserve
oral and written expression of them to the privacy of the conference
room or the circle of his associates. The opportunism to which some
have pointed as the essence of Hitler's policy was in fact an integral
part of his long-term theory of political action, and many of the most
extravagant and perplexing instances will be seen to fit most precisely
into his general view.

The objection might be raised, of course, that those who see a
plan in Hitler's steps will be tempted to read the evidence in a manner that supports their interpretation; but the unanswerable fact
remains that new evidence, as it comes to light, not only fits into but
in astonishing ways underlines the accuracy of that view. Thus the
publication in 1961 of what can only be called an apologia for Field
Marshal Keitel, who was executed at Nuremberg, includes an instance
of a revelation of war plans by Hitler in a 1935 military gathering that
moved the editor to comment on this new indication of Hitler's real
policy at a time when peaceful liquidation of the Versailles Treaty
was the officially proclaimed policy of the German government. A
number of other new examples of this kind will be cited in the course
of the narrative, while the proponents of contrary interpretations have
based them, not on the discovery of new evidence, but on attempts to

explain away or disregard the obvious meaning of documents long known.

In 1933 Hitler's ideology consisted primarily of two related systems of ideas, acquired and developed in chronological sequence. The doctrine of race took form first and is clearly delineated by 1923; the partly derivative doctrine of space came to be defined, in the formulation to which Hitler continued to adhere, in the immediately following years.

Hitler's conception of foreign policy in his first years of political activity, that is until November 1923, can be summarized as follows: Germany was not defeated in World War I but stabbed in the back by Jews and those inspired by Jews. These same elements now controlled Germany internally and maintained themselves in part by their subservience to those foreign powers who had been made the victors by that stab in the back. A preliminary to any successful foreign policy therefore must be an internal change, in fact a revolution. A nationally conscious group must assume power, ruthlessly eradicate whatever steps toward democratic government had been taken inside Germany, and rearm to provide the tools for an aggressive foreign policy. Such a policy must be directed primarily against France, Germany's eternal enemy. This might mean an alignment with Italy since that power was also opposed to French hegemony in Europe. The inclusion of postwar Austria in a greater Germany was also required; and other territories, not very clearly defined, would be annexed. War was an unavoidable step on the road to national recovery, and would be victorious, as there would be no repetition of the home-front laxness responsible for Germany's recent defeat.

These views were based on Hitler's doctrine of race, a vulgarized version of Social Darwinism that found increasing acceptance in Germany both in supposedly learned circles and, especially in the years between 1900 and 1914, among the masses. According to this doctrine, the history of mankind can be understood in terms of racial analysis, that is, in terms of the supposed racial components of different societies. The rise or fall of civilizations is due to their success or failure in maintaining racial purity; the internal divisions of society are racially determined; and the cultural achievements of some are the result of their racial characteristics. The rise and fall of Rome can thus be understood as the products of the racial purity of early Roman and the racial mixture of later Roman society. The political division of France in the age of the French Revolution reflects the division between the Romanic, i.e., racially "Westic" lower classes, and the Nordic descendants of the Franks who had unified and organized the country. The cultural accomplishments of civilizations are the product of their racial composition—the great artists of Renaissance times were all Nordics whose works reflect their own appearance, while the monstrosities of modern art only mirror the appearance of their creators. Botticelli must have been as slim as his famous Venus, Rubens must have been as corpulent as the figures he painted, and Picasso presumably has three eyes.

An especially significant facet of the racialist doctrine was its rejection of the biblical distinction between man and other creatures. With the most drastic implications—assuming that one was prepared to follow them to their logical conclusion—the new paganism argued that racial purity and selective breeding are the necessary instruments of progress in the human as in the animal world and insisted that social policy be oriented accordingly. The elimination of categories of people, like the elimination of categories of insects or plants, could be judged solely by standards of utility, not morality. It was within this framework that the allegedly alien racial stock represented by the Jews was particularly dangerous because of their wide distribution and imagined influence as well as the progress which their assimilation had made, especially in Germany.

The racial element also provides a basis for Germany's hope. Its defeat in the war was due not to its inherent weakness; on the contrary, its ability to hold out for so long against a world of foes was in part a reflection of its inherent racial superiority. A full recognition of this superiority and the willingness to draw from it the necessary conclusions for domestic policy would combine to produce a different outcome next time. That this "next time" would come was beyond question. France was the great enemy. In Hitler's view, however, the enmity of Germany and France was based on more than the obvious reasons of recent war and contemporary (1920–23) French hegemony. There was a racial angle of special virulence that greatly affected Hitler's perception of France and his policies toward that country.

A key element in National Socialist hostility to France was the role of the latter as the European home of the concept of human equality, and especially the extension of *Égalité* to the Negro. Because racialism in Germany focused most directly on the Jews, it has generally been overlooked that the next great danger to European racial purity was supposed to be the Negro, introduced into Europe and sponsored by France. Unquestionably the experience of the world war had intensified, if it did not create, this concern. The large-scale deployment on European battlefields of soldiers recruited in Africa had made a major impact on German thinking. Partly because so many Negroes had been included in the French army, and partly because of the presence of colored units among the French forces stationed in the Rhineland, this whole process came to be associated with France in German eyes. National Socialist publications of the 1920s were filled with attacks on the supposed negroidization of France, and Hitler found ways to connect this directly with the "Jewish menace." Thus enmity for France was ordained by more than political or territorial factors.

Hitler's views of other countries in these first years of his political activity were not yet as systematized as they were to become in the mid-1920s. In his writings and speeches of these years his doctrine of space, built on that of race, was to provide a whole series of prescriptions for foreign policy in general and for policies toward certain countries in particular. This principle of space therefore requires scrutiny.

Space, in Hitler's thinking, always referred to agriculturally usable land; the word is regularly employed in connection with the raising of food for the support of the population living on it. Hitler had no confidence in the possibility of increasing food production from available land. The struggle for existence in which the races of the world engaged, the basic element of life on earth, was fundamentally a struggle for space. In this struggle the stronger won, took the space, proliferated on that space, and then fought for additional space. Racial vitality and spatial expansion were directly related. A people always faced the question of bringing about a proper relationship between the space on which it lived and its population. In his view, a people could choose between adjusting the population to a given space or adjusting space to population. The adjustment of population to a fixed space meant emigration, birth control, abortion, and suicide—all leading to eventual racial decay as each occurred with higher frequency among the racially superior elements of the population. Furthermore, this course generally involved dependence on others, because of the need to import food, even for the population that had been intentionally held down. Only a weak people would choose this course, and they would become weaker in the process.

The desirable alternative course, which Hitler consistently advocated in *Mein Kampf* and his political speeches from 1925 on, was the adjustment of space to population by the conquest of additional land areas whose native population would be expelled or exterminated, not assimilated. The availability of such land areas would in turn encourage the good, healthy Nordic couples settled on them to raise large families that would both make up for the casualties incurred in the conquest of the territory and assure adequate military manpower for subsequent wars *they* would need to wage.

Two facets of this last point need emphasis. Wars cost casualties—Hitler knew this as well as his audiences—but this did not mean that wars should be avoided. They were the only way to gain the land required for racial survival, and therefore necessary. But they should be fought for an adequate purpose: an amount of land believed worth the casualties in a calculation that applied to the prospective German dead the same extreme instrumentalization Hitler applied to all. In Hitler's calculation, the German borders of 1914 were not such an adequate purpose and were not worth the sacrifices their recovery would require. Until 1933, therefore, he never ceased to attack as a ridiculously inadequate objective the idea of trying to regain the borders of 1914. In his second book, Hitler mentioned 500,000 square kilometers of additional space in Europe as his first goal. Since Germany's European territorial losses in the war had slightly exceeded 70,000 square kilometers, it is no wonder that he wrote in *Mein Kampf:* "The borders of the year 1914 mean absolutely nothing for the future of the German nation." The foreign policy Hitler advocated thus promised war for new land beyond Germany's prewar borders, and further specified that the land would be settled by German farmers.

The second aspect of this expansionist program requiring attention is its potentially limitless character. The specific and immediate conclusions Hitler drew from his theories of race and space will be reviewed in detail, but first this inherent long-term trend toward world conquest must be noted. Clearly, if space is to be adjusted to an expanded population by conquest, and such conquest again enables the population to expand and facilitates further conquest, the only possible limitations are utter defeat on the one hand or total occupation of the globe on the other. A gifted German scholar, Günter Moltmann, has already called attention to the tendencies in this direction to be found in *Mein Kampf* and has suggested that the more explicit statements of 1932–34, attributed to Hitler by Hermann Rauschning, may be accepted as consistent with them. Evidence that has come to light since Moltmann wrote shows that in the years between the periods reflected by *Mein Kampf* and by Rauschning's report Hitler himself recognized these implications. Rudolf Hess in 1927 informed Walter Hewel, who had been in Landsberg prison together with Hess and Hitler, that Hitler was of the opinion that world peace could come only "when one power, the racially best one, has attained complete and uncontested supremacy." It would then establish a world police and assure itself "the necessary living space. . . . The lower races will have to restrict themselves accordingly." The process was described aptly by Hitler himself in 1928: "We consider our [anticipated] sacrifices, weigh the size of the possible success, and will go on the attack, regardless of whether it will come to a stop 10 or 1,000 kilometers beyond the present lines. For wherever our success may end, that will always be only the starting point of a new fight."

The combined doctrines of race and space had significant implications for the day-to-day conduct for foreign affairs. Hitler was publicly explicit about these before 1933; their influence will be apparent in his record after 1933, although he no longer discussed them quite so publicly. It has already been shown that war was to be a key instrument of policy; not the last resort, but in some instances the preferred approach. This role of war as a deliberate prior choice, not the *ultima ratio,* was to have a profound influence on German diplomacy. It meant, for example, that if you decided that your opponent must give in absolutely or you would go to war, the process of negotiations would be one in which your demands would be constantly raised as deadlock approached, not reduced as the parties move toward a compromise.

A second way in which the doctrines affected the handling of international relations was their import for treaties. If treaties are to serve the struggle for space, their primary objective would be either the immediate gain of space by the partitioning of third countries or the postponement of troubles considered dangerous at the moment until they could be faced with safety. In either case, treaties were temporary instruments to be broken as soon as they were no longer useful in the struggle for space. Hitler assumed that there could be no alliance except on the basis of such gains for both parties. Once the prospect of gain was gone, or even obstructed by the treaty, it had to be dropped.

With this view of treaties in mind, one can readily understand National Socialist opposition to all multilateral treaty commitments. It is easier to make and break a treaty with one partner than to join and subsequently disengage oneself from a complicated multilateral structure. For this reason, as well as opposition to the doctrine of the equality of states, the National Socialists did not approve Germany's adherence to the Locarno Pact and the Kellogg Pact and were strongly opposed to Germany's entrance into the League of Nations. Hitler's repeated public denunciations of the League were paralleled by the frequent introduction of resolutions calling on Germany to leave Geneva by the National Socialist members of the Reichstag. As will be seen, after 1933 Hitler not only took Germany out of the League and tore up the Locarno Pact at what seemed to him the earliest possible moments, but he was to avoid most carefully any new type of multilateral commitment. . . .

The doctrines of race and space were not limited in their implications to general considerations of foreign policy aims and methods but had very specific import for the policies to be followed toward individual countries. The space Germany needed was to be found primarily in the East, in Russia. The major theme of the foreign policy sections of *Mein Kampf* and of most of Hitler's second book was this insistence on the conquest of territory toward the Urals. This theme, constantly reiterated in his speeches before 1933, was one in which Hitler's perception of Russia, primarily in terms of his doctrine of race, seemed to fit most precisely with the requirements of space policy. The land area the Germanic farmers would be settled on was inhabited by Slavs, an inherently inferior group. They were incapable of organizing a state or developing a culture. The only state organization ever successfully imposed on these inferior people had been established and maintained by individuals of Germanic racial stock whose russification had been no more real in the racial sense than the supposed germanization of Poles and Czechs had made real Germans of these groups. This stratum of good racial stock, however, had been weakened even in prewar Russia by political attacks from the developing Slavic bourgeoisie with its Pan-Slavic and anti-German ideology. The world war had drastically depleted the Germanic group: war always bears most heavily on the racially best elements who serve at the front while the racially inferior attempt to escape service. The enormous casualties Russia had suffered thus decimated the Germanic stock, especially in the officer corps in which they were heavily represented. The final blow came during the Bolshevik Revolution in which the last remnants were exterminated.

This process of elimination of the Germanic element in Russia had left behind an amorphous block of Slavs, ruled and exploited for the benefit of world capitalism by the Jews. Inherently, the Jews were even less capable of organizing and maintaining a state than the Slavs, and would in any case be destroyed on the triumph of Pan-Slavism among the Russian people. The remaining Slavic population, however, would constitute a permanently feeble and unstable society. The "Slavs have no organizational ability whatever," and a purely Slavic Russia would have no power; in fact, it would fall into dissolution. That recent events—World War I and the Bolshevik Revolution—had so weakened Russia, therefore, constituted a piece of "good luck" for the future of a Germany that would know how to profit from it. The vast number of Russians presented no problem in itself: Germany had defeated the great Russian armies in the war, and space and numbers alone were not important. Nobody, Hitler maintained, would ever arrive at the idea that there was any danger of Russian hegemony in the world, because there was no inner value —meaning no racial value—in the Russian population, however numerous. Since the reduction of the Russian population by slaughter and expulsion was implicit in his policies, it is not surprising that Hitler referred to the rural areas of Eastern Europe, notoriously suffering from overpopulation, as being thinly settled. Territorial conquest eastward was thus both necessary and simple, and the major areas to be conquered lay in Russia.

If Germany were to conquer Russian territory, it had to concern itself with the tier of new states that had gained their independence after the First World War because all the great powers of Eastern

Europe had been defeated in that conflict. Poland was the largest of these states. It should be noted that Hitler did not pay nearly as much attention to Poland as many of his German contemporaries. To them, regardless of political orientation, Poland was an abomination, temporary but most irritating. The Poles were, in German eyes, an Eastern European species of cockroach; their state was generally referred to as a *Saisonstaat*—a country just for a season; and the expression *polnische Wirtschaft*—Polish economy—was a phrase commonly applied to any hopeless mess. The general orientation of German foreign policy with its goal of a return to the borders of 1914, at least in the East, hoped for a new partition of Poland, probably in cooperation with the Soviet Union. There is no evidence to suggest that anyone who occupied a leading position in Weimar Germany recognized that the existence of a strong and independent Poland might have great advantages for Germany. Until the Germans had broken what were commonly known as the "chains of Versailles," they did not notice that the same chains had bound Soviet Russia. Official German policy called for permanent hostility to Poland, manifested in a trade war as well as constant friction over questions of minorities and revisionist propaganda.

In the Weimar period, German policy toward Russia was influenced to a great extent by the priority of revisionist hopes against Poland; in Hitler's view, policy toward Poland was incidental and subordinated to his aim of territorial aggrandizement at the expense of the Soviet Union. This certainly did not make him any friendlier toward the Poles than his predecessors, but he did not share their fixed objectives because he thought them inadequate. His desire for enormous territory rather than border revision automatically diminished the long-term importance of Poland and freed from rigid preconceptions Hitler's short-term tactics toward that country. . . .

If the doctrine of space led Hitler to seek territorial expansion eastward, the presumptive increase in strength that would accrue to Germany from such expansion added yet another reason to the many existing ones making for enmity between Germany and France. Surely France would do anything to prevent such an enormous increase in German might. On this assumption, it seemed safer to defeat France first, that is, before moving East, so that Germany would not have a dangerous enemy at its back while engaged in the great enterprise. The first great war Germany would fight, therefore, would be against France; the second would be against Russia. In fact, Hitler now asserted that in the long run the first war would prove useless unless it paved the way for the second.

As the concept of space reinforced enmity for France, so it accentuated a hitherto only slightly apparent difference in Hitler's attitude toward England. Until about 1923, England was regularly included with France among Germany's present and future enemies, but with greater emphasis on the enmity of France. Perhaps British opposition to the French occupation of the Ruhr stimulated a more fundamental differentiation between the two powers. England now appears in Hitler's view of the world in a separate category. His new attitude toward Great Britain was a mixture of admiration and hate, never entirely untangled. He thought he recognized in the British upper classes the product of a process of selective breeding not entirely unlike what he hoped to accomplish in Germany. Similarly, he often referred to the ability of a small number of Englishmen to control the Indian subcontinent as a model for his own vast schemes of conquered areas and subdued peoples. On the other hand, Jews were allowed to play a part in British society, Britain had a democratic form of government, and the people of England were oriented more toward trade and industry than toward agriculture. The Jews were imagined to have all sorts of great influence; by definition democracy destroyed responsibility and leadership in a society; and trade and industry were not only not as healthy occupations as agriculture but had a debilitating effect on the social structure. Nevertheless, the hegemony of France, apparently created by the Paris peace settlement, would strengthen France in world competition for trade and empire and was thus against the interests of Great Britain. Opposition to the strongest power on the Continent in defense of the European balance would logically place England alongside Germany in its conflict with France—even if that conflict eventually produced a Germany so strong that England would again turn against Germany, at a time when, presumably, it would be too late.

In Hitler's eyes, the only thing required to persuade England of the wisdom of an alliance with Germany would be the abandonment of Germany's world trade and naval ambitions. These had threatened England before the war, and he believed them responsible for British entrance into an alliance with her former enemies France and Russia against Germany. The new eastward-directed space policy that Hitler projected for Germany would entail finding food for Germany's people by competition for land in Europe instead of competition for trade in the world and would thus remove any basis for hostility between Germany and England. Furthermore, if France was one great danger to England, Russia with its expansionist possibilities in the oil-rich Near East and toward India was a second danger, while the rising trade empire of the United States was a third. With no cause for enmity with Germany, therefore, and with a shared hostility to France and Russia, there was no reason why England should not become an ally of Germany, at least temporarily. As has been mentioned, there are explicit hints in Hitler's second book that such an alliance might subsequently give way to renewed enmity, but that was a distant future in which Germany would have acquired the territory needed to take care of itself.

The new emphasis on *Lebensraum* strengthened the apparent wisdom of a German alliance with Italy. Hitler had favored such an alliance on purely pragmatic grounds: Italy's ambitions in the Mediterranean clashed with those of France, and this common hostility to France could furnish the basis for joint action. Hitler's plans for expansion eastward would upset France but not Italy. The divergent expansions of Italy and Germany constituted a potential tie between them; they would not bring the two powers in conflict with each other, but both could be achieved only over the opposition of France. The alliance between Germany and Italy that appeared to be the logical deduction from this set of facts was confronted by a negative factor in the form of a potential division between the two powers and a positive factor in the form of a potential additional tie. The potential tie was the ideological affinity of Italian fascism and national socialism; the potentially divisive factor was the question of South Tyrol.

Hitler was an early and continuing admirer of Mussolini and his program. The Fascist seizure of power in Italy seemed to him a harbinger of his own success. The attacks upon the Fascist leader by the liberal newspapers in Germany and elsewhere confirmed Hitler's assessment of their spiritual kinship. Personal admiration for Mussolini played an undoubted part in this, and the curious type of friendship Hitler developed for his distant hero was to outlast shocks that would have sundered most personal relationships. . . .

The very first contact between the two leaders in 1922 was used by Mussolini to bring home to Hitler the danger to German-Italian relations in the question of South Tyrol. The German agitation for revision of the peace treaties constantly called attention to those people of German background who had been transferred from Austria to Italy by the Treaty of St. Germain and were being subjected to a process of Italianization. In the 1920s, the German minority in South Tyrol was probably the one most subject to repression of their original nationality and thus a plausible object for attention by those German parties that claimed a monopoly in national patriotism. Italian insistence on the maintenance of the existing border on the Brenner made revision here incompatible with German-Italian friendship, and Hitler promptly decided that the question of South Tyrol must be sacrificed to the vastly greater interest in a German-Italian alliance. Although this was a most unpopular stand in Germany, where in any case public opinion was very anti-Italian because of Italy's alleged unfaithfulness to its alliance with the Central Powers, Hitler publicly defended a renunciation of South Tyrol. . . .

There was still one other potential source of difficulty between Germany and Italy, and on it Hitler was not prepared to make concessions so readily—the annexation of Austria. Hitler always argued that Austria and Germany should be joined in one country and never ceased to make this opinion public. The very fact that tactical considerations led him to renounce claims to South Tyrol probably made him all the more obdurate in regard to the *Anschluss*. It is clear from his writings—and later acts—that this desire was not due to any great love for the land of his birth. Rather, it was the desire to expand the racial base of the forthcoming German empire. He hoped that his renunciation of South Tyrol would ease Italy's objections to the *Anschluss*, and that the time would come when Italy would see no more reason to oppose a union of Austria with an anti-French Germany. . . .

If Austria was to be swallowed up completely, Hungary was another potential ally, even if not a very important one. A revisionist power opposed to Yugoslavia, which was backed by France and in turn opposed by Italy, Hungary might be fitted into the German alliance system. The National Socialists and other extremist groups in Bavaria had been in contact with similarly oriented elements in Hungary in the years before 1923, and there had been talks about simultaneous revolutions in both locations in November of that year. . . .

Another Central European country that figured in Hitler's perceptions and plans was Czechoslovakia. His analysis of prewar Austria dealt very extensively with the growing power of the Czechs in both Bohemia and Vienna itself, his attacks on the Habsburg dynasty were phrased to a great extent in terms of their failure to combat this trend, and his praise of the Pan-German movement was based heavily on the anti-Czech element in Georg von Schönerer's program. In Hitler's eyes, the nationality problem in Bohemia was the presence of Czechs in an area he believed appropriate solely for German settlement. He assumed that the Czech state would be hostile to Germany, and he kept in contact with sympathetically inclined elements among the German population of Czechoslovakia. When the time came, they were to be the tool of far-reaching schemes.

Yugoslavia appeared in Hitler's mental world primarily in two ways. First, he thought of Yugoslavia as an enemy of Italy and friend of France and thus as a possible partner of France in a war against Mussolini's Italy; and second, as the country of the Serbs who had followed their national interest realistically and persistently by working for the destruction of Austria-Hungary. It should be noted that in Hitler's assessment of people in terms of their racial awareness and value, this point constituted something of a plus mark for the Serbs. Hitler was, of course, aware of the struggle over the border between Austria and Yugoslavia in Carinthia, but there is nothing on his part to suggest any special interest in that issue. Other European countries appear to have played little part in Hitler's thinking before 1933; what references to them can be found will be mentioned in the context of their later relations with Germany.

Outside the European continent and its colonial extensions, the major areas of importance for German foreign policy were the Far East and the United States. Hitler's vision was primarily continental, and he paid very little attention to either area, a habit that was to continue until 1945. He was not especially interested in the Far East, a fact that was to be reflected in a more than usual confusion in German policies toward that area after 1933. Three facets of Hitler's perspective on Far Eastern affairs deserve mention. In the first place, there can be no question that he shared in some way the aversion to the people of Eastern Asia expressed in references to the Yellow Peril, widespread in those early years of the twentieth century when so many of Hitler's ideas were formed. His own racist orientation, of course, served only to intensify this attitude. Second, Hitler did not share the sinophilism current in the Germany of his day as a counterweight to the "Yellow Peril" fears. In the third place, he had somewhat kindlier feelings toward Japan. Though of "racially uncreative stock," the Japanese were at any rate very clever; and their aggressive moves in the Far East, which brought down upon them the attacks of the liberal press, were to their merit in Hitler's eyes.

The United States originally drew very little attention from Hitler. In his political speeches and writings Hitler echoed the denunciations of the United States in general and President Wilson in particular that were then current in Germany. He was sure that Jewish influence had been responsible for America's entrance into the war, but his references to the United States were few indeed. His interest was aroused, however, by American immigration legislation and by the very considerable importation of American automobiles into Germany. This latter fact drew Hitler's attention to the advantages of a large domestic living space, and thus market, for industrial as well as agricultural purposes. This evidence of American strength was related, in Hitler's eyes, to American immigration legislation. These laws seemed to Hitler, not without reason, to be basically racist in orientation. They reinforced a tendency he believed inherent in the process of migration from Europe to America: the best and most enterprising members of each community, i.e., the Nordics, emigrated to America. The United States was, therefore, not the melting pot of the American imagination but the great meeting place of the Nordics who maintained their racial purity by strict immigration laws. This gathering of the finest Nordic racial stock from each European country explained why the Americans had made such good use of their living space. With a racial headstart over the others— especially the European countries drained of their best blood by the same process that had made America strong—and with a vast area on which to proliferate, the American people were exceedingly dangerous and a real threat to German predominance in the world. Only a Eurasian empire under German domination could hope to cope with this menace successfully. A third big war was added to the original two; after the wars against France and Russia would come the war against the United States. One of the major tasks of the National Socialists would be the preparation of Germany for this conflict.

This assessment of the United States was to give way in the early 1930s to a far different one. Under the impact of the world depression and its effect on the United States—an effect Hitler thought permanent—Hitler concluded that the United States was really a very weak country. Turning again to a racial explanation, he came to believe that America was a racial mixture after all, a mixture that included Negroes and Jews. Such a mongrel society, in which "the scum naturally floated to the top," could not construct a sound economy, create an indigenous culture, or establish a successful political system. America was a weak country whose hope for strength had been destroyed in the past by the victory of the wrong side in the Civil War and whose hope for the future, if there were any, lay with the German-Americans. In any case, the United States could not interfere with Hitler's plans which, in confidential discussions, were now said to include Mexico and much of Latin America. Thus Hitler was to go forward in the 1930s, unconcerned about the United States and generally uninterested in it. The basic hostility remained, but concern about America's racial strength had vanished.

It should be noted that, with significant exceptions, the general nature of Hitler's views as summarized in the preceding pages was readily recognizable before his assumption of power. In fact, the rise of the National Socialist party was financed to a considerable extent by the thousands and thousands of Germans who paid admission to public meetings at which Hitler publicly proclaimed his belief in these ideas and policies. He tried to leave his audiences in no doubt about his meaning; on the contrary, he repeated the same ideas and even phrases over and over again. He assured them that, if granted power, he would ruthlessly and brutally establish a dictatorship in Germany, build up Germany's military might after its republican institutions and ideas had been swept away, and then proceed to lead his country as its absolute dictator in a series of wars. In promising a ruthless dictatorship, he did not hesitate to say explicitly that it would be like that of Italy and of Soviet Russia. In promising war, he was always personal and specific: "I believe that

I have enough energy to lead our people whither it must shed its blood [*zum blutigen Einsatz*], not for an adjustment of its boundaries, but to save it into the most distant future by securing so much land and space that the future receives back many times the blood shed," Hitler said on 23 May 1928.

Why did millions of Germans respond so enthusiastically to these appeals? Certainly the terrible cost of the war had left many Germans disillusioned with war and fearful of its repetition. But it should be noted that the disillusionment in Germany was not quite like that in Western countries. There were books expressing such sentiments as characterized Erich Maria Remarque's *All Quiet on the Western Front* in other countries than Germany, but one would find it exceedingly difficult to match outside Germany the literature glorifying war that was typified by the works of Ernst Jünger and was applied to the postwar period by the members of the Free Corps.

More important, perhaps, than this survival of militaristic attitudes was the psychological disorganization produced by defeat. Unaware of the real situation, the German people had seen their hopes tumble from the vision of victory to the reality of collapse in a few months of 1918. After the glory of a powerful state, after the immense sacrifices of war, their world had crashed down around them. In the preceding decades, while the peoples of England and France were painfully learning to govern themselves, the German people had been trained to think that this was neither possible nor desirable for them. In the chaos and despair of a defeated country, it was easier for many to mock the brave few who tried hard to reconstruct a self-respecting society than to take a hand in the difficult task of rebuilding. It was simpler to put one's faith in one man who would take care of everything than to assume a share of the responsibility for the agonizing choices to be made in daily political life. Those who agreed that one man was to lead and decide while they would obey and follow could not thereby escape the responsibility for his decisions; they simply accepted that responsibility in advance.

A further factor of great significance was the widespread acceptance of racial ideology among the people of Germany. Whether or not willing to agree to all its horrible implications, vast numbers were prepared to accept its premises. It is significant that in a country where academic persons were high in prestige, the pseudo-science of racism had made very rapid inroads in the academic community. Furthermore, it is clear from all accounts of National Socialist gatherings that anti-Semitism was the most popular part of Hitler's appeal to his audiences. If so many followed, it was in part that they were enthusiastic about the direction he wanted to take.

Certainly one should not overlook the belief of many that the National Socialists did not necessarily mean precisely what they said; that Hitler's more extreme ideas should not be taken seriously; that, once in power, the movement would find itself forced into a more reasonable course by the impact of responsibility and reality. Many of those who deluded themselves in this opinion were to argue after World War II that Hitler had deluded them. But he had not lied to them; they had misled themselves. In many instances this self-delusion was greatly facilitated by the hope that Hitler *did* mean what he said about destroying the Social Democratic Party and the trade unions, regardless of the methods used and the purposes for which this might be done. There was also the hope of some of the older generation of German leaders that the dynamism of national socialism could be harnessed to their own more limited goals. But above all there was the opposition of millions to the Weimar Republic, its ideals and its practices, and the whole tradition of liberalism and humanism to which they were related. The German people was to be the new all-powerful god and Hitler the all-powerful prophet; and already in January 1933 there were many who identified the two. He could lead Germany back to strength; he could overcome the psychological depression of past defeat and the economic depression of Germany's contemporary situation.

Many in Germany opposed Hitler's rise to power, some of them recognizing clearly the implications of his policies, especially in the field of foreign affairs. Before 1933 the millions who pushed Hitler forward, and the small clique who installed him in office, by no means constituted the whole population. But there were vast reservoirs of support for the new leader to draw on, and for many years the support was to increase rather than lessen. The national acceptance of the leadership principle implied the unconditional surrender of the country to the will of a leader who had explained for years what he would do with power when he secured it. His people were not to be disappointed. They would get all the wars he had promised, and he would remain faithful to the ideas he had preached until the bitter end.

III AGGRESSION AND APPEASEMENT

Esmonde M. Robertson
THE FIRST CHALLENGE

What was the relationship between Hitler's foreign policy and German military planning? To what degree did military problems determine German foreign policy under Hitler? These are two of the questions examined by Esmonde M. Robertson, formerly a research fellow at the Institut für Zeitgeschichte, and now lecturer in history at the University of Edinburgh. There were occasions when foreign policy had to give way before the military realities. One such case, examined in this excerpt from Robertson's Hitler's Pre-war Policy and Military Plans, 1933–1939 *(1963), was the need for Hitler to secure military sovereignty in Germany in order finally to achieve his foreign-policy goals.*

Apart from the Corridor and Austria, France had two further possible pretexts for intervention affecting Western no less than Eastern and Southern Europe: German violations of the Treaties of Locarno and Versailles. According to the Treaty of Locarno of 1 December 1925 Britain and Italy guaranteed both sides of the frontiers between Germany and France, and Germany and Belgium, together with the observance by Germany of Articles 42 and 43 of the Treaty of Versailles, proscribing the mobilization of troops and the construction of fortifications on the left bank of the Rhine and 50 kilometers on the right bank. In the event of a "flagrant" breach of the Treaty, Britain and Italy were bound to render France or Belgium immediate aid; a "qualified" breach would bring the cumbrous machinery of the League into operation. Hitler was determined that France would not catch him out over Locarno, and it will be seen later how until 1936 Germany adhered to her obligations in the Rhineland which she had contracted voluntarily.

In the German Foreign Ministry's view a move against Germany under Part V of the Treaty of Versailles was more probable than under Locarno. It applied to the whole Reich, not just to the West, and would be welcome, not merely to Belgium, but to Poland and Czechoslovakia. Part V prohibited the possession by Germany of heavy artillery, tanks, submarines, ships of over 11,000 tons and all

From *Hitler's Pre-war Policy and Military Plans, 1933–1939* (London, 1963), pp. 17–24. Reprinted with the permission of the publishers, Longman Group Limited and the Citadel Press, Inc. Footnotes omitted.

military aircraft. The German army (*Reichswehr*) was not to exceed 100,000 men, including 4,000 officers. Under Article 213 a commission of investigation could operate on German soil if Treaty infringements were suspected. Until the summer of 1934 German rearmament did not seriously exceed these limits, and it could only have had serious consequences if Hitler refused defiantly to recognize those future limits, proposed by the British and Italians, but not necessarily by the French.

On 16 March Ramsay MacDonald submitted a draft convention to the Disarmament Conference, according to which all European armies were to be transformed into militias of short-term service. Five years after the proposed convention came into force, French effectives, stationed in Europe, were to be reduced to 200,000 men, and at the end of the same period the number of German effectives raised to this figure. The truce in building capital ships, binding on the signatories of the London Treaty of 1930 until the end of 1936, was to be extended to other states, with the reservation that Italy might lay down one keel not exceeding 26,500 tons as a counter-balance to the French ship, the *Dunquerque*. While the plan envis-aged the reduction of military aircraft belonging to all states, Germany was not conceded the right to possess them.

Needless to say German military experts—who in any case were never enthusiastic about a militia—were reluctant to accept it, and the German Naval High Command were particularly outspoken. On 24 March Admiral Raeder informed Blomberg that the construction of the *Dunquerque,* which in speed and armament was greatly su-perior to the existing 10,000-ton German pocket battleships, "has fundamentally changed our strategic and tactical position." In reply Blomberg stated that in the course of negotiations at Geneva Ger-many could not possibly demand the right to construct vessels of 25,000 tons. He feared that if Germany pressed her claims for a more powerful fleet, it would be less easy to gain British support against France for recognition of increased land forces. In a later interview with Raeder, Blomberg declared that the German army of 200,000 men, as envisaged by the MacDonald Plan, was insufficient and that Germany could not dispense with submarines or military aircraft.

Early in May after much discussion on the MacDonald Plan, Hitler and his Cabinet had to decide whether to accept it as it then stood. At a Cabinet meeting of the 12th, Neurath, who had been kept informed on the progress of negotiations by the German delegate to the Conference, Nadolny, spoke against its acceptance but was apprehensive because of Germany's isolation. Even Italy, he claimed, was no longer backing Germany. Hitler was decidedly in favor of rejecting the plan. "Unless," he declared, "we were accorded heavy weapons any departure from the system of the *Reichswehr* was unthinkable. . . ." The threat of sanctions, in the event of Germany's leaving the Conference table, had to be faced courageously and the fact made known that their application would be regarded by Germany as tantamount to the tearing up of the peace treaties. A declaration would be issued indicating that Germany's further remaining in the League of Nations had been made "exceedingly doubtful by the actions of our opponents." In the discussion which followed Blomberg and Neurath stressed that a German representative should be present, but not negotiate, at Geneva. Hitler replied that he would only make his proposed declaration after consulting with Schacht, who was attending the preliminary meeting of the World Economic Conference in the USA and who was most certainly in favor of accepting the Plan. Hitler's advisors however were not of one mind: whereas Blomberg insisted on nonacceptance of the British plan, Nadolny was emphatically of the opinion that Germany had no alternative but to accept it.

The next day President Roosevelt appealed to the participants of the Conference to exclude offensive weapons from their armament, and Hitler was requested by Neurath to quote passages from this speech. In these changed circumstances Hitler duly made a public declaration on the 17th. But far from carrying out the bombastic threats of the 12th, the world listened to his famous "peace speech" (*Friedensrede*). In it he described the British plan as a "possible solution" provided it did not entail the destruction of Germany's existing defense forces. Germany, he said, agreed to the transitional period of five years and was prepared to renounce offensive weapons, provided the heavily armed Powers destroyed theirs within a specified period. Yet at the end Hitler made a carefully veiled warning. If violence were done to Germany by means of a "simple majority vote" she would, with a "heavy heart," have to draw the conclusion that her continued membership of the League of Nations was incompatible with her "national honor." Two days later Hitler instructed Nadolny to declare Germany's acceptance, despite the sacrifices involved, of the MacDonald Plan as the basis for a Disarmament Convention.

Before negotiations were resumed later in the summer Hitler had expressed himself equally willing to discuss a security plan, adumbrated by Mussolini in October the previous year. Mussolini's primary aim was to divert German ambitions from an *Anschluss* and from the annexation of the South Tyrol to the northeast of Europe. On 14 March 1933 his plans had matured; he proposed that Italy, France, Great Britain and Germany should work for the preservation of peace in the spirit of the Kellogg Pact and consider revision of the peace treaties in accordance with article 19 of the Covenant of the League. He also urged that the *equality of status,* theoretically conceded to Germany should, if the Disarmament Conference were to lead to only partial results, have effective application. Hitler, who was already quarreling with Dollfuss and who disliked any invocation of the League, told his leading Ministers on 23 May that Germany would only negotiate on Mussolini's plan if the Disarmament Conference broke down. But after much discussion, sometimes of a heated kind, Hitler accepted an amended version of the Pact which was initialed in an emasculated form on 7 June, and signed on 17 July. Since the Pact was soon to prove less acceptable to France and her allies than to Germany it was never ratified and a chance of tying Hitler down was missed.

Hitler, in expressing himself willing to accept both Italian and British mediation, however reluctantly, had accomplished two master strokes in diplomacy, and before considering the tactics he was to employ later at the Disarmament Conference it is necessary to examine the MacDonald Plan in relation to his intended program for future German rearmament. The technical difficulties of rearmament were very great, almost commensurate with the legal difficulties: the entire German economy had to be put on a firm footing. According to General Thomas, two Five Year Plans were adopted in 1928, the first to be completed by 1933 with the aim of supplying 16 divisions for defense against Poland, the second by 1937–1938 for 21 divisions and 300,000 men, a figure which on mobilization could be trebled and which was considered just adequate for defense against France. Although, owing to shortages of raw materials, the first program was never put into operation; a start was made after 7 April 1933 with the second; initial progress was, however, slower than expected, and a mere 10,000 to 20,000 additional men were recruited. The MacDonald Plan could therefore early in May be reviewed in a more favorable light. It would have allowed Germany 200,000 effectives, two-thirds of the number required in five years, and although Blomberg had already complained that this figure was too low his objections were not overriding: with a little hard bargaining and treaty evasion Germany might still find the extra 100,000 men. Renunciation of offensive weapons, above all of tanks and planes for tactical purposes, posed a more serious obstacle, but even these weapons could not yet be produced on a scale sufficient to make the plan completely unacceptable. Finally, since no direct supervision of the German military establishment was envisaged, the plan had at least one positive merit.

German acceptance of the MacDonald Plan was not, however, the main issue. The French were soon to express their dissatisfaction with it and seek: first, more stringent terms for a future convention; secondly, action under article 213 of the Treaty against illegal German rearmament. Their success depended on British support. Of the two issues the second constituted the greater danger to Germany, and the generals of the Defense Ministry did all in their power to forestall it. In a minute of 26 April 1933 a subtle distinction was drawn between leakages of evidence on rearmament from hearsay and that which could be proved from documents. But good internal security on the custody of documents was not enough. Despite the *Manchester Guardian* disclosures of 1926, many experiments of secret weapons were still carried out on Soviet soil. What if, in the changed political situation of the autumn of 1933, Russia played foul and handed over to France even some of the incriminatory documentary evidence which she unquestionably possessed?

Germany's position was distinctly unnerving. On 2 September it was learned in the Defense Ministry from what was described as a "reliable" source that France and Britain were sounding Russia on the possibility of divulging military information. This news had to be treated with great circumspection for French and Polish military personages were visiting Russia at that time, and the French Press was actually publishing details of what Germany was alleged to have been producing. On 18 September Schönheinz, the German Military Representative at the Disarmament Conference in Geneva, listed the allegations, and in case he were asked difficult questions inquired whether the facts contained in them were correct. He was told by the

Defense Ministry on 10 October that regrettably many of them were.

The French Government were well informed on the extent of German secret rearmament, and at a joint meeting of Cabinet Ministers in London on 25 September drew their British colleagues' attention to a dossier which they had prepared on the subject. The British, however, when sounded, were not prepared to assume obligations on sanctions, and thus the French were all the more determined on stricter terms than the MacDonald Plan. They proposed dividing a future convention into two periods of four years' duration: in the first, the efficiency of supervision should be tested; in the second, while a measure of rearmament would be permitted to those states with restricted armaments, a start would be made with the disarmament of the more powerful. While Hitler was opposed decidedly to such a radical amendment, he told Neurath on the 30th that he was still ready to negotiate on the MacDonald Plan as it originally stood even if "not all our wishes were fulfilled by it. . . ." It would be wrong, in his opinion, "to ask for more than we were able for technical, financial and political reasons actually to procure in the next few years." Early in October it was learned that the British were giving way to the French, and that the French were revising their original plan, but the precise details were still unknown. After a Cabinet Meeting of the 4th Hitler told Bülow that he and Blomberg were "agreed that we must not run the risk of negotiating at all on a new draft that was in the last analysis unacceptable to us. . . . It was time therefore, in order to prevent such a development, to revert to the 'original question' [Blomberg], to demand by ultimatum the disarmament of the others and to declare that we would leave the Conference as well as withdraw from the League of Nations in the event that the others rejected disarmament. . . ." Hitler also suggested delivering a major speech in order to appeal to world opinion, and the German Disarmament Delegation was instructed accordingly. By 12 October it was clearly evident that both the British and American Governments had acceded in all essentials to the French amendment. On the 13th Hitler described its terms somewhat tediously to his Cabinet. Germany, he said, could not arm the reserves which would have accumulated after four years, and there was no guarantee that the heavily armed Powers would start to disarm under the second part of the Convention. "Especially intolerable" were the provisions regarding supervision, "which technically can be carried out only with respect to us. . . ." It was therefore necessary for Germany to leave both the Disarmament Conference and the League. He would accordingly dissolve the Reichstag, order new elections and call upon the German people to "identify themselves through a national plebiscite with the peace policy of the Reich Government." Mussolini was to be the only foreign statesman to be informed in advance. Hitler had already obtained Hindenburg's approval for his decision, and there seems to have been no concerted opposition to it from his fellow ministers. It was confirmed by the Cabinet the next day and duly put into force.

Hitler in this the first of a succession of *faits accomplis* had won for his country greater freedom of action. German statesmen dreaded nothing more than those occasions when the British and French were closeted together in negotiations on German affairs behind their back, and events were to prove that they could achieve far more in separate negotiations with other Powers than when Geneva was a general clearing house for diplomatic business.

Hitler's success at home was no less notable. However much he detested and vilified the Weimar statesmen, he now made it clear, in his appeals to the German electorate, that his policy was merely the logical fulfillment of theirs. But he possessed the confidence which they lacked. On 24 October 1931 the leaders of the *Reichswehr* trembled at the possibility of winning no concession at the conference: they were convinced that "90 percent of the German people" would feel failure to be a "hard blow." Yet Hitler, having returned completely emptyhanded, won almost universal acclamation. In the plebiscite of 12 November, 95.1 percent of the electorate concurred in his decision. He was now indisputably master of his own house, and by winning mass enthusiasm had taken the first step towards the restoration of military sovereignty.

Jean-Baptiste Duroselle

FRANCE AND THE RHINELAND

The remilitarization of the Rhineland destroyed the last restriction on Germany left by the Treaty of Versailles. It was a severe injury to French security because the German army had regained a jumping-off place for an invasion of France. In this essay, Jean-Baptiste Duroselle, director of the Centre d'Etude des Relations Internationales and professor of contemporary history at the Sorbonne, examines the remilitarization of the Rhineland from the French point of view, utilizing the documents from the files of the Ministère des Affaires Étrangères. In retrospect, some historians have claimed that this was the moment when Hitler should have been challenged.

. . . We learned at the Nuremberg trials that on May 2, 1935 Hitler had given orders for the preparation of plans for the reoccupation of the Rhineland "by lightning surprise." We also know that on February 27, 1936, the Franco-Soviet Pact was ratified in the French Chamber of Deputies by 353 votes to 164, that on March 1 Hitler decided to act, and that the German Minister of War, General von Blomberg, gave the necessary orders on March 2. . . .

The Level of Government Policy

There are three problems to be considered: The extent of advance information; the extent of preparations for a response to possible German action; the decisions taken.

Information. In his speech of May 21, 1935, Hitler confined himself to denouncing the Franco-Soviet Pact as a violation of Locarno and in no way implied that Germany would take advantage of it to remilitarize the Rhineland. The German press subsequently followed this line. The French ambassador in Berlin, André François-Poncet, tells us that after an interview with Hitler on November 21, 1935 he warned the French government of the possibility of remilitarization. We have no documents to confirm this statement and we can begin our analysis only with January 1, 1936. The documents reveal that,

From "France and the Crisis of March 1936," translated by Nancy L. Roelker, in French Society and Culture since the Old Regime, edited by Evelyn M. Acomb and Marvin L. Brown, Jr. Copyright © 1966 by Holt, Rinehart and Winston, Publishers. Reprinted by permission of Holt, Rinehart and Winston, Publishers.

in fact, François-Poncet hesitated greatly in his evaluation of the situation. On January 1, for instance, he said that Hitler had reiterated "what he had already told me often, namely that he did not intend to challenge the agreements of 1925." In the long report on the general situation and outlook for the future that François-Poncet drew up on January 2, only two lines (out of 241) allude to the Locarno Pact. In the following weeks François-Poncet returned to this theme from time to time, but in general he did not seem to expect immediate action. . . .

When Hitler received François-Poncet on March 2, he did not fail to protest the ratification, but he reassured the French ambassador by proposing negotiations. Moreover, François-Poncet on the morning of March 6, one day before the catastrophic act, cites an informant who "does not believe that Hitler is preparing to reoccupy the zone at a date in the very near future." The ambassador repeated this opinion in a telegram sent at 9:25 p.m.

If the principal informant of the French government remained so vague and was anxious to believe that a forceful coup was improbable, this was not the case with the French consuls in Cologne, (Jean Dobler) and Düsseldorf (Noël Henry), the French ambassador in Berne, Count de Clauzel, or the French military attaché in Germany. On the other hand, French Ambassador Laroche wrote from Brussels on March 2, "information in the hands of the Belgian government does not indicate that we should consider that the German government plans a threatening move for the moment." A note from the General Staff of the army, dated March 7—the day of the occupation—furnishes three bulletins, two from the French Intelligence announcing the reoccupation for March 12 or 15 and for April 1, respectively, and one issued by the press announcing it for March 7. (Parenthetically, this is no credit to the French Intelligence.)

In any case, whatever the hesitations and uncertainties, the French government could not avoid foreseeing the *possibility* of German reoccupation of the Rhineland in the near future. Moreover, Foreign Minister Flandin, who succeeded Laval on January 24, was perfectly conscious of the fact, as was the Deputy Director for Political Affairs at the Quai d'Orsay, René Massigli, to whose role we shall later return. Flandin says so in his memoirs. The *Documents diplomatiques français* confirm his allegations. . . .

This leads us to pose a second problem. If the risk was clear, well-known, even studied, what preparations had the French government made to deal with it?

Preparations.   The account of the weeks preceding March 7 in the diplomatic and military documents is extremely disillusioning. It reveals that, while the Quai d'Orsay was aware of the problem, General Maurin, Minister of War, and the high military authorities generally, had not made a single preparation worthy of the name and obstinately refused to envisage a response to possible German action. The interim government of Albert Sarraut, which was in power between Laval's Rightest cabinet (resigned January 22) and the beginning of the Popular Front (June 1936), either did not know of or was unwilling to be concerned with the problem.

As early as January 21, Laval had written to the then Minister of War, Jean Fabry, to inform him of the threat of German action, but he did not ask anything about what French forces could do to oppose it. The Minister of War and, especially, the General Staff were blindly hostile to the ratification of the Franco-Soviet Pact. A note of January 27, found in the war archives shows that they foresaw the results of ratification would be: (1) to furnish Hitler "a pretext to abandon the commitments of Locarno"; (2) to drive Germany and Poland together—"the military alliance with Poland seems incompatible with the Russian alliance. We must choose"; and (3) to push Belgium into a policy of neutrality.

In his correspondence with Flandin, General Maurin seems to have done everything possible to avoid answering precise questions. On January 29 he confined himself to a declaration that the demilitarization of the Rhineland was imposed by the treaties. This was news to nobody. . . . On February 6 a note to the Ministry of War made explicit that in case of the entry of German troops into the demilitarized zone, the French government

> *even while apprising the Council of the League of Nations, is free to act by military means if such measures appear necessary. Each of the signatory powers is indeed obliged to intervene, without waiting for the decision of the League council, if it considers that an act of unprovoked aggression has occurred and that immediate action is necessary. Nothing in the Treaty obliges the French government to subordinate its own moves to an exchange of views with London or Rome.*

Nevertheless, of course it must make sure "in advance, that the nature of the decision is understood, at least in London."

Armed with this precise plan, to which he adhered without reservations, Flandin attended a meeting on February 7 at the Ministry of War. Present were General Maurin, François Piétri, Minister of the Navy, and Marcel Déat, Minister of Air, attended respectively by General Gamelin, Admiral Durand-Viel, and Generals Pujo and Picard. It should be noted that the High Military Commission (created in June 1935 and composed of approximately the same people) had met on January 18 and that the then Minister of War, Fabry, had proposed at the close of the meeting that the High Commission study the agenda for its next meeting. The February 7 meeting was the equivalent of one of the High Military Commission.

After long discussion of relatively minor matters, Flandin put the question: "It is time," he said, "to define in a very clear manner the probable means of remilitarization, and, on the other hand, what countermeasures we can assume we should take." According to minutes in the archives of the Navy, the military ministers merely changed the subject—an elegant way of refusing to answer without saying so.

In his memoirs Flandin is more precise.

> *My statement was received with much reticence by the Ministers of National Defense and their colleagues. I had asked a specific question . . . the Minister of War declared, to my great surprise, that the mission of the French army was conceived entirely in terms of the defensive, that it had nothing in preparation and was still less ready for use in a military intervention.*

General Gamelin said that it was up to the French government to decide.

> *I then asked, in anticipation that the Government might decide on armed resistance, that measures of implementation be prepared in advance and that a new meeting of the High Military Commission be planned to this end.*

Flandin says that he transmitted his wishes to the next meeting of the Cabinet. He was about to go to Geneva for a meeting of the Council of the League of Nations, where he would meet British Foreign Secretary Eden, to whom he wished to submit a precise plan. The Cabinet merely authorized him to declare "that the French Government would put its military forces (including Navy and Air) at the disposition of the League of Nations in order to oppose by force a violation of the Treaties." This vague decision seemed to rule out unilateral action by France. In any case, a meeting of the High Military Commission would be held "in order to translate the decision taken by the Government into acts."

On February 12 General Maurin wrote to Flandin, describing the measures he envisaged. They were ridiculous. "The sudden reoccupation of all or part of the demilitarized zone would necessarily involve certain precautionary measures on our part." Precautions, because reoccupation might be followed by a German attack. No direct response to reoccupation itself was planned. On the contrary, General Maurin seemed so afraid of attack that he envisaged "the reduction to a minimum of the number of measures actually planned in the case of the threat of a sudden attack, so as to avoid any valid pretext for a clash." Hence, no recall of available troops or reservists.

Flandin replied to this letter on February 14. "The operations you list," he said, "are incomplete, and you confine yourself to mere allusions to the most important measures, which are to be reserved for government decision, pending further notice." "I agree with you," he added, "on the necessity of this decision. But what measures are we talking about? The government should decide the principle behind these measures, their implementation being reserved for further deliberation."

What was Maurin's answer, in a letter dated February 17? He seemed to pretend not to understand. First, his general attitude was wholly negative. "It would seem that to use our right to occupy the demilitarized zone runs the risk of being contrary to French interests. . . . We risk appearing as the aggressor and finding ourselves left to face Germany alone." This last phrase is pregnant with meaning and we shall return to it. Then Maurin replied obliquely to the question. Flandin had asked him to outline precise measures of eventual *response,* but he replied in the abstract with a list of *precautionary* measures: warning, stronger warning, security, reliance on protection forces. Nothing is said of possible intervention.

Furthermore, the military chiefs met without the ministers on February 19 and the decisive word was pronounced by Gamelin. He considered that "it is not proper to envisage that France alone could occupy the demilitarized zone, but precautionary measures would be called for." He then said "everything must be done to maintain the causes of the Treaty of Versailles relative to the demilitarized zone, at least until such time as the influence of the depletion of our military reserves ceases to make itself felt, that is, until about 1940 or 1942." Do anything, that is, except the most essential thing. . . .

Did Flandin continue the correspondence with Maurin? No trace has been found. Déat, Minister of Air, wrote to Piétri, Minister of the Navy, on March 2 to inform him of measures that should be taken, but again they were only precautionary ones.

It is abundantly clear that, through blindness or unwillingness, the leaders in charge of national defense had not, before March 7, planned a single measure or prepared a single move toward a response in terms of force by France to an imminent German move using force. Even the idea of general mobilization, which from March 7 on was to be used as a bugbear, was never mentioned before that date. Although it was fairly well warned, the French government was absolutely unprepared for action.

Hence, finally, the decision not to act.

The Lack of Decision. First, let us outline, as far as possible, the timetable of official steps taken by the French government between March 7 and March 11.

On March 7, François-Poncet, who learned of the German decision at ten-thirty in the morning, protested solemnly while awaiting "the evaluation and decision of the government of the Republic." He sent another telegram at three o'clock in the afternoon concluding, "personally, it seems to me difficult for the French government to accept the *fait accompli* deliberately created by the German government without a vigorous reaction." But what could this reaction have been?

On the same day there was no meeting of the whole Cabinet in Paris but there were two meetings attended by some members of the Cabinet. One, late in the morning, was attended by Premier Sarraut, Foreign Minister Flandin, Minister for League of Nations Affairs, Paul-Boncour, Minister for Colonies, Georges Mandel, and generals Gamelin and Georges. Paul-Boncour and Mandel declared themselves resolutely in favor of decisive measures. But, wrote General Gamelin, "we stayed in the realm of generalities." Paul-Boncour said to him, "I'd like to see you in Mayence as soon as possible." Gamelin replied, "That is another matter. I ask nothing better, but I must have the means." Sarraut asked Gamelin if France could act alone.

Gamelin replied that at first "we would have the advantage," but that a long war would bring out German superiority. . . .

At three o'clock in General Maurin's office, generals Gamelin, Georges, and Colson, together with those in charge of equipment, decided on the disposition of matériel.

At five o'clock, Gamelin saw the Secretary-General of the Quai d'Orsay, Alexis Léger, who "is still of the opinion that we should react and act energetically. The British and the Belgians will be inclined to yield, but they will be obliged to follow us."

At six o'clock there was another meeting in Flandin's office, with Déat, Piétri, and their staff leaders, Pujo and Durand-Viel, in addition to those who had been present at the morning meeting. "Renewed theoretical discussion, but we did not seem to be planning firm solutions, at least not immediately." The only decision taken was to move two divisions from the Rhône Valley toward the Maginot Line by truck and railroad.

The next morning, Sunday, March 8, the Cabinet met. It is very difficult to know exactly what was said, because in the first-hand accounts there is great confusion between the Cabinet meeting of March 8 and that of March 9. We know for certain that Flandin spoke and that it was decided (1) to send a message to the Secretary-General of the League of Nations and (2) to call a meeting of the signatories of the Locarno Pact—excluding Germany—in Paris the next day. When Foreign Secretary Eden let it be known that he had to make a statement of general policy in the House of Commons, however, the meeting was postponed to Tuesday, March 10.

What is also certain is that at the Cabinet meeting of March 8 the government took no decision to act at once. Nevertheless, the atmosphere seemed to favor firmness, which permitted Premier Sarraut to make his famous radio speech that night, in which he declared that France would not negotiate under pressure. Notably, he said, "we are not disposed to leave Strasbourg exposed to German guns." It is known that this speech had been drawn up at the Quai d'Orsay. Massigli formulated the phrase. He had underlined it. He and Flandin had pointed out its implications to the Premier. The fact that Sarraut agreed to read it seemed to indicate that he expected to galvanize public opinion and that the Cabinet had not yet debated the heart of the problem: Was France going to intervene alone and at once?

There is therefore reason to believe that the Cabinet meeting of

Monday, March 9 was of capital importance. . . . The first-hand accounts of the debate (those of Flandin, Paul-Boncour, Sarraut, and Maurin) are contradictory.

According to Flandin and Paul-Boncour, after Flandin had asked what military measures were planned,

> *the Minister of War, then indicated, to my profound stupification, that all that had been planned was to place in position the security troops of the Maginot Line and to move two divisions stationed in the valley of the Rhône toward the eastern frontier. And he added that in order to intervene with military force in the Rhineland, the General Staff demanded general mobilization. General mobilization, within six weeks of election would be a crazy move!*

Paul-Boncour, Minister in charge of League of Nations Affairs, also expressed surprise. According to his account, Mandel, Flandin, and he himself

> *declared ourselves very clearly in favor of military action; two others present, messieurs Guernut and Stern, agreed. The rest showed by their statements, their reservations, or their silence either that they were opposed or that they felt it had serious disadvantages.*

Flandin thought that Premier Sarraut was also in favor of immediate military action.

Then the debate "continued, conscientious, but painful and without enthusiasm." And, reports Paul-Boncour, Flandin then concluded, "I see, Monsieur le Président, that one must not press the point." Sarraut himself thought Paul-Boncour was wrong in saying ten years later that the decisive opportunity had been lost through weakness.

The interpretation of General Maurin was more significant. . . . On two points he contradicted Flandin and Sarraut: He said (1) that no voice was raised in favor of immediate war and in any case not that of Mandel; and (2) on the contrary, someone said, "nobody here wants war" and nobody else protested.

Maurin thus suggests that Paul-Boncour and Flandin used hindsight to endow themselves with the gift of prophecy. Nevertheless he notes that after he had mentioned the inclusion of protection forces in his plan, Sarraut asked, "And what then?" And then he replied, "that depends on what the government wants to do." Paul-Boncour asked about the recall of available troops and Maurin replied, "But what do you want us to do with them?" He was convinced that if they were called up simply as a threat, Hitler would hold to his position.

Maurin also says that he mentioned a limited operation in the Saar region. But what then?

> *Nothing would be gained unless we forced Germany to repudiate Hitler . . . therefore it would mean war and unless we are to strike out senselessly a general mobilization would have to be planned. This is what led me to discuss a general mobilization in the Council of Ministers, but I never said that it ought to be immediately ordered.*

One point remains clear despite these disagreements: In Maurin's words, "at this meeting of the Council of Ministers, in the end we decided nothing."

Two days had already been lost. On Monday March 9 the Germans, uncertain the day before, began to be confident. François-Poncet reports that between nine in the morning and two in the afternoon ruling circles in Berlin were anxious because of "the energetic and definite attitude of the French government." But then they quickly realized that the French government was neither energetic nor definite. On March 11, François-Poncet was able to write, "As of today the great majority of Germans no longer expect a strong reaction from France and her allies."

Nevertheless one last inclination to military action showed itself on March 10 and 11. On March 10 at 9:00 p.m., a meeting was held in the private rooms of Premier Sarraut, attended by the three ministers of defense and their chiefs of staff. In an atmosphere of free discussion the possibility of using the left bank of the Saar for bargaining purposes was taken up. In the files of the General Staff there was a plan drawn up by Colonel Vaulgrenant, designed to replace Plan D, Part Four, of October 22, 1932, dealing with the reoccupation of the Saar. This plan, dating from the period when the German army had not been reconstructed, was to reoccupy the entire Saar with three divisions of infantry, one of cavalry and one brigade of Senegalese. On the evening of March 10, 1936, only the left bank of the Saar—between Saarbrücken and Merzig—was in question. The force envisaged was ten divisions of infantry, one of cavalry, and the special armaments and services of an Army Corps, that is, one-third of the available defensive forces.

During the discussion, according to the account of Gamelin himself, the military men showed that they did not favor such an operation. They did not ask for the immediate calling-up of three classes of reserves. "If Germany yields, everything will be easy." But if Germany resisted, it would mean war, and a general mobilization was called for. "With Germany mobilizing its superior resources in manpower and industry, France would need allies." Maurin supported Gamelin. Piétri and Déat couldn't imagine such an operation without the support of the League of Nations—this was tantamount to burying it.

Indeed, the note of March 11, formulated by Gamelin and signed by Maurin, which Sarraut received in the late morning, constituted a long list of difficulties to be overcome and conditions to be met before action could be taken. Moreover, it specified that the operation "could not be launched until a week after the decision was taken." It was to be implemented within the framework of the League of Nations, with 1.2 million men to be mobilized and a general mobilization anticipated.

The High Military Commission, meeting at three in the afternoon of this same day, hardly touched upon these questions.

It may be said that on this day, March 11, the die was cast. France had not taken independent action, a right given her by Article 4 of the Locarno Treaty, and there was no chance of obtaining anything more than verbal support from Great Britain and Italy, the powers associated with her in the treaty. The British government—despite Eden's reluctance—had already decided to follow an appeasement policy. They thought it possible to sign further pacts with Hitler along the lines of the Naval Accord of June 1935. The German aim to revise the treaties in order to correct injustices therein seemed to them to have some merit. Of course, they disapproved the methods Hitler used—force and the unilateral repudiation of treaties—but they thought Hitler would become more tractable once his object had been obtained. The idea that they were rewarding aggression did not occur to them any more than it did to Sir Samuel Hoare and Pierre Laval when they cooperated in the partition of Ethiopia in December 1935. Moreover, Great Britain and Italy were much more concerned with the Ethiopian problem than with the Rhineland. To Mussolini, even though he had not yet begun to ally himself with Hitler's Germany, the mere idea of intervention seemed impractical so long as the bulk of his forces were fighting in East Africa.

This does not alter the fact that for three or four days France had a critical responsibility and that she was unwilling to carry it out. . . .

The new fact brought out by the *Documents diplomatiques français* is the extent of the responsibility of the military chiefs, especially Maurin and Gamelin. Of course they did what they believed to be their duty. What is noteworthy is that they thought the German army was already stronger than the French army, at least for purposes of a long war. They therefore wanted to avoid action by France alone at all costs and they did not realize that if she *did* act, France's allies would be obliged to follow suit.

Finally, the French military chiefs were victims of the currently dominant military strategy, developed under the influence of the principal leaders of the 1918 victory, especially Marshal Pétain and General Weygand. As early as 1921, Pétain had said, "The defensive is an infinitely superior position to the offensive, because action kills." The French army, trusting in the Maginot Line, was unwilling to venture beyond it. The General Staff condemned the new theory of action based on tanks, advocated by General Étienne in 1922 and General Doumenc in 1928, which had been developed in two books, Guderian's *Achtung Panzer,* published in 1931 and Charles de Gaulle's *Vers l'armée de métier,* published in 1934 and much discussed in the press. We are forced to agree with Charles Serre, that for the High Command, "inaction had become the supreme wisdom."

In addition, at the time, almost all Frenchmen also preferred a course of nonaction.

Keith Eubank

APPEASEMENT AND APPEASERS

Those who advocated the policy of appeasement have been assigned much of the responsibility for the outbreak of war in 1939. But appeasement as a policy did not originate simply in response to Hitler's aggressions, argues Keith Eubank in this selection excerpted from his The Origins of World War II. *Appeasement was then regarded as sensible and in agreement with public opinion.*

Since 1945, the word "appeasement" has become a derogatory term to be hurled at any statesman willing to negotiate with an opponent. However, at one time, it was a term applied to a policy that was not only publicly approved, but also praised. While appeasement has most often been associated with Neville Chamberlain, he did not actually originate the policy, but inherited it from his predecessors. It was not a policy created suddenly in the 1930s to buy off Hitler and Mussolini. It had originated in the minds of Englishmen who believed that World War I need never have come and that the outbreak of the war was entirely accidental. These Englishmen believed that both Britain and Germany shared responsibility for the outbreak of the war—an idea nurtured by revisionist historians who argued that the Treaty of Versailles was unjust and should be revised.

But appeasement also stemmed from a lack of faith in the British cause in World War I and from a firm resolve to prevent Europe from accidentally becoming entangled in another world war. Englishmen who looked with favor on the German educational system, on German industrial development, and on German social legislation became appeasement-minded. There was no one man or group of men who can be considered responsible for appeasement. Rather, a combination of forces—the horrors of the trenches, the disillusionment over the Treaty of Versailles, and the reluctance to burden Germany with total responsibility for the war—generated and fostered the policy.

Their guilt feelings over the Treaty of Versailles inclined the appeasers to take a soft line whenever Germany complained about the

From *The Origins of World War II* (New York, 1969), pp. 71–80. Reprinted by permission of the publisher, Thomas Y. Crowell, New York. Footnote omitted.

severity of the treaty restrictions. In the early 1920s, French insistence on complete fulfillment of the Versailles treaty alarmed the appeasers who feared that France would force Germany to take up arms again. Consequently, they argued that war could be prevented only by nonfulfillment of the treaty terms.

British opposition to the French occupation of the Ruhr in 1923–1924 had the effect of preventing the enforcement of the Treaty of Versailles. At the same time, it rescued Germany from being torn apart by the separatist movements that had begun to develop. When French troops withdrew from the Rhineland, the appeasers, as well as the Germans, had won a great victory; if France could not enforce the treaty, then it would never be enforced, and without enforcement, revision of the treaty—the appeasers' goal—would be easier.

J. Ramsey MacDonald, who became Prime Minister in 1924, helped clear up the difficulty that resulted from the Ruhr occupation by pushing the Dawes Plan through to completion. Under his leadership, a conference in London in the summer of 1924 brought Frenchmen and Germans together to consider the reparations problem. The nations who met at the London Conference agreed to end the Ruhr occupation and to assist German recovery with a loan—but they refused to help France and Belgium, both of whom had suffered heavier damage than had Germany. With these concessions granted, Germany agreed to pay the reparations at a reduced rate. Because Britain and its allies treated the former enemy as an equal, appeasement became more firmly established.

Stanley Baldwin, who in 1924 succeeded MacDonald as Prime Minister, was well-acquainted with the habits of the British electorate, but he paid as little attention as possible to foreign affairs, preferring to postpone unpopular decisions on the chance that they would solve themselves. Truly ignorant of foreign affairs and socially uneasy with foreigners, he could neither comprehend nor deal with the impending conflict in Europe, and so resolved on peace at any price. He was well aware of the German breaches in the Treaty of Versailles, but he unhesitatingly accepted the Locarno Pact. It did seem at the time that the final solution to Europe's postwar problems had been reached at Locarno. Many of the appeasers envisioned the treaty as creating a new spirit that would bring peace to Europe. Because Germany had freely participated in a conference and had willingly signed an agreement, the appeasers were convinced that they had replaced the ineffective Treaty of Versailles with an agreement that could be maintained.

When Hitler came to power, the arguments in favor of appeasement increased. Whatever faults the new Germany might possess, the appeasers believed that it could not have been as great a threat as the threat of Communist Russia. And, as long as the new Germany was not Communist, it could serve as a barrier to Russia. They believed that German rearmament should be accepted and changes must be made in the Treaty of Versailles.

By 1937, when Neville Chamberlain became Prime Minister, appeasement had become entrenched as British foreign policy. He was not a naive man as many would want to paint him, but actually a seasoned politician. Son of the famous Joseph Chamberlain, Neville had trained for a career in business. He understood contracts, accounts, and production schedules better than the intricacies of European diplomacy. He was conscientious but lacking in imagination; and his brusque and obstinate manner did not gain him popularity. Convinced that the techniques of business would succeed in international diplomacy, Chamberlain approached Hitler and Mussolini as he would a fellow businessman, offering them deals that would be mutually advantageous.

Distrustful of career men in the Foreign Office, he relied too much on his narrow background and on men whose grasp of European affairs was minimal. Men such as Hoare, Simon, Halifax, and Wilson were poor choices for advisors. Both Hoare and Simon had been failures at formulating foreign policy, and Halifax's ignorance of European affairs had made him ill-prepared to be Foreign Secretary. The last member of the quartet, Sir Horace Wilson, was a very capable civil servant, an expert in labor disputes with the title of "Chief Industrial Adviser to the Government," but in foreign affairs he was strictly an amateur. Given an office in No. 10 Downing Street, he acted unofficially for Chamberlain, often presenting his views in behind-the-scenes meetings with German officials.

Chamberlain would not listen to Eden, the Foreign Secretary he had inherited from the Baldwin cabinet. The Prime Minister believed that diplomats wasted time in red tape, and that he must handle his own foreign policy in order to avoid this problem. When he took office, he had resolved to end the policy of drift and inaction that had typified the Baldwin administration; and to do this, he believed he had to act quickly and independently on policy matters. It was to be expected that he would clash with Eden, who preferred more traditional ways of dealing with the Fascist powers.

The difficulties between Chamberlain and Eden came into the open over a proposal made by Franklin Roosevelt that the diplomatic corps in Washington meet to consider an agreement on the basic principles of international conduct. This agreement would include decisions on the reduction of armaments, methods of promoting economic security, and measures for protecting neutrals in wartime. Chamberlain objected strenuously to this plan; he was certain that it would not only fail but also ruin all his efforts at appeasement. Without informing Eden of his move, Chamberlain requested Roosevelt to postpone putting his plan into effect. Eden, who thought he saw excellent possibilities in the Roosevelt proposal, had no success in convincing Chamberlain to change his mind. Although he has generally been condemned for rejecting the President's impractical scheme, Chamberlain, because of Roosevelt's previous unwillingness to commit the United States to any international responsibility, had some justification in believing the efforts would come to naught. The only important result of Roosevelt's proposal was to strain the relations between Chamberlain and Eden to the breaking point.

The breaking point came almost immediately—on the question of Ethiopia. In hopes of separating Mussolini from Hitler, Chamberlain wanted immediate discussions over recognition of the Italian conquest of Ethiopia. Eden preferred to negotiate on a *quid pro quo* basis: Mussolini could withdraw his troops from Spain, and then Britain would recognize the conquest of Ethiopia. When Chamberlain rejected Eden's recommendation entirely, the Foreign Secretary resigned.

Edward, third Viscount Halifax, who followed Eden as Foreign Secretary, was much more to Chamberlain's liking. A country gentleman, a former Viceroy of India, and a High-Church Anglican with deep spiritual convictions, Halifax was completely unsuspecting when confronted with men such as Hitler and Mussolini. He had never bothered to read *Mein Kampf,* and he believed that the men who had warned against Hitler were exaggerating. But this was the man whom Chamberlain wanted as Foreign Secretary—a faithful servant of the King who would not object to whatever brand of appeasement Chamberlain wanted to practice.

Before he took office, and despite the protests of Eden, Halifax was sent on his first errand for Chamberlain. In November 1937, Halifax accepted an invitation from Hermann Goering to attend the Sporting Exhibition in Berlin. On November 17, the English country gentleman met with Hitler at Berchtesgaden; but he almost wrecked the meeting at the outset by mistaking Hitler for a footman, stopping short of handing the dictator his hat. Halifax was in agreement with Hitler on the inequity of the Treaty of Versailles, but he wanted the potentially dangerous questions arising from the treaty—Danzig, Austria, Czechoslovakia—handled in a peaceful way. He promised that the British government would not "block reasonable settlements . . . reached with the free assent and goodwill of those primarily concerned." This was just short of an invitation for Hitler to do whatever he wanted in Central Europe. Hitler had already—in the Reichschancellery meeting—announced plans for expansion; but now, thanks to Halifax (and Chamberlain), he had the means for taking the territory he wanted. If he could make his moves appear to be in accordance with the wishes of the people in the territories occupied, he would have British consent.

The policy that resulted in this invitation to Hitler had developed considerably since Versailles. In retrospect, appeasement had so managed to root itself into British foreign policy as to make it extremely difficult—if not impossible—for Chamberlain to have taken any other approach. Under Lloyd George, with his attempts to make Wilson lighten the Treaty of Versailles, appeasement became the keystone of British foreign policy. All of Lloyd George's successors followed his example: Andrew Bonar Law denounced the French occupation of the Ruhr in 1923; MacDonald, in his first administration, got the French out of the Ruhr, and in his second administration, preached disarmament of Britain and its allies as a means of satisfying German complaints about military inequities; and Baldwin aided the growth of appeasement by making the Anglo-German Naval Agreement the crowning diplomatic achievement of his third government.

By the time Chamberlain came to office in 1937, appeasement would no longer satisfy Hitler (whom Chamberlain regarded as a German politician with strong feelings about the Versailles treaty and the suffering German people). Nevertheless, Chamberlain prescribed a more vigorous form of appeasement than had his predecessors,

pushing for intensive discussions and, if necessary, face-to-face negotiations between heads of state. Appeasement to Chamberlain did
not mean surrendering to Hitler's demands, however, but it meant
finding ways of satisfying those demands by wise concessions that
would avoid further dangers to peace. Chamberlain honestly believed
that world peace could be guaranteed by economic prosperity, by
ending existing economic difficulties; and he believed that these
troubles could be solved by reducing military expenditures and by
balancing national budgets. Germany, he believed, would become
more peacefully inclined if southeastern Europe were opened to
German economic exploitation, thereby ridding the country of the
need for a massive army and providing the German economy with a
market. This fact has often been minimized in evaluating the years
before the war. For Chamberlain practiced appeasement, not out of
cowardice or fear, but out of a positive belief that appeasement
would open the way to peace for all.

Chamberlain did not deliberately appease Hitler in order to turn
his aggressive activities away from the West and toward the Soviet
Union—Chamberlain was not as cunning as that. True, he distrusted
the Russians, but he believed that another world war would devastate
Europe and leave Communists in control. To Chamberlain as well as
the other appeasers, the greatest evil of all—the evil to be avoided
at all costs—was war. One world war was sufficient to make the appeasers fearful of what the outcome of such a major conflict might
be.

The appeasers did ignore one important fact: a policy of appeasement could end only with Germany restored to its former strength.
Given the German population, industry, educational system, and—
above all—geographical position, appeasement must result in German domination of Central Europe and perhaps in an attempt to
dominate all of the Continent as well. The appeasers' sins were the
sins of all the post-1919 generation, who read Keynes, regretted the
Treaty of Versailles, sorrowed for Germany, and admired Mussolini
for running trains on time. They took too optimistic a view of the
Germans, always conceding the benefit of the doubt in hopes of
bringing peace. Through improved Anglo-German relations, they
sought to avoid direct conflict. Although they would later be reviled
for their actions, the appeasers did perform a vital task: their efforts
for peace proved without a doubt that Hitler could not be trusted
and eventually convinced Britain that war was necessary and just.

The Hossbach Memorandum

A STRATEGY CONFERENCE?

All studies of Hitler's foreign policy at one time or another refer to a conference that Hitler called in the Reich Chancellery on November 5, 1937 because of a quarrel over raw materials among the armed services. Hermann Goering, chief of the Luftwaffe, was taking more than his fair share. Hitler used the conference to comment on some of his ideas about future German policy. Was he considering possible courses of action or was he explaining the strategy he intended to pursue in the future? Three of those present— Neurath, Blomberg, and Fritsch—who voiced criticism of Hitler's ideas, were soon dismissed. The only record of this meeting was composed some days later by Hitler's military adjutant, Colonel Friedrich Hossbach.

MEMORANDUM

Berlin, November 10, 1937.

Minutes of the Conference in the Reich Chancellery, Berlin, November 5, 1937, from 4:15 to 8:30 p.m.

Present: The Führer and Chancellor
Field Marshal von Blomberg, War Minister
Colonel General Baron von Fritsch, Commander in Chief, Army
Admiral Dr. h. c. Raeder, Commander in Chief, Navy
Colonel General Göring, Commander in Chief, *Luftwaffe*
Baron von Neurath, Foreign Minister
Colonel Hossbach

The Führer began by stating that the subject of the present conference was of such importance that its discussion would, in other countries, certainly be a matter for a full Cabinet meeting, but he— the Führer—had rejected the idea of making it a subject of discussion before the wider circle of the Reich Cabinet just because of the importance of the matter. His exposition to follow was the fruit of thorough deliberation and the experiences of his $4\frac{1}{2}$ years of power. He wished to explain to the gentlemen present his basic ideas concerning the opportunities for the development of our position in the

Reprinted from *Documents on German Foreign Policy, 1918–1945*, series D, Vol. I (Washington, 1949), pp. 29–39.

field of foreign affairs and its requirements, and he asked, in the interests of a long-term German policy, that his exposition be regarded, in the event of his death, as his last will and testament.

The Führer then continued:

The aim of German policy was to make secure and to preserve the racial community [*Volksmasse*] and to enlarge it. It was therefore a question of space.

The German racial community comprised over 85 million people and, because of their number and the narrow limits of habitable space in Europe, constituted a tightly packed racial core such as was not to be met in any other country and such as implied the right to a greater living space than in the case of other peoples. If, territorially speaking, there existed no political result corresponding to this German racial core, that was a consequence of centuries of historical development, and in the continuance of these political conditions lay the greatest danger to the preservation of the German race at its present peak. To arrest the decline of Germanism [*Deutschtum*] in Austria and Czechoslovakia was as little possible as to maintain the present level in Germany itself. Instead of increase, sterility was setting in, and in its train disorders of a social character must arise in course of time, since political and ideological ideas remain effective only so long as they furnish the basis for the realization of the essential vital demands of a people. Germany's future was therefore wholly conditional upon the solving of the need for space, and such a solution could be sought, of course, only for a foreseeable period of about one to three generations.

Before turning to the question of solving the need for space, it had to be considered whether a solution holding promise for the future was to be reached by means of autarchy or by means of an increased participation in world economy.

Autarchy

Achievement only possible under strict National Socialist leadership of the State, which is assumed; accepting its achievement as possible, the following could be stated as results:

    A.   In the field of raw materials only limited, not total, autarchy.

        1.   In regard to coal, so far as it could be considered as a source of raw materials, autarchy was possible.

        2.   But even as regards ores, the position was much more

difficult. Iron requirements can be met from home resources and similarly with light metals, but with other raw materials—copper, tin—this was not the case.
3. Synthetic textile requirements can be met from home resources to the limit of timber supplies. A permanent solution impossible.
4. Edible fats—possible.
B. In the field of food the question of autarchy was to be answered by a flat "No."

With the general rise in the standard of living compared with that of 30 to 40 years ago, there has gone hand in hand an increased demand and an increased home consumption even on the part of the producers, the farmers. The fruits of the increased agricultural production had all gone to meet the increased demand, and so did not represent an absolute production increase. A further increase in production by making greater demands on the soil, which already, in consequence of the use of artificial fertilizers, was showing signs of exhaustion, was hardly possible, and it was therefore certain that even with the maximum increase in production, participation in world trade was unavoidable. The not inconsiderable expenditure of foreign exchange to insure food supplies by imports, even when harvests were good, grew to catastrophic proportions with bad harvests. The possibility of a disaster grew in proportion to the increase in population, in which, too, the excess of births of 560,000 annually produced, as a consequence, an even further increase in bread consumption, since a child was a greater bread consumer than an adult.

It was not possible over the long run, in a continent enjoying a practically common standard of living, to meet the food supply difficulties by lowering that standard and by rationalization. Since, with the solving of the unemployment problem, the maximum consumption level had been reached, some minor modifications in our home agricultural production might still, no doubt, be possible, but no fundamental alteration was possible in our basic food position. Thus autarchy was untenable in regard both to food and to the economy as a whole.

Participation in World Economy

To this there were limitations which we were unable to remove. The establishment of Germany's position on a secure and sound foundation was obstructed by market fluctuations, and commercial treaties afforded no guarantee for actual execution. In particular it had to be remembered that since the World War, those very countries which had formerly been food exporters had become industrialized. We were living in an age of economic empires in which the primitive urge to colonization was again manifesting itself; in the cases of Japan and Italy economic motives underlay the urge for expansion, and with Germany, too, economic need would supply the stimulus. For countries outside the great economic empires, opportunities for economic expansion were severely impeded.

The boom in world economy caused by the economic effects of rearmament could never form the basis of a sound economy over a long period, and the latter was obstructed above all also by the economic disturbances resulting from Bolshevism. There was a pronounced military weakness in those states which depended for their existence on foreign trade. As our foreign trade was carried on over the sea routes dominated by Britain, it was more a question of security of transport than one of foreign exchange, which revealed, in time of war, the full weakness of our food situation. The only remedy, and one which might appear to us as visionary, lay in the acquisition of greater living space—a quest which has at all times been the origin of the formation of states and of the migration of peoples. That this quest met with no interest at Geneva or among the satiated nations was understandable. If, then, we accept the security of our food situation as the principal question, the space necessary to insure it can only be sought in Europe, not, as in the liberal-capitalist view, in the exploitation of colonies. It is not a matter of acquiring population but of gaining space for agricultural use. Moreover, areas producing raw materials can be more usefully sought in Europe in immediate proximity to the Reich, than overseas; the solution thus obtained must suffice for one or two generations. Whatever else might prove necessary later must be left to succeeding generations to deal with. The development of great world political constellations progressed but slowly after all, and the German people with its strong racial core would find the most favorable prerequisites for such achievement in the heart of the continent of Europe. The history of all ages—the Roman Empire and the British Empire—had proved that expansion could only be carried out by breaking down resistance and taking risks; setbacks were inevitable. There had never in former times been spaces without a master, and there were none today; the attacker always comes up against a possessor.

The question for Germany ran: where could she achieve the greatest gain at the lowest cost.

German policy had to reckon with two hate-inspired antagonists, Britain and France, to whom a German colossus in the center of Europe was a thorn in the flesh, and both countries were opposed to any further strengthening of Germany's position either in Europe or overseas; in support of this opposition they were able to count on the agreement of all their political parties. Both countries saw in the establishment of German military bases overseas a threat to their own communications, a safeguarding of German commerce, and, as a consequence, a strengthening of Germany's position in Europe.

Because of opposition of the Dominions, Britain could not cede any of her colonial possessions to us. After England's loss of prestige through the passing of Abyssinia into Italian possession, the return of East Africa was not to be expected. British concessions could at best be expressed in an offer to satisfy our colonial demands by the appropriation of colonies which were not British possessions—e.g., Angola. French concessions would probably take a similar line.

Serious discussion of the question of the return of colonies to us could only be considered at a moment when Britain was in difficulties and the German Reich armed and strong. The Führer did not share the view that the Empire was unshakable. Opposition to the Empire was to be found less in the countries conquered than among her competitors. The British Empire and the Roman Empire could not be compared in respect of permanence; the latter was not confronted by any powerful political rival of a serious order after the Punic Wars. It was only the disintegrating effect of Christianity, and the symptoms of age which appear in every country, which caused ancient Rome to succumb to the onslaught of the Germans.

Beside the British Empire there existed today a number of states stronger than she. The British motherland was able to protect her colonial possessions not by her own power, but only in alliance with other states. How, for instance, could Britain alone defend Canada against attack by America, or her Far Eastern interests against attack by Japan!

The emphasis on the British Crown as the symbol of the unity of the Empire was already an admission that, in the long run, the Empire could not maintain its position by power politics. Significant indications of this were:

a. The struggle of Ireland for independence.
b. The constitutional struggles in India, where Britain's half measures had given to the Indians the opportunity of using later on as a weapon against Britain, the nonfulfillment of her promises regarding a constitution.
c. The weakening by Japan of Britain's position in the Far East.
d. The rivalry in the Mediterranean with Italy who—under the spell of her history, driven by necessity and led by a genius—was expanding her power position, and thus was inevitably coming more and more into conflict with British interests. The outcome of the Abyssinian War was a loss of prestige for Britain which Italy was striving to increase by stirring up trouble in the Mohammedan world.

To sum up, it could be stated that, with 45 million Britons, in spite of its theoretical soundness, the position of the Empire could not in the long run be maintained by power politics. The ratio of the population of the Empire to that of the motherland of 9:1, was a warning to us not, in our territorial expansion, to allow the foundation constituted by the numerical strength of our own people to become too weak.

France's position was more favorable than that of Britain. The French Empire was better placed territorially; the inhabitants of her colonial possessions represented a supplement to her military strength. But France was going to be confronted with internal political difficulties. In a nation's life about 10 percent of its span is taken up by parliamentary forms of government and about 90 percent by authoritarian forms. Today, nonetheless, Britain, France, Russia, and the smaller states adjoining them, must be included as factors [*Machtfaktoren*] in our political calculations.

Germany's problem could only be solved by means of force and this was never without attendant risk. The campaigns of Frederick the Great for Silesia and Bismarck's wars against Austria and France had involved unheard-of risk, and the swiftness of the Prussian action in 1870 had kept Austria from entering the war. If one accepts as the basis of the following exposition the resort to force with its attendant risks, then there remain still to be answered the questions "when" and "how." In this matter there were three cases [*Fälle*] to be dealt with:

Case 1: Period 1943–1945

After this date only a change for the worse, from our point of view, could be expected.

The equipment of the army, navy, and *Luftwaffe,* as well as the formation of the officer corps, was nearly completed. Equipment and armament were modern; in further delay there lay the danger of their obsolescence. In particular, the secrecy of "special weapons" could not be preserved forever. The recruiting of reserves was limited to current age groups; further drafts from older untrained age groups were no longer available.

Our relative strength would decrease in relation to the rearmament which would by then have been carried out by the rest of the world. If we did not act by 1943–45, any year could, in consequence of a lack of reserves, produce the food crisis, to cope with which the necessary foreign exchange was not available, and this must be regarded as a "waning point of the regime." Besides, the world was expecting our attack and was increasing its counter-measures from year to year. It was while the rest of the world was still preparing its defenses [*sich abriegele*] that we were obliged to take the offensive.

Nobody knew today what the situation would be in the years 1943–45. One thing only was certain, that we could not wait longer.

On the one hand there was the great *Wehrmacht,* and the necessity of maintaining it at its present level, the aging of the movement and of its leaders; and on the other, the prospect of a lowering of the standard of living and of a limitation of the birth rate, which left no choice but to act. If the Führer was still living, it was his unalterable resolve to solve Germany's problem of space at the latest by 1943–45. The necessity for action before 1943–45 would arise in cases 2 and 3.

Case 2

If internal strife in France should develop into such a domestic crisis as to absorb the French Army completely and render it incapable of use for war against Germany, then the time for action against the Czechs had come.

Case 3

If France is so embroiled by a war with another state that she cannot "proceed" against Germany.

For the improvement of our politico-military position our first objective, in the event of our being embroiled in war, must be to overthrow Czechoslovakia and Austria simultaneously in order to remove the threat to our flank in any possible operation against the West. In a conflict with France it was hardly to be regarded as likely that the Czechs would declare war on us on the very same day as France. The desire to join in the war would, however, increase among the Czechs in proportion to any weakening on our part and then her participation could clearly take the form of an attack toward Silesia, toward the north or toward the west.

If the Czechs were overthrown and a common German-Hungarian frontier achieved, a neutral attitude on the part of Poland could be the more certainly counted on in the event of a Franco-German conflict. Our agreements with Poland only retained their force as long as Germany's strength remained unshaken. In the event of German setbacks a Polish action against East Prussia, and possibly against Pomerania and Silesia as well, had to be reckoned with.

On the assumption of a development of the situation leading to action on our part as planned, in the years 1943–45, the attitude of France, Britain, Italy, Poland, and Russia could probably be estimated as follows:

Actually, the Führer believed that almost certainly Britain, and probably France as well, had already tacitly written off the Czechs and were reconciled to the fact that this question would be cleared up in due course by Germany. Difficulties connected with the Empire, and the prospect of being once more entangled in a protracted European war, were decisive considerations for Britain against participation in a war against Germany. Britain's attitude would certainly not be without influence on that of France. An attack by France without British support, and with the prospect of the offensive being brought to a standstill on our western fortifications, was hardly probable. Nor was a French march through Belgium and Holland without

British support to be expected; this also was a course not to be contemplated by us in the event of a conflict with France, because it would certainly entail the hostility of Britain. It would of course be necessary to maintain a strong defense [*eine Abriegelung*] on our western frontier during the prosecution of our attack on the Czechs and Austria. And in this connection it had to be remembered that the defense measures of the Czechs were growing in strength from year to year, and that the actual worth of the Austrian Army also was increasing in the course of time. Even though the populations concerned, especially of Czechoslovakia, were not sparse, the annexation of Czechoslovakia and Austria would mean an acquisition of foodstuffs for 5 to 6 million people, on the assumption that the compulsory emigration of 2 million people from Czechoslovakia and 1 million people from Austria was practicable. The incorporation of these two States with Germany meant, from the politico-military point of view, a substantial advantage because it would mean shorter and better frontiers, the freeing of forces for other purposes, and the possibility of creating new units up to a level of about twelve divisions, that is, one new division per million inhabitants.

Italy was not expected to object to the elimination of the Czechs, but it was impossible at the moment to estimate what her attitude on the Austrian question would be; that depended essentially upon whether the Duce were still alive.

The degree of surprise and the swiftness of our action were decisive factors for Poland's attitude. Poland—with Russia at her rear—will have little inclination to engage in war against a victorious Germany.

Military intervention by Russia must be countered by the swiftness of our operations; however, whether such an intervention was a practical contingency at all was, in view of Japan's attitude, more than doubtful.

Should case 2 arise—the crippling of France by civil war—the situation thus created by the elimination of the most dangerous opponent must be seized upon *whenever it occurs* for the blow against the Czechs.

The Führer saw case 3 coming definitely nearer; it might emerge from the present tensions in the Mediterranean, and he was resolved to take advantage of it whenever it happened, even as early as 1938.

In the light of past experience, the Führer did not see any early end to the hostilities in Spain. If one considered the length of time which Franco's offensives had taken up till now, it was fully possible that the war would continue another 3 years. On the other hand, a 100 percent victory for Franco was not desirable either, from the German point of view; rather were we interested in a continuance of the war and in the keeping up of the tension in the Mediterranean. Franco in undisputed possession of the Spanish Peninsula precluded the possibility of any further intervention on the part of the Italians or of their continued occupation of the Balearic Islands. As our interest lay more in the prolongation of the war in Spain, it must be the immediate aim of our policy to strengthen Italy's rear with a view to her remaining in the Balearics. But the permanent establishment of the Italians on the Balearics would be intolerable both to France and Britain, and might lead to a war of France and England against Italy—a war in which Spain, should she be entirely in the hands of the Whites, might make her appearance on the side of Italy's enemies. The probability of Italy's defeat in such a war was slight, for the road from Germany was open for the supplementing of her raw materials. The Führer pictured the military strategy for Italy thus: on her western frontier with France she would remain on the defensive, and carry on the war against France from Libya against the French North African colonial possessions.

As a landing by Franco-British troops on the coast of Italy could be discounted, and a French offensive over the Alps against northern Italy would be very difficult and would probably come to a halt before the strong Italian fortifications, the crucial point [*Schwerpunkt*] of the operations lay in North Africa. The threat to French lines of communication by the Italian Fleet would to a great extent cripple the transportation of forces from North Africa to France, so that France would have only home forces at her disposal on the frontiers with Italy and Germany.

If Germany made use of this war to settle the Czech and Austrian questions, it was to be assumed that Britain—herself at war with Italy—would decide not to act against Germany. Without British support, a warlike action by France against Germany was not to be expected.

The time for our attack on the Czechs and Austria must be made dependent on the course of the Anglo-French-Italian war and would not necessarily coincide with the commencement of military operations by these three States. Nor had the Führer in mind military agreements with Italy, but wanted, while retaining his own independence of action, to exploit this favorable situation, which would not occur again, to begin and carry through the campaign against the Czechs. This descent upon the Czechs would have to be carried out with "lightning speed."

In appraising the situation Field Marshal von Blomberg and Colonel General von Fritsch repeatedly emphasized the necessity that Britain and France must not appear in the role of our enemies, and stated that the French Army would not be so committed by the war with Italy that France could not at the same time enter the field with forces superior to ours on our western frontier. General von Fritsch estimated the probable French forces available for use on the Alpine frontier at approximately twenty divisions, so that a strong French superiority would still remain on the western frontier, with the role, according to the German view, of invading the Rhineland. In this matter, moreover, the advanced state of French defense preparations [*Mobilmachung*] must be taken into particular account, and it must be remembered apart from the insignificant value of our present fortifications—on which Field Marshal von Blomberg laid special emphasis—that the four motorized divisions intended for the West were still more or less incapable of movement. In regard to our offensive toward the southeast, Field Marshal von Blomberg drew particular attention to the strength of the Czech fortifications, which had acquired by now a structure like a Maginot Line and which would gravely hamper our attack.

General von Fritsch mentioned that this was the very purpose of a study which he had ordered made this winter, namely, to examine the possibility of conducting operations against the Czechs with special reference to overcoming the Czech fortification system; the General further expressed his opinion that under existing circumstances he must give up his plan to go abroad on his leave, which was due to begin on November 10. The Führer dismissed this idea on the ground that the possibility of a conflict need not yet be regarded as so imminent. To the Foreign Minister's objection that an Anglo-French-Italian conflict was not yet within such a measurable distance as the Führer seemed to assume, the Führer put the summer of 1938 as the date which seemed to him possible for this. In reply to considerations offered by Field Marshal von Blomberg and

General von Fritsch regarding the attitude of Britain and France, the Führer repeated his previous statements that he was convinced of Britain's nonparticipation, and therefore he did not believe in the probability of belligerent action by France against Germany. Should the Mediterranean conflict under discussion lead to a general mobilization in Europe, then we must immediately begin action against the Czechs. On the other hand, should the powers not engaged in the war declare themselves disinterested, then Germany would have to adopt a similar attitude to this for the time being.

Colonel General Göring thought that, in view of the Führer's statement, we should consider liquidating our military undertakings in Spain. The Führer agrees to this with the limitation that he thinks he should reserve a decision for a proper moment.

The second part of the conference was concerned with concrete questions of armament.

Hossbach

Certified Correct:
Colonel (General Staff)

Christopher Thorne
THE FIRST CONQUEST

Christopher Thorne, a member of the faculty of the University of Sussex, in
The Approach of War *(1967) has written a study of the diplomatic history
of the last two years of peace. Those two years were filled with crises, and
each seemed to bring Europe closer to the brink of war. The selection
excerpted below tells the story of the Austrian* Anschluss *when Hitler gained
his first conquest without fighting a battle. It was a prelude to more conquests, but most of them would not be so peaceful.*

"Destiny," according to Hitler, had appointed the frontier region between Germany and Austria as his birthplace, and certainly the
merging of those two states was the most likely of his conquests. It
was also the most improvised in its execution, an apparent lesson
of the easy triumphs to be obtained by ruthless pressure and swift
action in the face of a critical but passive Europe.

The break-up of the Habsburg Empire towards the end of the Great
War had briefly seemed to offer an end to the nineteenth-century
problem of relations between the Germans in the Empire and those
who came to be gathered in Bismarck's Reich; but when in November
1918 the former, six and a half million strong, declared themselves
part of the new German Republic, self-determination was denied
them. By the treaties of Versailles and Saint-Germain the Allies prohibited the union, and in 1922 Austria, in return for international
financial assistance, had to affirm that she would in no way alienate
her independence. A projected Austro-German customs union had
similarly been quashed in 1931 at French insistence, and in the following year fresh loans were accompanied by an extension of the
assurance given in 1922.

It was an unhappy situation for the small Republic. Legal obligations and financial necessity clashed with dissatisfaction over a
peace settlement which, in Schuschnigg's later words, "we considered an injustice which we could and would not recognize as a
lawful treaty." While friction between the successor and the disin-
herited states of the Danube basin prevented the possibility of some

From *The Approach of War,* by Christopher Thorne (New York, 1967), pp. 35–50.
Reprinted by permission of St. Martin's Press, Inc., and Macmillan London and
Basingstoke. Reference notes omitted.

wider association in that direction, union with Germany remained attractive, perhaps all the more because forbidden fruit. Pan-German sentiments were strongly implanted in men like Karl Renner and Dollfuss on either side of the center, as well as in the right-wing of Austrian politics; until January 1933 the great majority of the Austrian people were not averse to the idea of the *Anschluss.*

The advent of Nazi Germany, though making the project more practicable, diminished its respectability. Many of the anti-Semitic and anti-Slav roots of National Socialism were far from alien to Austrian soil (it is a movement, commented one Viennese professor, "which puts the Prussian sword at the disposal of Austrian lunacy") and in the confused struggle for power during the early 1930s Berlin, as well as Rome, was still used by Austrian politicians as a potential source of influence. But with Dollfuss as Chancellor strong measures were adopted against the Nazi party, and the failure of the *putsch* in which Dollfuss was murdered in 1934 helped drive it further underground for the time being.

Yet the internal weaknesses of Austria remained. No national identity had developed since 1918 to overcome the ambivalence of being German as well as Austrian. "Already in 1934," wrote Dollfuss's successor, "I was sure of one thing: never again a war against Germany as in 1866," and he assured von Papen that "he was well aware that the historical position of Vienna had come to an end and that the focal point of the German mission now lay in Berlin"; there were many besides the new Chancellor who, neither Nazi nor unswerving Monarchist, were lured by the dream of an autonomous Vienna becoming the cultural heart of a wider fatherland which might also include the South Tyrol. Nor was there sufficient loyalty to Austria to heal the breach between the anticlerical socialism of Vienna and the "Austro-Fascism" of those who had triumphed in the brief but bitter civil war of 1934. "Both Government and Socialist leaders knew that the decisive hour for Austria was approaching; both felt that the danger could be met only by uniting forces. But it was too late; the chasm of mutual distrust could no longer be bridged." Ironically, it was only in the last days before Hitler struck that many Austrians began to see themselves as one people.

By then, their country's external protectors had faded away, and the British, French, Hungarian and Italian agreements of 1934 and 1935 to consult if her integrity were endangered counted for nothing.

Even before the Stresa front had disintegrated Mussolini was remarking that he "could not always be the only one to march to the Brenner," and Schuschnigg himself, reflecting the antipathy of many of his countrymen, had made it clear that Italian troops would never be welcome beyond that point. A political agreement which was signed between Austria and Germany in 1936 was, in reality, a token of Rome's diminishing determination; when Goering sounded Mussolini on the *Anschluss* in January 1937 the latter disliked the ominous and abrupt manner in which it was done, but he declared that he would not be bound by his "watch on the Brenner," and when Schuschnigg arrived in Italy in the spring he was treated with a certain reserve. In September Mussolini was Hitler's guest, and impressive displays of German strength reminded him where his interest lay. Though still unwilling to witness the complete disappearance of Austria, he made no protest two months later when Ribbentrop, on signing the anti-Comintern pact, remarked that the question must be settled, and Ciano in his diary defined the task of the Italian Minister in Vienna as "that of a doctor who has to give oxygen to a dying man without the dying man's heir noticing." "In case of doubt," he added, "we are more interested in the heir than in the dying man."

Only Czechoslovakia of Austria's other neighbors need be watched carefully if Germany moved, and even she had been prevented by the contrast in regimes from drawing closer to Vienna in the face of a common danger. Stoyadinovitch of Yugoslavia had talked to Ciano of the *Anschluss* as "inevitable," and assured the Nazi leaders in January 1938 that his country would never fight over "a purely domestic question . . . [wherein] a people wished to be united." If Admiral Horthy, Regent of Hungary, feared the disappearance of an independent Austria, he too had advised the Germans that they "only needed a little patience in this question," while from further afield the Foreign Minister of Poland came to swell the reassuring chorus which gladdened the ear of Berlin. As the French Foreign Minister, Delbos, traveled gloomily around Eastern Europe in December 1937, he found no more evidence of a determination to stand firm than he had in London a week before. Even he had privately indicated a readiness to see "a further assimilation of certain of Austria's domestic institutions with Germany's," and Chautemps, his Premier, "could see no way to prevent Hitler from swallowing Austria in the relatively near future."

It had long been evident that Britain would not fight for Austrian independence. Eden, moving towards his final break with Chamberlain over Italy, apparently told Ribbentrop in December that the question "was of much greater interest to Italy than to England," whose people "recognized that a closer connection between Germany and Austria would have to come about sometime," though they wished force to be avoided. Despite Eden's later strictures, this was scarcely different language from that used by Halifax to Hitler during his November visit to Germany. England realized, said Halifax on that occasion, "that one might have to contemplate an adjustment to new conditions, a correction of former mistakes and the recognition of changed circumstances," and though insisting upon peaceful methods he specifically mentioned Danzig, Austria and Czechoslovakia. Any further encouragement needed was being supplied by Henderson, whose talk of Germany's right to absorb Austria and dominate the whole Balkan and Danube area was widely reported among the diplomatic community.

Few doubted that some developments would occur over Austria before very long. The Austrian Nazi party had survived their 1934 setback stronger than ever, despite internal squabbles and Hitler's order that "a new method of political penetration" must take the place of terrorism. The "Gentleman's Agreement" of 1936 whereby Austria, "recognizing herself to be a German State," had had her sovereignty acknowledged by Germany, had further diluted the ruling Fatherland Front by the inclusion of members of the pan-German opposition in the government, and had not eased the pressure of Nazi propaganda from within and from across the border. When all paramilitary formations, including the Italian-oriented *Heimwehr,* were dissolved shortly afterwards, another potential weapon in the struggle for survival was thrown away. Outwardly and reassuringly conservative and Catholic, the time-serving Franz von Papen was in Vienna as German Minister "to undermine and weaken the Austrian Government," urging Schuschnigg that "Austria, with heart and soul . . . support the struggle of the German world for its existence," reinforcing the demands being pressed on behalf of the "moderate" Nazis by the naive traitor, Seyss-Inquart (appointed Councillor of State in July 1937), diverting attention by his own counter-charges from the "very incriminating" documents which police had discovered in the Austrian Nazi headquarters in the spring of that year. "National Socialism," wrote von Papen to Hitler, "must and will overcome the new Austrian ideology."

With Schuschnigg ready to compromise and still trusting Seyss-Inquart as a fellow Catholic and a gentleman, it was a satisfactory situation for Hitler. Rebuking the eager Goering in September 1937 he stated that "Germany should cause no explosion of the Austrian problem in the forseeable future, but . . . should continue to seek an evolutionary solution," and his existing military plans were contingent only upon an attempt in Vienna to restore the Habsburgs. Yet the temptation to succeed by one swift stroke remained, and his readiness to do so should a suitable occasion arise was made clear to his Foreign Minister, War Minister and service commanders on 5 November. Though the so-called Hossbach conference has attracted its full share of controversy, no satisfactory arguments have been advanced to alter the conclusion that in its explicitness and its anti-Western rather than anti-Bolshevik framework here was a significant moment in the development of Nazi expansionism. Taken in conjunction with the changes of the following February, when Ribbentrop replaced Neurath at the Foreign Ministry, Hitler became his own War Minister in place of Blomberg, and servility rather than ability was rewarded in other military and economic posts, the harangue of 5 November marked "a real turning point in Hitler's prewar policy."

Germany, said Hitler, must seek greater space in Europe, and her problems "could only be solved by means of force [which] was never without attendant risk." Two "hate-inspired antagonists, Britain and France," had to be reckoned with, but he was determined to settle matters "at the latest by 1943–45"; earlier action might be made possible by French internal strife—"then the time for action against the Czechs had come"—or a French war against Italy. Should war with the West come first, then Austria and Czechoslovakia must be overthrown simultaneously to protect Germany's flank, but he believed "that almost certainly Britain, and probably France as well, had already tacitly written off the Czechs." The annexation of both neighbors which could thus be anticipated would provide increased foodstuffs, improve Germany's frontiers, and free her forces "for other purposes."

Though the conditions envisaged by Hitler were not to materialize, the new readiness for action was transmitted to the armed forces by Blomberg in December:

> *Should the political situation not develop, or only develop slowly in our favor, then the execution of operation "Green" [an attack against Czechoslovakia while adopting a defensive posture in the West] will have to be postponed for years. If, however, a situation arises which, owing to Britain's aversion to a general European War, through her lack of interest in the Central European problem and because of a conflict breaking out between Italy and France in the Mediterranean, creates the probability that Germany will face no other opponent than Russia on Czechoslovakia's side, then operation Green will start before the completion of Germany's full preparedness for war. The military objective . . . is still the speedy occupation of Bohemia and Moravia with the simultaneous solution of the Austrian question in the sense of incorporating Austria into the German Reich. In order to achieve the latter aim military force will only be required if other means do not lead or have not led to success.*

"Today we are faced with new tasks," declared Hitler to the Nazi Old Guard in November, "for the *Lebensraum* of our people is too narrow. The world seeks to evade the examination of these problems and the answering of these questions. But that it will not be able to do."

The use of the army against Austria was still no more than an alternative, but Ribbentrop, urging Hitler in January that "every day that our political calculations are not actuated by the fundamental idea that England is our most dangerous foe *would be a gain for our enemies,*" had proclaimed that "in case of a quick success [in Central Europe] I am fully convinced that the West would not intervene." Goering, too, was working for an early solution by putting pressure on Guido Schmidt, Schuschnigg's Foreign Minister. Moreover Nazi extremists in Austria, setting an example later to be followed in Czechoslovakia, Memel and Danzig, were striving to bring on a crisis. In the summer of 1937 Berlin had attempted to bring them under firmer control, but on 25 January Austrian police raids uncovered plans to provoke repression on a scale which would bring in the German Army, with the convenient murder of von Papen providing a further justification. Seyss-Inquart, too, though he deplored the reckless indiscipline of the extremists, had come to despair of obtaining further rapid concessions from Schuschnigg, and had to be ordered by Goering not to resign as Councillor of State at the turn of the year.

Schuschnigg's reaction to the chilling news of the Nazi plot, however, was to seek further compromise. "The incident," wrote Papen to Hitler, "made the Federal Chancellor conscious of the impossibility of letting the present state of affairs continue. He is most eager for the personal meeting contemplated, and in Glaise's[1] opinion would also be prepared to change his attitude fundamentally." Schuschnigg, in fact, dreaded the thought of meeting Hitler, even though some measure of reassurance was provided by the smooth promises of von Papen that the 1936 agreement would be the basis of the talks "which would in no case be to the disadvantage of the Austrian Government." The Chancellor privately observed that a psychiatrist would have been a more suitable visitor than himself, and that he would go to Berchtesgaden "only in order to forestall a 'coup' and to gain time until the international situation should improve in Austria's favor."

But Hitler had apparently forgotten the proposed meeting, engrossed as he was in the internal crisis concerning Blomberg, Fritsch, and the replacement of Neurath, and it was only when von Papen, shaken by dismissal from his Vienna post, arrived at Berchtesgaden on 5 February that the project was revived. The news which reawakened Hitler's interest and restored von Papen to his former position was of fresh signs of nervous Austrian weakness. Instead of preparing a denunciation of illegal Nazi activities, Schuschnigg was undermining his own position in advance by conceding to Seyss-Inquart an end to discrimination against "moderate" Austrian Nazis, and their participation in "the development of military, economic and political relations with the Reich." On the eve of the visit now fixed for 12 February he went even further, and through Zernatto, Secretary of the Fatherland Front, put forward suggestions for cooperation over press facilities, the closest collaboration between the Austrian and German armies, the appointment of specific Nazis to the Council of State, and the incorporation of certain tenets of National Socialism "into the political ideology of the new Austria." Swiftly the trusted Seyss had these good omens conveyed to Berchtesgaden where they arrived before Schuschnigg on the morning of the 12th. The visitor's own proposals would be used against him.

The interview which followed was the most forceful intimation an outsider had yet received that Hitler was not a statesman but a gangster. Summoning his generals to heighten the tension and mod-

[1] Edmund Glaise-Horstenau, a crypto-Nazi member of Schuschnigg's Cabinet.

erating his verbal assault only briefly, when the murder of Dollfuss was mentioned, he lashed a deferential Schuschnigg with "the uninterrupted high treason of Austrian history," boasted of his "mission" as "perhaps the greatest German of all history," threatened that possibly one day his visitor "would wake up in Vienna to find the Germans there—just like a spring storm," and issued a deadline of that afternoon by which a prepared agreement on Austro-German relations must be signed. When Schuschnigg pointed out that he could not commit his President in advance he was eventually given three days in which to confirm the protocol he now signed; its provisions included the alignment of foreign policies, the inclusion of Seyss-Inquart in the government as Minister of the Interior with control over security, complete freedom for National Socialists, and their incorporation in the ruling Fatherland Front. While the barest of communiqués was issued to the world, Hitler ordered that the impression be given that serious military preparations were in hand against Austria, and on the 15th the required ratification was to be forthcoming. As the visitors drove away, however, they were assured by von Papen that next time would be different, for "the Fuehrer could be absolutely charming." A month later one of the soldiers who now opened a barrier to let them pass was guarding Schuschnigg in a cell he left only to clean SS latrines with his own towel.

In the terrible position in which Schuschnigg found himself after Berchtesgaden he behaved with a mixture of acquiescence and defiance easy to understand but difficult to commend. He scarcely fostered that "improvement in the international situation" which apparently had been his aim. The full truth of what had happened reached the British and French governments only gradually and informally (at a dinner on 14 February Schuschnigg told the French Minister that Hitler, "a madman with a mission," had been most brutal) and Vienna followed up an anodyne Austro-German communiqué issued on the 15th by privately seeking to prevent protests and questions from the democracies which might further enrage Hitler. In Paris the uneasiness that was manifest nonetheless was accompanied by a sense of helplessness and was sharply rebuffed when François-Poncet sought assurances from Ribbentrop over what the latter declared to be solely a domestic affair; in London Chamberlain's attention was firmly fixed upon the need to begin talks with

Mussolini and thereby repair the "endless chances" missed by Eden, who resigned on 20 February; in Berlin Henderson was still on hand, not only to convey an invitation to Hitler to consider a new colonial division in Africa (partly at Portuguese and Belgian expense), but to hint that his own support for the *Anschluss* was nearer the opinions of his government than were the anxious protests of his colleague in Vienna. Mussolini and Ciano for their part swung with pompous impotence between acceptance of the *Anschluss* as "inevitable" and anxiety over the consequences of "Germany at the Brenner," between renewed hope aroused by stirrings of Austrian patriotism and despairing attempts to offset in advance their coming loss of face by obtaining an agreement from the compliant hands of Chamberlain. Austria, partly through her own actions, stood alone.

How long this precarious state of affairs would have lasted had Schuschnigg not belatedly decided upon defiance is uncertain. Reassuring reports had reached Berlin on 18 February that "the collapse is so complete that . . . a number of decisive positions can be captured within the succeeding weeks," and Keppler, Hitler's Special Commissioner for Austrian affairs, repeated early in March that "more and more concessions" could be wrung from Schuschnigg. When disgruntled Austrian Nazi extremists like Tavs and Leopold were reported as planning fresh provocation and working against Seyss-Inquart they were told by Hitler that though "the need for intervention by force might still arise," their actions "had been insane." "He wanted the evolutionary course to be taken," he declared to them in private on 26 February, and "did not now desire a solution by violent means if it could at all be avoided, since the danger . . . in the field of foreign policy became less each year and German military power greater each year."

On Wednesday, 9 March, however, with a suddenness and intensity born of despair, determining not "to wait with fettered hands until . . . we should be gagged as well," Schuschnigg attempted to regain some freedom of action. Already on 24 February he had made a stirring appeal to Austrian patriotism. Now, with his new Minister of the Interior openly identifying himself with an equally open Nazi revolt in Styria, he called upon his countrymen to vote on the following Sunday for "a free and German, independent and social, Christian and united Austria." Mussolini, consulted beforehand, advised against so rash a move. In Berlin, an astonished Hitler, informed through

Austrian Nazi channels a few hours before the news became public, "bordered on hysteria," for as the enthusiasm which greeted Schuschnigg's announcement suggested, the plebiscite was likely to give the latter an overwhelming vote of confidence; this was all the more certain since an age limit of 24 would exclude young Nazi zealots. It was of no significance when on the 10th Seyss-Inquart allowed himself to be persuaded by Schuschnigg to support the move; his role as puppet was about to be made clearer than ever. Keppler was already in Vienna with instructions to prevent Sunday's event taking place or at the least have a question on the *Anschluss* added, while the intention to invade "should other means fail," avoiding provocation but "breaking ruthlessly" any resistance encountered, was embodied in a directive prepared on the 10th and issued from Hitler to the armed forces the next day. Any Czech forces encountered were to be regarded as hostile, Italians as friends.

Frantically, the *Wehrmacht* prepared an assault so improvised that it was to leave along its path a trail of stranded vehicles; it was time for the kill, and none reveled more in the moment, then or later, than the Reich's Chief Game Warden, Hermann Goering. Hitler himself was still not committed to use force, as the opening sentence of his first directive showed, but during the night of the 10th–11th the Nazis in Austria learned that the Fuehrer had given them "freedom of action" and would "back them in everything they did." It was the method, not the intention, that was still to be decided.

Austrian independence was not to outlive Friday, 11 March. Schuschnigg was woken at 5:30 a.m. with the news that Germany had closed the frontier and was massing troops, and the threat became clearer when Seyss-Inquart and Glaise-Horstenau, obeying instructions they had received by letter from Hitler that morning, declared that unless the plebiscite were called off they would resign. As the three men faced one another within the Vienna Chancellery, eager preparations for Sunday's plebiscite filled the warm streets outside with bustle and a scattering of leaflets. At about 2:30 p.m. Schuschnigg decided to give way, only to be pursued further by a series of telephone calls which Goering, with Hitler's approval, put through to Seyss, Keppler and others in Vienna from 2:45 p.m. onwards. Seyss, with his colleagues, was ordered to demand Schuschnigg's resignation, to get himself appointed Chancellor, and to dispatch to Hitler a telegram requesting assistance in restoring order. By 4 p.m.

Schuschnigg had again surrendered, and when President Miklas "resolutely and at times pathetically" refused to appoint Seyss in his place, deadlines were issued under the threat that "200,000 men standing in readiness at the border" would otherwise march and that resistance would be "summarily dealt with by our tribunals." Schuschnigg, still caretaking as Chancellor, further diminished any likelihood of resistance by authorizing announcements that the plebiscite had been postponed and that the entire Cabinet, except Seyss-Inquart, had resigned; he followed this by personally broadcasting at 7:50 p.m. that the army was withdrawing in order to avoid "shedding German blood" and that the country was "yielding to force."

As Seyss confirmed to Goering by phone that a vacuum now existed, Hitler hesitated no longer. As late as 6 p.m. he had been wavering, and on premature news that Seyss had been appointed had withdrawn his order to march; now, at 8:45 p.m., he gave the word to invade the following morning. Three minutes later Goering dictated to Keppler the text of the telegram Seyss was to send asking for help, ignoring Keppler's remark that "everything was quiet and orderly": "He does not have to send the telegram. He has only to say that he did. You get me?" By now Nazi thugs were swarming insolently though the Chancellery and baying in the streets outside; others were seizing control in the provinces. When in the small hours of the morning Seyss-Inquart pathetically attempted to limit the consequences of his treachery by suggesting that invasion was no longer necessary, Hitler decreed that it was too late, and at dawn the German troops crossed the frontier to be greeted with flowers. In the afternoon the Fuehrer made his homecoming in person to so tumultuous a welcome that on the 13th he decided to settle immediately for more than a union of states under common leadership. That day, as the mass arrests and pillaging began, Austria was declared to be a province of the German Reich. "Destiny" was on the march. If brutality had accompanied its progress—Schuschnigg's broadcast on the evening of the 11th, let alone the reports of diplomats and correspondents, made this quite clear—who could argue in the face of the 99 percent vote of approval soon bestowed by the Austrians themselves?

In any event, the other European Powers had by then openly or tacitly acquiesced. On the 11th an anxious Hitler had almost begged for the Duce's approval now that he "could no longer remain pas-

sive" in the face of Austro-Czech collusion and anarchy in his homeland, swearing to prove a steadfast ally and to respect the Brenner
frontier forever; when Prince Philip of Hesse telephoned from Rome
at 10:25 p.m. to convey Mussolini's friendly response he was swamped
by the jubilant relief at the other end of the line. Already on that day
a request for advice from Schuschnigg to his former protector had
met with evasion and coldness, and an even blunter rebuff greeted
French inquiries as to the possibility of a joint stand. "After sanctions, the nonrecognition of the Empire, and all the other miseries
inflicted on us since 1935," wrote Ciano of the West, "do they expect
to rebuild Stresa in an hour with Hannibal at the gates?" Italy would
keep her distaste and disquiet to herself.

Even this was scarcely needed to decide the democracies against
action. France, without a government between the 10th and the 13th,
might issue the strongest warnings and protests, but she could not
move without Britain as well as Italy close beside her, and Britain's
response to Hitler's action went no further than apologetic indignation. On the 10th, it is true, Halifax solemnly warned Ribbentrop, who
was back in London to pay his farewell calls as Ambassador, that aggression might eventually precipitate a general conflict and that
though he himself "did not believe in plebiscites much" he attached
"the utmost importance" to the Austrian one being carried out "without interference or intimidation." Ribbentrop, however, was not
merely placing his usual overconfident gloss on matters when he
reported to Hitler that Britain would do nothing "of her own accord"
to help Austria (though a "plausible justification" for German action
was needed for public opinion). Sir Horace Wilson on the same day
was indicating to Erich Kordt of the German Embassy that while "he
hoped very much that [Germany] would succeed as much as possible
vis-à-vis Czechoslovakia and Austria without the use of force, the
prerequisite . . . was, of course, that the other side also played fair,"
and he did not dissent when Kordt retorted that Schuschnigg's
plebiscite was itself not "fair." Similarly, at a Downing Street luncheon
in Ribbentrop's honor on the 11th Chamberlain was more interested
in future agreement than current difficulties. "Once we have all got
past this unpleasant affair," he remarked privately to his guest, "and
a reasonable solution has been found, it is to be hoped that we can
begin working in earnest towards a German–British understanding."
Though the atmosphere of cordiality was shattered by the arrival of

telegrams indicating the pressure being put on Schuschnigg at that moment, and though an excited and indignant Halifax in particular warned that a setback in relations must follow the use of such "intolerable" methods, Chamberlain agreed that the plebiscite had best be postponed, and remarked that "personally he understood the situation."

The development of events necessitated further protests, of course, and one was forthcoming later that day "against such use of coercion backed by force against an independent State in order to create a situation incompatible with its national independence." But when Schuschnigg asked for immediate advice he was told that "His Majesty's Government cannot take responsibility of advising the Chancellor to take any course of action which might expose his country to dangers against which [they] are unable to guarantee protection." Given the need to sound Mussolini this was doubtless a necessary, though cheerless, reply, and Rome ensured that it would not be improved upon; it was of no consequence anyway, since when the message arrived Schuschnigg had already resigned.

There was little more that could be done. Goering, still anxious on the 11th about British reactions, must have been somewhat reassured by Henderson's agreement "that Dr. Schuschnigg had acted with precipitate folly," and the ensuing rebuke Halifax delivered to his Ambassador for allowing personal views to "diminish the force" of official protests no more helped Austria than it prevented Henderson from repeating his behavior on later occasions. The disbelieving laughter of the Opposition which greeted Mr. R. A. Butler's assurance in the Commons that "solemn representations" were being made in Berlin to secure the withdrawal of the German Army and moderate treatment for Austrian Jews, socialists and Catholics was entirely justified. Chamberlain himself could write privately that "it was now perfectly evident that force was the only argument Germany understood," and could announce in the Commons on the 14th that a fresh review would be made of the British defense program, but as has been suggested this did not mean what Churchill hopefully assumed at the time, that "the scales of illusion had fallen from many eyes . . . in high quarters." The Czech crisis was about to show as much.

IV FROM MUNICH TO MOSCOW

Laurence Thompson
THE MUNICH CONFERENCE

Laurence Thompson, a journalist, has written one of the best revisionist studies of the Munich crisis. In his book he challenges many of the legends that have grown up around the Munich crisis. Thompson shows that President Eduard Beneš of Czechoslovakia was not as heroic and Neville Chamberlain not as foolish as some historians have made them appear. He reveals that the Czechoslovak army was overrated and would have been overwhelmed by the German army, a view that is contrary to that advanced by the opponents of the Munich agreement. Under these circumstances, the result of the Munich Conference is not so shocking.

Munich, once the capital of the proud and independent kingdom of Bavaria, still has the civilized air of a capital city, with its opera houses, theaters, concert halls, centers of government. The patrician towers of rococo churches contrast pleasantly with the elaborate bourgeois decorations and noisy jollity of the city's celebrated beer halls where Hitler found his first political following. Munich is as yet a city, bearing the marks of its princely past, and with a blunt, tangy character of its own. It has not yet sprawled into one more provincial parking lot for commuters' motor cars.

The taxi drivers of Munich now speak English with an American accent because of a war which the Munich Agreement delayed but had no hope of averting. There is still an American military presence discreetly outside Munich, but the sight of an American uniform in the center of the city is almost as rare now as it was in 1938, when the principal representatives of Britain's successor as a world power were its foreign correspondents, driving from hotel to lush hotel to read in a casual phrase of Goering, an unguarded look from Daladier, the chances of war or peace.

The city swarmed with journalists, with photographers and newsreel camera teams jostling outside the discreet Hotel Regina for a shot of Chamberlain, all teeth and starched wing collar, or of Goering entering the Vier Jahreszeiten in one of a changing series of dazzling uniforms which, Daladier noted censoriously, emphasized the General's fatness.

From *The Greatest Treason: The Untold Story of Munich* (New York, 1968), pp. 237–251. Copyright © 1968 by Laurence Thompson. Reprinted by permission of William Morrow and Company, Inc., and A. D. Peters and Co. Ltd.

The delegations, indeed, could be divided into the uniformed and the nonuniformed. The Italian diplomats with Mussolini outshone the gold-braided brilliance of the soldiers. The Duce himself, chest thrown out, wore a uniform which seemed, to the lounge-suited Daladier, rather too small for his well-developed figure. Even the Führer was dressed in khaki tunic, swastika armband, long black trousers reaching down to rather old black shoes. The representatives of democracy looked like black beetles among these butterflies. Daladier, in François-Poncet's phrase, "a broad-shouldered, sunburnt man with his head sunk on his shoulders, his forehead furrowed with lines"; Chamberlain, like an elderly English lawyer, "greying, bowed, with thick eyebrows and protruding teeth, a blotchy face and his hands reddened by rheumatism."

These notables drove in big official Mercedes cars through streets decorated with swastikas and flags of the four nations—but not of a fifth; Czechoslovakia officially did not exist—and streamers proclaiming *"Willkommen."* They were cheered, the same hopeful cheers which had greeted Daladier at Le Bourget, where women held up their babies and shouted, "Long live Daladier! Long live peace!" and which Chamberlain had heard at Heston, where his entire Cabinet had assembled to smile at the cameras and ostentatiously display their solidarity. Resign? Such a thought had obviously never occurred to any one of that confident, happy group of servants in the popular cause of peace.

Léon Blum in the Socialist *Populaire* had spoken for everyone that morning: "The news of the Munich meeting has aroused an immense wave of faith and hope. . . . It would indeed be a crime against humanity to break off the negotiations or make them impossible. The Munich meeting is an armful of wood thrown on to the sacred hearth just at a time when the flame was dying down and in danger of going out."

In Britain, just in case anybody forgot what was going to happen if the flame went out, copies of a Home Office pamphlet, "The Protection of Your Home Against Air Raids," came plopping through suburban letter-boxes.

The most memorable thing about the Munich Conference was its confusion. With less than twenty-four hours for preparation, the logistics broke down at every point. The British delegation found it quicker to send a message by car from the conference room to their hotel than to telephone. There were no arrangements for a formal note of the proceedings to be taken, no chairman, only the most sketchy agenda. The truth is that the Führer was not interested in arrangements. In his opening remarks, he made quite clear to his guests what was expected of them.

"In my speech at the Sportpalast," he said, "I stated that whatever happened I should enter Czechoslovakia on October first at the latest. The objection was raised that this act would have a violent character. Very well, let us take advantage of the fact that we are gathered here to remove this character from it. But it must be done quickly!"

Nobody felt in a position to dispute this statement.

The conference was held in the Führerhaus, a new building on the great open square of the Koenigsplatz, which had a Greek façade superimposed upon a squat Teutonic body. It belonged to the Nazi Party, not to the German nation, but none of the older and civilized halls in Munich were big enough to accommodate the expected throng of diplomats, soldiers, journalists and hangers-on. The principal feature of the Führerhaus was a central hall a hundred feet wide, sixty-five feet high, from which an imposing stone staircase led to suites of rooms above. In one of these rooms, a buffet had been laid out, served by footmen in knee-breeches and silver-buckled shoes. Chamberlain was the first to arrive at the Führerhaus. Then came Daladier, who, such was the state of distrust that now existed between the British and French, had had no previous consultation with Chamberlain. Mussolini made a delayed entrance at the head of a train of uniforms, and was ostentatiously greeted on the great staircase by the Führer in person, although they had parted only a short time before. Mussolini's handshakes for Daladier and Chamberlain were pointedly brief and cold. "There is a vague sense of embarrassment," noted Ciano, "particularly on the part of the French. I talk to Daladier, then François-Poncet about trivial things. Then to Chamberlain, who says he wants to talk to the Duce. The Duce, coldly, does not take advantage of the opening, and the conversation peters out."

The Führer left his guests little time to eat, drink and chat, but shepherded them firmly into a big, rectangular room set with a round table, some armchairs, and a sofa. Schmidt, who had to take a note of the proceedings, complained that, as usual at the Führer's conferences, the table and chairs were too low for him to write comfortably. The Führer, however, liked low chairs, and it was his conference. Without waiting for his guests, he slumped into the first chair he came to, on the left of the door, leaving the rest to seat themselves where they liked. Schmidt sat down on the Führer's right. Chamberlain sat next to Schmidt, with Wilson on his other side. Mussolini and Ciano, crumpling their uniforms, lounged on a sofa. Daladier and Alexis Léger of the French Foreign Ministry sat facing the Führer.

When they had settled themselves, the Führer expressed a few perfunctory thanks to his guests for their presence. Then he launched into the familiar tirade, voice raised, clenched fist punching into open palm: distress and misery of Sudeten German population . . . barbaric persecution . . . no end to flood of refugees . . . unbearable situation . . . immediate decision . . .

Mr. Chamberlain, Wilson noted primly, replied suitably, as did M. Daladier and Signor Mussolini. But of course they did not reply suitably, although Daladier made some show of standing up for the Czechoslovaks and, according to his own account, threatened to walk out, as everybody did on their first encounter with the Führer.

"I should like the Chancellor's intentions to be made perfectly clear," Daladier said. "If, as I understood him, he means to destroy Czechoslovakia as an independent state and purely and simply join it to the Reich—to annex it—I know what remains for me to do. There is nothing left but for me to return to France."

That was not the Chancellor's present intention, and Mussolini quickly intervened: "No, no, there's a misunderstanding. That isn't what the Führer meant to say. On the contrary, he has dwelt on the fact that apart from the Sudeten districts, Germany doesn't claim any part of Czech territory."

Mussolini spoke French, as well as German and English; Hitler, German only. During this exchange, Hitler never took his eyes off Mussolini. When the translation had been made, he himself broke in: "No, Monsieur Daladier, I have expressed myself badly. I don't want any Czechs. If you offered me the lot, I wouldn't accept a single one."

As a matter of cold fact, 800,000 Czechs came under German rule as a result of German interpretation of the Munich Agreement. But for the moment there were sighs of relief, the Führer was springing no surprises in the manner of Godesberg, nobody was going to have to walk out with consequences too appalling to contemplate.

These preliminaries out of the way, Mussolini produced a little thing he happened to have in his pocket, the memorandum drafted for him by Weizsaecker, Goering and Neurath, "a short compromise proposal," as he modestly described it.

The Anglo-French terms accepted by the Czechoslovak Government involved the transfer to Germany of areas in which more than half the inhabitants were Sudeten Germans, with an adjustment of the frontier to be carried out by an international body including a Czechoslovak representative, and an international guarantee of the new boundaries. The areas to be transferred included most of the Czechoslovak fortifications, but no time limit was set for the transfer.

At Godesberg, Hitler added a time limit, October 1, for the transfer of the area which included the bulk of the fortifications. This area was to be handed over with all its installations, communications, and goods intact. A second area was to be subject to plebiscite and subsequent adjustment by a German-Czech or international boundary commission.

The British compromise proposal put to Hitler on September 28 offered occupation by October 1 of Asch, and those parts of the Egerland which were on the German side of the fortifications; an immediate meeting of an Anglo-German-Czech boundary commission; and the handover on October 10 of further areas to which that commission had agreed.

The compromise Mussolini now produced required the evacuation of the largest area, including the fortifications, to begin on October 1, with a guarantee from Britain, France and Italy that the handover would be completed by October 10 without destruction of any of the installations. This first handover would be followed by a plebiscite under international supervision and an international commission to determine the final frontiers.

The key to all this, of course, was the fortifications. Once those were surrendered, the Czechoslovaks had no chance in a fight even if they had the will. It was Colonel Moravec's complaint against the Czechoslovak politicians that they would not defend the fortifications, and they were too afraid of public opinion to reach an agreement with Germany. So it was left to Chamberlain and Daladier to do it for them at Munich. It cannot be claimed that these defenders of democracy behaved very heroically, but they should not be left to bear the odium alone.

When Mussolini's compromise had been produced, discussion of it rambled on for some time. Chamberlain was concerned about the guarantee. How could Britain, France and Italy give a guarantee, he asked, if there were no Czechoslovak representatives present to accept it on behalf of their Government?

Hitler was standing no nonsense of that kind: "If we have to ask the Czechs for their consent to every detail we shall still be at it in a fortnight's time. In the present state of tension the slightest delay would be terribly dangerous."

Always the unspoken threat over their heads: "I shall march in, and then what will you do?"

Chamberlain nevertheless stubbornly insisted that there must be no guarantee. The British, he said, regarded the word "guarantee" as meaning a great deal.

On this point—it was about the only one—he eventually got his way. Britain, France and Italy did not have to guarantee that the Czechoslovaks would evacuate the territory by October 10 without destroying anything. They agreed that it should be done, and held the Czechoslovak Government responsible for doing it.

Chamberlain turned to another point: what was the meaning of the regulation in the German memorandum stating that no cattle should be taken out of the evacuated territory? Did this mean that the farmers would be expelled but that their cattle would be retained?

Chamberlain has of course been ridiculed for talking about cattle at such a time. Nevertheless, farmers are more interested in their cows, shopkeepers are more interested in their stock-in-trade, and householders are more interested in their furniture than any of them are in fortifications. Perhaps this is wrong, but it is so.

The Führer agreed with Chamberlain's critics. He swept these insignificant people and their cattle out of his way: "Our time is too valuable for us to waste it over trifles of this kind."

This was the man speaking who could contemplate the Final Solution, the extermination of the Jewish race; the great Romantic of the Berlin bunker, making his own splendidly defiant ending without regard to its effect upon unimportant people who bother about cattle. It is comforting to recall that, so far, the farmers and their cattle have always won in the end.

At three o'clock the conference adjourned to consider in their separate groups the Italian proposals. Hitler left the Führerhaus first, looking straight in front of him, driving off alone to his flat in Prinz-regentenstrasse. Daladier followed, and almost got into Mussolini's car by mistake. When he found his own, Goering climbed in beside him, and they drove off together, Goering laughing heartily.

When a French journalist asked Daladier during this adjournment what were his impressions, he answered carefully: "I have no impression. . . . When I say that I have no impression, it must be understood that I do not say I have a bad impression. On the contrary, the mere fact that we are all four here is in itself a good sign, as I see it."

It was about the best that could be said.

The British had arranged for a conference with the French at a quarter-to-four to formulate a joint approach to the Italian memorandum. The French did not appear. They were, according to Ivone Kirkpatrick of the British delegation, resolved to reach agreement at any cost. It seems more probable that, with Gallic logic, they saw no point in quibbling about cows when Chamberlain was clearly bent on surrendering the fortifications, without which, Gamelin had told Daladier, Czechoslovakia would "cease to be an effective military asset."

The four delegations met again at a quarter-to-six, and there followed hours of chaos, with small multilingual working-parties drafting clauses which then got lost and had to be laboriously agreed upon again. The Italian Ciano found it agreeable: "This allowed a more intimate way of thinking, and it broke the conversational ice." Hitler showed his opinion of these proceedings by sitting moodily apart, from time to time glancing ominously at his watch. He crossed and uncrossed his legs, folded his arms, and glared round the room, wriggling on his sofa. At intervals, with an obvious effort, he joined in a conversation, only to relapse quickly into silence. On one of these conversational forays, he angled for an invitation to Paris from Daladier, with whom he talked "as between two ex-soldiers." Daladier claims to have been surprised and to have thought of the Parisians' expressions if he returned with Hitler and Goering in his plane. Unsatisfactory as the British were as allies, however, he does not seem to have contemplated swapping horses yet again.

Mussolini was bored by the vaguely parliamentary atmosphere. He strode up and down, up and down, hands in pockets, or allowed himself to be buttonholed by Chamberlain for what Wilson described as "some useful conversation." But Mussolini, like Daladier, remained steadfast to his ally.

A banquet had been arranged at the Führerhaus for eight o'clock. Chamberlain and Daladier had been invited, but preferred to dine at their hotels. There was, they explained, so much still to do, and colleagues in London and Paris had to be consulted by telephone. Without these skeletons at their feast, the Germans and Italians were able to enjoy themselves. Mussolini became expansive on the subject of democracies: "The fools! If they had simply extended their sanctions to cover oil, in a week they would have made it impossible for me to conquer Abyssinia!" It was perhaps fortunate that he did not know the British Mediterranean Fleet, upon which enforcement of oil sanctions would have depended, had only enough ammunition at the time to fire for fifteen minutes.

While the banquet proceeded, wild rumors circulated among the assembled journalists. There was a last-minute hitch, Chamberlain was flying back to London to consult his Cabinet, this would certainly mean war. Goebbels' representative at Munich stilled the rumors, however, by announcing rather prematurely that agreement had been reached on all the main points. Only one difficulty had arisen: how the terms of the agreement were to be transmitted to the Czechoslovaks.

It was still five weary hours before the legal experts had finished their drafting. A little before two o'clock on the morning of September 30, the Munich Agreement was ready to be signed. It followed closely the Italian proposals: evacuation of the ceded areas was to begin on October 1 and be completed by October 10. The conditions governing the evacuation would be laid down by an international commission consisting of representatives of Germany, Britain, France, Italy and Czechoslovakia. This commission would also determine the areas in which a plebiscite was to be held, and the final frontier lines. An annex repeated the Anglo-French offer to join in an international guarantee of what remained of Czechoslovakia. The German and Italian Governments agreed to join the guarantee "when the question of the Polish and Hungarian minorities has been settled."

François-Poncet glanced through the agreement, flushed, and said aloud: "That is how France treats the only allies who have remained faithful to her." Mussolini congratulated a stone-faced Daladier:

"You'll be cheered when you get back to France." Hitler looked glum. Perhaps he was thinking how much better it would have been to squash these democratic black beetles once and for all.

The four statesmen lined up to append their signatures to this document. The photographers filed respectfully in. The newsreel men set up their cameras and switched on their lights. It was then found that the imposing inkwell provided was as empty of ink as the conference had been of conferring.

Ink was fortunately procured, and the agreement signed. Frederick T. Birchall of *The New York Times* was in consequence able to tell the world that "all four seem to have worked together with a thoroughness of purpose and speed in execution that restore to the practice of conferences some of its lost prestige."

There then arose, as Wilson delicately put it, the question, "What to do about the Czechs?" A British suggestion that Daladier, as Prime Minister of Czechoslovakia's ally, should personally take the agreement to Prague was turned down by that statesman. The British were now determined, however, that there should be no more shuffling off of French responsibilities on to British shoulders, and it was decided that Daladier and Chamberlain together should see Dr. Mastny, the Czechoslovak Government's official representative, and hand over the document to him. This meeting took place, according to Wilson, in the Prime Minister's room in the Hotel Regina at about quarter-past two in the morning.

"I gave M. Daladier the prepared copy (with map) so that he might hand it to M. Mastny," Wilson recorded pointedly.

Mastny read the document, and asked a number of questions. "He was given a pretty broad hint," wrote Wilson, "that—having regard to the seriousness of the alternative—the best course was for his Government to accept what was clearly a considerable improvement upon the German Memorandum."

Accustomed though he was to being given pretty broad hints by Goering, Ribbentrop and every other bully, Mastny could not keep back his tears. François-Poncet consoled him: "Believe me, all this is not final. It is only a moment in a piece of history that is beginning and in which everything will soon be called into question once again." One would like to believe that François-Poncet did say it, and did not simply invent it for his memoirs.

Daladier was brusque and embarrassed. Chamberlain could not

hide his yawns. He was, he said, tired, but pleasantly tired. He had, after all, achieved what he had set out to achieve, which was to prevent war.

The French and British Prime Ministers got away from the weeping Mastny as quickly as they decently could. Perhaps rather more quickly.

A telegram was soon on its way to the British Minister in Prague: "You should at once see President and on behalf of His Majesty's Government urge acceptance of plan that has been worked out today after prolonged discussion with a view of avoiding conflict. You will appreciate that there is no time for argument; it must be a plain acceptance."

At half-past six that morning, Hencke, the German chargé d'affaires in Prague, wakened Krofta, the Czechoslovak Foreign Minister, with a telephoned summary of the Agreement and with an invitation to send representatives to the first meeting of the international boundary commission. This was to be in Berlin at five o'clock that afternoon. Beneš was being made to pay dearly for May 21 and September 13.

At nine o'clock, Mastny reached Prague with the full text and took it straight to Beneš. At half-past nine, Beneš telephoned Alexandrovsky, the Russian Ambassador. He said the great powers had sacrificed Czechoslovakia to Hitler in the most shameful way, and for their advantage. The final settlement of formalities had been left to Czechoslovakia. This meant that Czechoslovakia was faced with a choice. Either she could start a war with Germany, in which Britain and France would be against her, or at least their Governments would try to influence public opinion by representing Czechoslovakia as the cause of war. Or she could capitulate. Beneš said he did not know what the attitude of Parliament and the political parties would be, but he inquired about the attitude of Russia either to fighting or to capitulation. He asked for a reply by six or seven o'clock that evening.

This was a dying kick, if indeed it was a kick at all, and not just something Beneš wanted written into the record. He had a very good idea what the attitude of the political parties was likely to be, since, if Beran is to be believed, he had been telephoning the leaders during the night, giving them a military assessment of the situation produced by Husarek, the new Chief of Staff. According to Beran,

Husarek's appreciation was that on the outbreak of war, Germany, Poland and Hungary would attack, Bohemia and Moravia would be quickly cut off from Slovakia, and "despite heroic efforts from the army, they would be thrown on their own resources and not be in a position to resist for long. Therefore, to go to war would be almost synonymous with suicide."

Communications between Prague and Moscow were such that Alexandrovsky was told he could not get a telephone call through until five o'clock that evening. He therefore telegraphed Beneš's inquiry, then went up to Hradcany Castle to find out what he could about the situation.

At the castle, two meetings were going on simultaneously. The first was attended by Beneš, members of the former Hodza Government, and the party leaders. The second involved General Syrovy and his ministers, the nominal Government, which Syrovy opened with the pronouncement that they were faced with a choice between being murdered or committing suicide.

Krofta followed Syrovy with a report on the Munich terms. Theoretically, he said, it would be possible to reject them, but then there would be a German invasion and a war in which no one would be on their side. Poland would also attack. It was doubtful whether Russia would help, or if she did, whether her help would be of any use. On the other hand, they could accept the agreement, and perhaps avert the worst by negotiations.

One member of the Government, Zenkl, the Lord Mayor of Prague, asked for the recall of Parliament, but was silenced by the customary argument: Parliament could not be recalled in time, there must be an immediate decision, it was a matter of acceptance or rejection.

At half-past eleven this meeting adjourned, assembling again a quarter of an hour later to hear the President of the Republic. Minister Zenkl caused some concern by ostentatiously absenting himself from this second meeting. As one of his colleagues remarked, nobody should be allowed to break the unity they had maintained until now, or to oppose the Government at such a critical time. In short, if there was to be another Defenestration of Prague, Minister Zenkl should be prepared to be thrown out of the windows with the rest of them.

Beneš made his report: he had no other course but to propose acceptance of the ultimatum. If they did not accept it, they would,

of course, fight an honorable war, but they would lose their independence and people would be exterminated. The leaders of the political parties saw matters in that light. If the Cabinet were now to
agree with them, then there would be complete unanimity.

One by one, these unhappy men made their little speeches. If
they accepted, said the first, it must be firmly insisted upon that the
Germans should not use force. The President of the Republic, said
another, must restrain the Communists. If the Commander-in-Chief
assured them that no defense was possible, said a third, he had no
option but to agree to the Munich terms.

The President of the Republic said he would regard these statements as agreement. He solemnly called on Government, State and
People to rise above this crisis. History, he said, would judge.

At midday, Alexandrovsky, waiting in the office of the President's
principal secretary, was told that in deference to the decision of the
Government, no answer to Beneš's inquiry was now required from
Moscow.

It is, of course, impossible to reconcile this statement to Alexandrovsky with the record of how the question of Russian help was
put to the Government by Krofta, or of the manner in which the Government reached its agreement. But Beneš and his colleagues were
men under almost intolerable strain.

The news of surrender was kept from the people of Czechoslovakia until five o'clock that evening, and came at the end of a broadcast by Syrovy. When they heard it, some wept, some got drunk, a
few shot or gassed themselves. The rest, thanks to Beneš and Chamberlain, went on living.

Keith Eubank

THE RIDDLE

After 1938 it became popular to equate appeasement with surrender. Chamberlain and Daladier were condemned for capitulating to Hitler without calling his bluff. If they had not surrendered to his bluff, he would have been forced to back down; they missed an opportunity to defeat Hitler without a world war. The reasons for the Anglo-French decision to choose appeasement instead of war are part of the "riddle of Munich."

In the story of the Munich Agreement there is a riddle. Was it only surrender to Hitler's bluff? If Britain and France had stood fast, resolute in their determination to resist, would Czechoslovak independence and world peace have been saved? Or was the Agreement unavoidable under the circumstances? Was it a "tragic necessity?"

To denounce the Munich Agreement as cowardly surrender is simple, but there is more to the tale. Other forces sent Chamberlain and Daladier to Munich. They did not go there out of sheer folly. They made the journey because it seemed the only alternative to a war no one wanted.

In 1938 the Munich Agreement seemed sensible to many who fancied themselves sane, sober, and Christian. It was far better than another world war. Because the Sudetens wanted to become a part of Germany, they seemed a poor excuse for bloodshed. The Treaty of Versailles was wicked; another world war was unthinkable. If appeasing Hitler with the Sudetenland avoided a world war, peace was preferred. There seemed to be no way to prevent German armies from overrunning Czechoslovakia.

There was an attempt to scientifically sample public opinion during the September crisis. This sampling revealed that 70 percent of those contacted in one London borough reacted favorably to Chamberlain's flight to visit Hitler on September 15. At the time of the Godesberg meeting, the opposition to Chamberlain had risen to 40 percent, according to a similar sampling; but the opposition dropped on September 30 to 10 percent, with 54 percent favoring him and 26 percent expressing no opinion. After September 30, however, the

From *Munich*, by Keith Eubank (Norman, 1963), pp. 278–287. Copyright © 1963 by the University of Oklahoma Press. Reprinted by permission. Footnotes omitted.

chorus of approval seemed proof of public assent, regardless of the wisdom of the Agreement. Every sign in France and Great Britain indicated the satisfaction of the man in the street with the Munich Agreement. The few dissenters were drowned out by those who wanted peace and had no wish to die for Czechoslovakia. To the politicians the Munich Agreement seemed justified by public opinion.

Of these politicians, none has been more condemned for the Munich Agreement than Chamberlain. He did not accept the Munich Agreement out of cowardice but because he was unwilling to drag the nation into a world war over an issue that did not seem worth the loss of countless lives. He doubted that the nation would have followed him into a war to coerce a minority who wanted to exercise the right of self-determination. He preferred to seek a formula satisfying Hitler's political demands and then to solve the Anglo-German economic problems because these were to him the most important.

To the end of his life, Chamberlain believed that his policy had been the only one possible in 1938, given the spirit of the time and the hostility of the Opposition. But the excuse of a strong Opposition meant little within the House of Commons where the Tories had a safe majority.

Chamberlain was strengthened in his resolution to appease Hitler by the pathetic condition of the French government and the Premier. Although Daladier accurately evaluated Hitler's aggression, he would not lead his nation into a war over Czechoslovakia. He blamed everyone else for the sins of France: British lack of armaments, Britain's refusal to support France, Polish hostility towards Czechoslovakia, Russian legalism over the alliance, and United States' isolationism. It was sheer folly, he told the National Assembly in 1946, to fight Germany alone: France could be engaged to fight Germany only within a coalition.

In 1938, France was alone except for the help provided by the British fleet. There was no mighty coalition. There had been hopes that, if war with Germany ever came, Poland, Russia, and Czechoslovakia would attack Germany from the east while the French armies remained behind the Maginot Line; but in 1938, Poland was hostile and Russia preferred to watch rather than act. To save Czechoslovakia, France would be forced to mount an attack.

When the French government had concluded the 1935 alliance with Czechoslovakia, no one considered that France would ever be called upon to fulfill her obligations by attacking Germany. The alliance would provide a Czech attack on Germany, not a French one. Appalled at the bloody prospect of assaulting Germany in 1938, French politicians and generals deserted Czechoslovakia, using the Munich Agreement. The generals tried to excuse their desertion by launching a campaign to expose the inferiority of the Czech armed forces.

If France had ever seriously intended to aid Czechoslovakia, she would have made plans for an invasion of Germany. Such plans never existed, and without an invasion of Germany to draw off Hitler's armies, the Czech forces were doomed. No plans for an attack on Germany existed in 1938, because French strategy was defensive. The war of 1914–18 seemed to have proven the superiority of the defense over the offense. As a symbol of this philosophy, the Maginot Line had been constructed to withstand the expected German offensive.

Behind the Line the armies of France would be secure; casualties would be slight while French guns decimated the enemy. The Line made defensive strategy imperative; it nullified the Czech alliance; it confounded all hopes of a French offensive against Germany. If the French armies stayed on the defensive, however, the Czech armies would be left alone to face the German attack. The armies of France would become involved in the war only if Germany attacked the Maginot Line, but Hitler planned to attack only in the east.

There had not even been any planning with the Czech general staff. When General Ludvík Krejčí, the Czechoslovak chief of staff, proposed to Gamelin, on June 18, 1938, that joint studies be made to insure unity of decision, Gamelin referred the question to his government. No action was ever taken because the French High Command had no intention of any offensive action to draw German troops away from the Czechoslovak frontiers. They followed the teachings of Marshal Henri Pétain, who believed that defensive strategy reinforced by the Line made alliances unnecessary.

There had not been any joint planning with the British general staff. Whatever plans the French may have had in September, 1938, were not passed on to the British, who only knew that French plans were based on defense rather than offense and that they would not leave the Maginot Line.

The failure of the staffs to confer was also a result of policy of the British chiefs of staff, who feared that talks with the French would anger the Germans when Chamberlain was seeking appeasement and would involve the British forces in commitments they could not fulfill. For similar reasons, cabinet instructions forbade any discussions of strategic plans with French generals. Until March, 1939, neither general staff had any definite idea of the strategic planning of the other.

Any plan to aid Czechoslovakia required a massive striking force —heavy tank divisions, possessing powerful engines, and long-range artillery with armor-piercing shells—poised on the western frontiers of Germany prepared to thrust deep into the vitals of the Nazi empire and draw off the German forces fighting in Bohemia and Moravia. Such an offensive force did not exist in 1938, mainly because of the attitudes of certain French generals and Daladier. In September, 1938, the French army had two light, armored divisions capable only of limited reconnaissance and protection for the infantry from other infantry but not from tanks. With heavy armored divisions and a resolve to attack, French forces would have broken through Germany and saved Czechoslovakia. Without these forces, Czechoslovakia was doomed.

Given the help of thirty to forty Czech divisions in 1938, France was stronger than Germany, but this strength was useless without an offensive strategy and plans for an invasion of Germany. Had war come in 1938, the French armies would have remained along the Maginot Line, facing only eleven German divisions, while the bulk of Hitler's forces slaughtered the Czechs.

The French air force would have provided little help in a war. It was antiquated, weak, and crippled by defensive strategy. In September, 1938, France had only seven hundred planes, and none was modern. The *Luftwaffe* had over twenty-eight hundred planes, and more than one thousand of these were bombers.

France lacked the industrial facilities necessary to sustain her air force in a modern world war. Between 1936 and 1938, the French government had ordered 761 planes, a month's production in Germany in 1938, and by September 1938, only 83 had been delivered.

The faith of the French in their air force was not improved by the reports of so eminent an authority as Colonel Charles Lindbergh. Appearing in Paris and London amid the September crisis, he preached peace at any price because the *Luftwaffe* was the strongest air force in the world and would "flatten out cities like London, Paris, and Prague."

The condition of the French air force was one more excuse that Daladier used to evade responsibilities which could have brought war. Another excuse was the condition of the British armed forces. Of these, only the Royal Navy approached a state of combat readiness when mobilized in 1938. However, there was no way for the fleet to aid Czechoslovakia because the seacoasts of Bohemia existed only in Shakespeare's mind.

The British army could offer no more than two divisions for service on the Continent, and Chamberlain was loath to promise even this. In 1938 only five, fully equipped, regular army divisions had been planned. They were to be trained for fighting a colonial war. Such a force would be unfit for offensive warfare against Germany. Noticeably lacking was any large force of mechanized armor, sufficient to pierce the German defenses and race to the aid of the Czechoslovak armies.

As late as November, 1938, the Chancellor of the Exchequer forbade the increase of the army to six divisions, using the argument of economy. One chief of staff observed that the Chancellor "was primarily concerned to insure that we had enough money left to pay the indemnity after losing the war."

After the occupation of Prague, the British army undertook to prepare thirty-two divisions—a force comparable in size to the Czechoslovak army which had been surrendered to Hitler without a fight. If Hitler had been faced in 1938 with thirty-two British divisions, thirty-five Czech divisions, and over one hundred French divisions, prepared to drive through Germany with all their strength, protected by a mighty air armada, there would not have been a Munich Agreement.

Of the three British military services, the status of the Royal Air Force had the most decisive influence on British policy in the September crisis. The R.A.F. did not measure up to the needs of the time either in defense or offense. In 1938 the R.A.F. could fight a German air force that had existed in 1936. The *Anschluss* forced the cabinet to approve a first-line expansion to twelve thousand planes, to be ready within two years. This planned increase was known as *Schedule L;* only 10 percent of the plan had been completed by the September crisis. This plan was consistent with the practice of expanding first-line aircraft without creating the reserves, administration, and auxiliary services necessary to withstand a long conflict.

In September, 1938, less than thirty fighter squadrons were ready for duty. Only five of these were equipped with modern Hurricane fighters and none with Spitfires. In all there were 759 fighters, and the majority were outdated and so slow that German bombers could evade them easily. Although 93 Hurricanes were available, they were unable to fight above fifteen thousand feet even in summer because the guns could not be heated. Pilots for these squadrons were in short supply. The administration, reserve planes, and auxiliary services were lacking for a long war. The situation was similar in the bombing squadrons—insufficiency in modern planes, personnel, airfields, and servicing facilities. The R.A.F. was unfit for a world war.

Other means for air defense were lacking. Only 126 antiaircraft guns were available for the defense of London in September, 1938, and only 334 for the whole of the British Isles. The radar chain was incomplete, and the personnel were untrained in its use. Except for hastily dug trenches in parks, sufficient air-raid shelters were lacking. Estimates of the probable number of killed and wounded that might result among the civilian population from air raids appalled the British government. Within sixty days of the first air assault, 600,000 dead were expected, creating an additional problem in the disposal of so many bodies. To build sufficient coffins would have required over twenty million square feet of timber. Hospitals would have been clogged with over 1.2 million wounded. Psychiatrists anticipated three to four million mental casualties within six months of the outbreak of war. There were no plans whatsoever to feed the population during the air attacks.

The inability of the British armed forces to wage modern war against Germany was known only too well within the government. When Chamberlain faced Hitler at Munich, the armaments and troops necessary to fight Germany did not exist, nor did the means to protect the civilian population. Thus it seemed wise to appease Hitler with the Sudetenland, for he could take all of Czechoslovakia if he desired while Britain could not stop him.

The riddle of the Munich Agreement is not solved by the testimony of the German generals, given after the war, that Germany was unprepared for a world war in September, 1938, and would not have fought had Britain and France resisted. Although Germany was unprepared for a world war in September, 1938, her armed forces were ready for a war against Czechoslovakia. Germany could not have held out against the Anglo-French forces in the West if they had been prepared to invade Germany, but emphasis on defensive strategy, lack of modern arms, and the Maginot Line made these forces ready to sit out the war.

At the Nuremberg trials, the German generals argued that their armies would have been delayed by the Czechoslovak fortifications, but if they had been willing to suffer losses they would probably have gotten through. Czechoslovak forces planned a withdrawal to avoid being outflanked on the old Austrian frontier where the fortifications were slight. Such strategy would have succeeded if the Anglo-French forces had been ready to sweep into Germany.

Now we know that the German armed forces were not as well prepared in 1938 as they were in 1939 or 1940, but they were ready for a war against Czechoslovakia—a limited war on one front. There was no need to worry about war on two fronts, because the British had little with which to fight, and the French had no intention of attacking Germany.

Now we realize that the intelligence estimates of the size of the *Luftwaffe* were exaggerated; however, in combat readiness, it far exceeded that of the Anglo-French air forces. Intelligence estimates were colored by the effects of the Douhet theory that bombers could score a swift, knockout blow. The Spanish Civil War increased the fears of total destruction from the air.

Although the *Luftwaffe* lacked heavy, long-range bombers to pound London and Paris, there were enough planes to overwhelm the Czech air force. Only a skeleton force would have been needed on the western front where there was no intention of attacking Germany. Hitler's forces could have defeated Czechoslovakia at will, aided by the Poles and Hungarians, if they cared to share in the loot.

If war had come in 1938, would the story have ended differently? If the Czechoslovak army had not been forced to divert too many troops against Poland and Hungary, probably the German armies would have been delayed a little longer in their conquest. Their ultimate victory, however, would have been certain, given time to wear down the Czech resistance and willingness to sustain casualties. Czechoslovakia would have received no direct aid from Britain and France and even less indirect aid than Poland received in 1939.

While the Germans conquered Czechoslovakia, Anglo-French troops would have remained on the defensive within the Maginot Line.

If Hitler had then taken only the Sudetenland, without direct aggression against Britain and France, these governments would have been sorely tempted to make peace. This policy would have seemed logical and moral because Hitler was only taking what many believed had been torn from Germany by the Versailles Treaty.

If a general European war had come in 1938, the fall of France could have come a year earlier. The R.A.F. would not have been ready for the Battle of Britain if it had come in 1939, for *Schedule M,* the plan under which the fighters for the Battle of Britain were produced, was not drawn up until October, 1938, as a result of the Munich Agreement. It is doubtful if the Hurricanes and Spitfires could have been built in sufficient numbers to be ready for an earlier battle. Time was needed to bring *Schedule M* to completion. Time was needed to complete the radar chain which provided the eyes and ears of the R.A.F. in 1940. Had the Battle of Britain been fought in 1939, there is serious doubt that the R.A.F. could have withstood the *Luftwaffe.*

Arguments over the feasibility of war in 1938 prove little, however, because few in positions of responsibility in France and Britain wanted war over Czechoslovakia. Waging war would have meant that war had been accepted as the only alternative to a worse fate. In September, 1938, this did not seem to be the case either to the British and French peoples or to their governments.

If they would oppose Hitler, they must be resolved to go to the brink of war and beyond if necessary, but only Hitler was resolved to press on to war if such were necessary. Neither France nor Britain was resolved to stand fast against Hitler if war were the consequence. They were without the will and the means to resist. To those who prided themselves on their realism, there was no excuse for a world war and every excuse for appeasement.

When the four powers met at Munich, only Germany was prepared to pay the cost of victory—war. The governments of Britain and France wanted to avoid war over the Sudetens because such a cause was unworthy of the cost. Appeasement of Hitler through the Munich Agreement seemed worthwhile if it avoided a world war which Britain and France never wanted and for which they were unprepared in armaments and in spirit.

Here is the answer to the riddle of the Munich Agreement: to wage war required sufficient cause, a will to war, and the men and armaments. Because these were lacking in 1938, Chamberlain and Daladier had no other choice than to sign the Munich Agreement.

Leonard Mosley
THE FALL OF CZECHOSLOVAKIA

During his career as a journalist, Leonard Mosley covered the Spanish Civil War, Nazi Germany, World War II in Africa and Yugoslavia, as well as in Normandy where he dropped on D-Day with a British airborne division. His On Borrowed Time *(1969), from which this selection is taken, focuses on the events from the Czechoslovak crisis through the outbreak of war; it is based on archival research as well as on Mosley's personal contacts. He is a strong supporter of the thesis that World War II could have been prevented by shelving appeasement in favor of resistance to Hitler's demands. It was the fall of Czechoslovakia, described in this selection, that undermined appeasement and revealed Hitler's duplicity.*

In Adolf Hitler's mind there had never been any doubt that Czechoslovakia would eventually come completely under the control of the German Reich; it was merely a question of how and when. In the months following his easy victory at Munich he had come to believe that Chamberlain and Daladier, with the misguided connivance of Mussolini, had tricked rather than appeased him, and that a more forthright and determined attitude would have given him the whole of Bohemia and Moravia instead of merely the Sudetenland. Long after the event, he continued to complain that Chamberlain was "that fellow [who] cheated me of my entry into Prague," and the more he saw of the supine attitudes of the Western democracies, the more he regretted not having been tougher.

But the Führer was shrewd enough to see that with patience he would get all he wanted, and without having to fight for it. Was that, however, really what he had in mind? Would the fact that the new

Czechoslovakia was practically pleading to be regarded as an obedient satellite of the Reich satisfy his needs? For Hitler had needs, as far as the Czechs were concerned: a need to see himself in control of their destinies, since he suspected that as non-Germans they despised him; a need to demonstrate to the world that though they proclaimed themselves so-called democrats and liberals, they would do his bidding at the crack of a whip. In his attitude toward the peoples of Central and Eastern Europe, Adolf Hitler remained an Austrian and was as arrogant a racialist as Emperor Franz Josef of the Austro-Hungarian Empire had been.

The new government in Prague never made any bones about its willingness to be considered a puppet state, and each time its Foreign Minister, Chvalkovský, was summoned to Berlin, he bent his small head in submission and pleaded to be helped and understood by the overlords of Greater Germany. He attacked the English and French; he sneered at the United States; he presented statistics to prove that the Jews and Communists were being driven out of Czech life. When pressed, he would admit that the change from freedom and democracy to wholehearted dependence on the Reich was perhaps not as swift as it might be, and that there were some Czechs who were not completely cooperative, but he added, "I hope that the Führer will have a good word for the Czechs sometimes. That could do wonders."

And yet if the remainder of Czechoslovakia fell into Germany's hands, just like that, what would be the triumph? Eduard Beneš had once defied Germany from the heights of Hradčany Castle in Prague; Hitler had seen pictures of him in the palace, which dominated the swift-flowing Vltava River. It was a building and a site that appealed to his sense of the dramatic. It was here that German kings had once ruled, waged wars, received vassals and settled the destiny of Central and Eastern Europe. But how could he ever usurp the seat once occupied by the hated Beneš if a subservient Czech state simply went on doing what the Germans told it to do?

But by March the Czechs provided him with the excuse he was seeking to turn a servile satellite into a dependency needing his "protection."

Some months earlier, in November 1938, the Germans and Italians had presided over a congress in Vienna to settle the eastern frontier of Czechoslovakia. Hungary in particular was seeking large tracts of territory which would extend far beyond those areas of Slovakia and Ruthenia where the majority of the population was Magyar. Encouraged by the Italians, with whom they had a long-standing alliance, they even went so far as to threaten to occupy the city of Bratislava, the ancient capital of Slovakia. Since Bratislava (or Pressburg, as the Germans called it) was just across the Danube from Austria and not many miles from Vienna itself, this was too much for Adolf Hitler. In any case, like most Austrians, he was fundamentally anti-Hungarian and was contemptuous of their cowardice during the Munich crisis. Why should they eat the meal they had refused to help to cook? Hence he ordered Ribbentrop to resist the Hungarian demands and to support the Slovak delegates in their pleas for the retention of their capital and territory—and so it was decided, to the ill-concealed disappointment of the Hungarians and Italians.

In approving the frontier in favor of the Slovaks, Hitler had only one idea in mind: to bring about the final disintegration of the Czechoslovak state. Ribbentrop had made it clear to the Slovak leaders, headed by Monsignor Jozef Tiso,[1] that they were being saved from the Hungarians in order to become independent and to break off their relations with the Czechs under President Emil Hácha in Prague. In the weeks that followed, however, not only did the Slovaks show no signs of breaking away; the Czechs made it clear that they would not be allowed to do so by moving troops into the area, especially into Bratislava, and threatening to use force against any Slovakian coup d'état.

On the evening of March 9, 1939, a message reached President Hácha as he was having supper with his daughter in Hradčany Castle. His Foreign Minister wanted to see him urgently.

The tiny gnome who now represented the external relations of Czechoslovakia was perspiring visibly when he came into the President's study, and it was obvious that he was extremely nervous. From Chvalkovský's hand a piece of paper fluttered, and he stammered several times before he could begin speaking. He had important news, he said. A message had just come through from Bratislava, and he feared that they were in for trouble unless they moved swiftly. The paper came from a most reliable source in the city, Klinevsky, the chief of police and head of intelligence in Slovakia.

---

[1] Political priests were an old tradition in this part of Europe. The Roman Catholic Premier's principal political opponent, Karol Sidor, was also of the priesthood.

Hácha reminded the Foreign Minister that he could not see well in such poor light and asked him to read it.

Chvalkovský did so. "I have to report that from the most reliable sources of information inside the Cabinet itself, a coup d'état is being prepared by Tiso and Durčansky [Minister of Communications in the Slovak federal government]. They have already been in contact with Seyss-Inquart and Bürckel in Vienna [Seyss-Inquart was the Nazi governor of Austria, and Josef Bürckel Gauleiter of the district abutting the Slovakian frontier], who have agreed to cooperate. Arms are being smuggled into Bratislava by the Nazis and will be given to the Hlinka Guard [the Slovak fascist group] and the German minority under Kerminski, their leader. They will conduct demonstrations and threaten a rising if Tiso does not declare Slovakia's independence of Prague. Tiso will bow to the demands of the people, and will sever his connection with the central government on March tenth."

There was a long silence, broken only by the crackle of paper as Chvalkovský folded the message. Finally the Foreign Minister coughed. What should be done?

The old man shook himself as if he had been asleep; he was old and tired and frightened.

There was only one thing to be done, he answered, if the state was to be saved from disintegration: act at once. The rebellion must be put down. The orders must be sent through at once to the army. Tiso and Durčansky must be arrested. A new Cabinet should be formed at once—under Karol Sidor, of course. At least he was reliable.

There was silence again. Chvalkovský waited, but the old man was sunk in gloom. After a few minutes he slowly tiptoed out of the room and motioned to Hácha's devoted daughter, Mrs. Milada Radlova, waiting outside, to tend to him.

Later that night in Bratislava, Czech army officers called on Monsignor Tiso in his office in the old rathskeller overlooking the bridge across the Danube leading to Austria, and politely informed him that he was under arrest.

Tiso seemed astonished. "What is the reason?" he asked.

They told him that they did not know the precise reason but believed it was to prevent the coup d'état he was planning.

"What coup d'état?" Tiso asked. "I know nothing about it. I am loyal to Prague."

The priest was taken to a monastery some fifty miles from the city, where a cell had been prepared for him and a guard stationed at the gates.[2] Then the army officers set off to find Durčansky. But warned of the orders for his arrest, more aware of what was going on than Monsignor Tiso, Durčansky had already crossed the Danube.

Meanwhile Klinevsky, the Bratislava chief of police and Prague's "reliable" intelligence chief in Slovakia, was on the telephone with Bürckel to report that all had gone well: the Prague government had swallowed the bait. For it was in connivance with Durčansky and the Germans that Klinevsky had drawn up the report for Hácha of Monsignor Tiso's planned coup d'état. It was completely false.

The trap had been set for Prague. Now all that was needed was the order to spring it. . . .

General Wilhelm Keitel, Chief of the Armed Forces High Command, had been waiting for orders since the end of February. He knew the signs; German newspapers had begun to fill with all the old stories. The savage Czechs were on the rampage again, but this time they were not only persecuting innocent German minorities; they were also bullying and brutalizing the Slovaks. Not a day passed without the *Völkischer Beobachter,* the official Nazi newspaper, reporting that a pregnant Slovak mother had been cold-bloodedly kicked in the stomach by a Czech soldier, or a Slovak student had been insulted by a Czech professor.

"The Führer repeatedly announced that he had put up with as much as he could stand and did not intend to stand impotently by," Keitel wrote later. "I gathered that the so-called 'cleaning up' of rump Czechoslovakia was drawing near. Although when I asked the Führer he would neither admit his ultimate intentions nor give me any kind of date, I took the necessary steps to see that the War Office was assured of being able to unleash a swift and sudden invasion should the need arise."

In early March, Hitler had called a meeting of his two senior generals, Keitel and Brauchitsch, the Commander in Chief of the Army,

2 Twenty-four hours later the monks let Tiso out and he made his way back to Bratislava.

and told them flatly that he had resolved upon military intervention in Czechoslovakia. He called it a "pacification operation" and said that it would not require any military conscription over and above that provided for in the orders still in force from the crisis of the previous autumn. But even now he did not give his generals a date.

"I put my own money on 'the Ides of March,'" wrote Keitel. "Apart from 1937, it had always been the date since 1933 that Adolf Hitler had chosen to act on. Was it always coincidence or superstition? I am inclined to believe the latter. . . . Sure enough, on March 12 the advance orders went out to the army and air force to stand by for a possible invasion of Czechoslovakia at six o'clock on the morning of March 15; no forces were to approach within six miles of the frontier before then. None of us soldiers learned what circumstances were to be invoked for the unleashing of such an attack."

When he heard the news, Keitel went to his office in the Bendlerstrasse and at once sent out a top-secret memorandum to his senior generals telling them to be ready. Within thirty minutes a copy had been received by Admiral Canaris, and was also being scanned by his assistant, Colonel Oster. . . .

Canaris handed over the Keitel memorandum to Oster, who did not need to be told what to do. He already had several contacts with the British Secret Service.

On March 11 the head of the British Secret Service telephoned from his office in Whitehall and asked for an immediate appointment with Sir Alexander Cadogan, Permanent Undersecretary at the Foreign Office. The two men met, and Sir Alexander was handed a decoded message from Germany which read:

> The German army will invade Bohemia and Moravia at six a.m. on March 15. Irregular forces will cross the frontier some hours ahead of this but these will be for diversionary purposes and are not to be confused with the main operation. An ultimatum of short duration will be handed to the Czech authorities and to the Chief of the Czech Armed Forces ordering them to lay down their arms, ground their aircraft and return to barracks, but this will not be delivered until the last possible moment. The main element of the operation is surprise.

In view of the stupefaction and indignation which the British Prime Minister was subsequently to display over the events of the next few days, the history of what happened to this message is worth noting. In the first place Sir Alexander Cadogan, who must have been told by his intelligence chief the source of the message, seemed to show surprisingly little alarm. To be sure, he wrote in his diary that "it made my hair stand on end," and he did say that he would show it to the Foreign Secretary and the Prime Minister at once. But thereafter he allowed Halifax to depart for various engagements around the country. As for Chamberlain, apparently it did not occur to him to summon the Cabinet for a briefing or to call in his service chiefs and discuss the situation with them. . . .

In a private apartment on the outskirts of Bratislava, a group of frightened men were holding a meeting early on Sunday morning, March 12.

Karol Sidor, Premier of the Slovak government, had held his first Cabinet meeting the evening before in the rathskeller in the center of the city, close to the Danube, and quickly learned something of the situation which he and his people were facing. At ten o'clock, halfway through the discussion, the doors were suddenly flung open and into the room marched Seyss-Inquart, Gauleiter Bürckel and five men whose uniforms and insignia identified them as generals in the German army. They had driven across the Danube from Austria and, as Seyss-Inquart explained to the mortified Slovaks, they hadn't much time to spare, for there was a great deal to do back in Vienna. Events were on the march.

All he had come to say, Seyss-Inquart went on, was that the Slovak government should not delay in proclaiming its independence. The Führer was not uninterested in the fate of Slovakia, but that fate was not likely to be a happy one if there was any more procrastination in Bratislava. His friends were—indicating the generals—witness to the fact that the German army was not far away.

Then he stalked out, the generals following, though Gauleiter Bürckel stayed behind to whisper to Sidor, "The Führer has decided to settle the fate of the Czechs once and for all. For God's sake, don't waste any more time in proclaiming independence—otherwise I can't tell you what will happen to you!"

The Slovakian Premier promised to keep the warning in mind, but stated firmly that neither he nor his colleagues could make a decision without first consulting Prague. He spent the rest of the night talking to Chvalkovský on the telephone, getting nowhere. Then, having decided that the rathskeller was too near the Danube and Austria, he asked his Cabinet to come to his own apartment at eight o'clock in the morning. He was about to put the issue to them when Klinevsky, the chief of police, rushed in. "You'll have to get out!" he said. "I have information that the Hlinka Guard knows you are meeting here and may attack you at any moment."

Sidor said that if so, they could not carry on government business in Bratislava. They were too near the Germans and their *francstireurs.* They should move the seat of government to Trnava, a small town twenty miles farther from the border.

Klinevsky told him that this was impossible; German troops had taken up positions on all routes leading from the city, and they would never get through.

Where, then, could they meet in safety? Sidor asked plaintively. Klinevsky suggested going to the *Slovak* offices. *Slovak* was the chief newspaper of Monsignor Tiso. Since he was such a bitter opponent of Premier Sidor, no one would guess that they would hold a Cabinet meeting there.

They finally agreed on this, but when the panicky members of the Cabinet filed into the editor's office, whom should they find sitting there but Monsignor Tiso himself, fresh from his monastery-prison. Without any formality he told his visitors that Gauleiter Bürckel had just delivered a telegram to him from Adolf Hitler summoning him to Berlin at once.

Sidor said firmly that Tiso must refuse to go, since it was no longer his responsibility. Tiso replied that he could not refuse—for Slovakia's sake. Bürckel had told him that if he did not comply with the Führer's request, two German divisions would occupy Bratislava; they were just across the river now. Furthermore, the Hungarians would be given carte blanche; Hitler had already promised them Ruthenia. If Tiso did not go to Berlin, Hitler would let them take eastern Slovakia as well.

Klinevsky agreed that the priest should go. Hitler might hate the Czechs, but he was Slovakia's friend. There was everything to gain by his going.

Tiso added that what he had most to gain was time. There was no train to Vienna before Monday morning, the next day. He could not possibly be back before Tuesday evening to deliver whatever decision the Führer decided to make. This gave the others time to consult Prague, and time for Prague to consult Warsaw—for Poland would certainly not be uninterested in their fate—and the situation might well be different by the time he returned.

Different it was, but not quite in the way Tiso had hoped, for the Germans had shrewdly anticipated his thinking. When the Monsignor's train arrived in Vienna just before noon on Monday morning, March 13, two Gestapo officers were waiting for him. They saluted him and politely invited him into a waiting car. Forty minutes later he was in a plane on his way to Berlin, and his former deputy, Durčansky, was in the seat beside him. At six-forty that evening they were led into the Reich Chancellery to meet the Führer.

Outside, Berliners were buying the evening newspapers and staring at the flaring red headlines. "GERMAN BLOOD FLOWS AGAIN IN CZECHIA" read the one on the front page of the *Völkischer Beobachter.* It was just like old times.

Inside the German legation in Prague, the minister was reading a secret telegram which had just been delivered to him from Berlin:

> With reference to telephonic instructions given by Kordt today, in case you should get any written communication from President Hácha, please do not make any written or verbal comments or take any other action but pass them on here by cipher telegram. Moreover I must ask you and the other members of the legation to make a point of not being available if the Czech Government wants to communicate with you during the next few days.

The message was signed by Joachim von Ribbentrop, the German Foreign Minister.

Up the hill, in Hradčany Castle, President Hácha asked once more whether there had been any reply to his calls to Bratislava.

Foreign Minister Chvalkovský shook his head. The lines must be cut; they could get no answer at all. When Hácha suggested that they perhaps should consult the Germans and ask for their advice, Chvalkovský replied drily that the way events seemed to be leading them, any consultation would have to be by written message. The German embassy also did not seem to be answering that evening. . . .

Intelligence reports were now coming into Whitehall from Prague, Warsaw, Bratislava and Berlin forecasting that the German army would march into Czechoslovakia on March 15, and each of these were sent by Cadogan to Halifax and by Halifax to Neville Chamberlain. . . .

"I am disappointed in Slovakia," said Adolf Hitler. "The way your people have been behaving lately, they might almost be Czechs."

He was addressing Monsignor Tiso and Durčansky in the Reich Chancellery on the evening of March 13. Across the room, facing them and seated beside the Führer, were Joachim von Ribbentrop, General Wilhelm Keitel and an assortment of Foreign Ministry officials. The two Slovaks bowed their heads and listened politely; they had a feeling that they were not expected to say a word.

For half an hour Adolf Hitler had been ranting about the sins of Prague, which had become a "hotbed of unrest" since the détente at Munich. He had no longer any patience with them; their future must be settled once and for all. But Slovakia—he had expected better things of their country. In the past year he had been forced to face a difficult decision—whether or not to permit the Hungarians to occupy Slovakia, as they had repeatedly requested. At first he had thought that this was what the Slovaks themselves wished. Their country was far away; he had more important things on his mind. It was only when the Munich crisis arose that he was dissuaded, for then it was put to him that Slovakia wished to conduct her own affairs . . . But what happened? He had sent Wilhelm Keppler as his envoy to Slovakia, and to him Sidor had declared that he was a soldier of Prague and would oppose separation from the Czech union. If Hitler had known this earlier, he would not have antagonized his friends the Hungarians, and would have let events take their course.

The Führer had begun pacing up and down the room, and now he suddenly swung around on Tiso. He had let the Slovaks come to Berlin in order to get the question settled quickly. He had no interests east of the Carpathians; he didn't care what happened there. But he demanded to know what the people of Slovakia really wanted. There were signs of internal instability, and that he would not tolerate. He had let them come to Berlin so that they could hear his decision. It was not a question of days but of hours. He had said that if Slovakia wanted her independence, he would support this endeavor and even guarantee it. He would stand by his word, but only so long as Slovakia made it quite clear that this was what she wanted. If they hestitated or if they refused to dissolve their connection with Prague, he would leave Slovakia to the mercy of events.

Hitler then turned to his Foreign Minister and asked him if he had anything to add.

Ribbentrop said that he only wanted to emphasize what the Führer had just said—that it was a matter of hours and not days. Thereupon he handed a message to the Führer which, he said, he had just received. Hitler read it aloud; it reported Hungarian troop concentrations along the Slovakian border. There, he said, they could see that events were moving fast and that he was no longer responsible for them.[3] Slovakia must decide, and decide quickly.

Now at last the Slovaks were allowed to speak. Monsignor Tiso swallowed hard and said how grateful he was to the Führer for the words he had spoken. For some time he had been longing to learn how the Führer felt toward his country and people. Now he knew, and he wanted to assure the Führer that he could rely on Slovakia. He wished to apologize for saying that the impression made by the Führer's words had been so deep that he was unable at this moment to clearly express his opinion or to make a decision. Might he withdraw with his friend—pointing to Durčansky—and think over the whole question? But he assured the Führer that they would show him that they were worthy of his care and interest in their country.

Hitler nodded. "All right, but don't waste any time. You can settle the details with my staff." He indicated that they were dismissed, and they quickly left the room.

At eight o'clock on Tuesday morning, March 14, deputies of the Slovak Diet, apprised by Tiso that they were threatened by Hungarian troops on one side and German on the other, voted to break with Prague and declare their independence. It was, of course, a sham,

---

[3] The Hungarians were, in fact, moving because they had been given permission by Hitler to occupy Carpathian Ruthenia, Slovakia's neighbor to the east. Just before the meeting with Tiso, Hungary's Regent, Admiral von Horthy, had telegraphed his thanks and gratitude to Hitler. "The dispositions have already been made," he wrote. "On Thursday, March 16, a frontier incident will take place, which will be followed by the big blow on Saturday. I shall never forget this proof of friendship, and your Excellency may rely on my unshakable gratitude at all times."

and Hitler demonstrated it by announcing that he would "protect" the new state.

The Führer was satisfied. Slovakia was taken care of. Ruthenia could be left to the Hungarians. Of the former sovereign state of Czechoslovakia, only Bohemia and Moravia now remained to be dealt with.

President Hácha received the news in Hradčany Castle just before noon, by way of an army field telephone. The commander of the Czech troops in Bratislava was urgently requesting instructions.

"Tell him to do nothing—nothing whatsoever," said the President to General Syrový, who was now his Minister for War. Then, turning to Chvalkovský, he said, "I think the time has come for us to consult our friends"—he hesitated slightly over the word—"in Germany. You had better ask the legation if the Führer can receive us, and as soon as possible. Tell them that we urgently need his advice."

He was to get much more than advice. . . .

As the special train from Prague sped across the whitening hills of Bohemia, President Hácha slept for the first time in days. His daughter Milada had tucked a rug around him to keep out the draft, and as his mouth fell open and he began to snore she smiled at him fondly. Like her father, she had no qualms about what would happen when they got to Berlin. After all, had not the Four Powers, Germany included, guaranteed the integrity of the Czechoslovakian state? Surely it could be in nobody's interest to allow it to fall to pieces. Adolf Hitler would know what to do to bring all this unrest and chaos under control.

The train stopped briefly at Pilsen, the last Czech city before the new frontier with Germany, and Chvalkovský stepped out and asked for news from a liaison officer on the platform. "We have heard nothing," the officer said. "There seems to be something wrong with the telephone." Although Chvalkovský did not say so to President Hácha, he guessed that the lines had been cut. Indeed they had—all but one, as Chvalkovský later discovered.

What Chvalkovský could *not* guess was that while they rode eastward toward Germany and darkness began to fall over Bohemia, Nazi troops were filtering across the Czech border. Zero hour for the invasion proper was still twelve hours away, but in Moravská Ostrava, on the Polish border in the north, a crack squad from the Leibstandarte Adolf Hitler[4] was moving toward the small Czech town of Vítkovice. Vítkovice had one of the most modern steel mills in Europe, and the Germans wanted to make sure of acquiring it intact. So the troops were on their way ahead of time, just in case the Poles, faced with a disintegrating Czechoslovakia, were tempted to make a grab for this plum. . . .

It did not seem to have occurred to Hácha that by going to Berlin he was walking into a trap. It is true that he was an old man and that once having accepted the facts of Munich and the political domination of Germany over Central Europe, he thought that since Czechoslovakia was no longer a danger to Germany, it was not now a target of Hitler's ambitions. Was his country not in the National Socialist German orbit already? Did she not do exactly what she was told? In any case, had not Adolf Hitler declared to the great statesmen of Europe that he did not want the Czechs in Germany, and had he not joined in a guarantee of the independence of the country with Britain, France and Italy?

All this may have convinced the unwary old man that there was nothing to fear. But his astuter advisers should surely have warned him; they could have spelled out for him the ominous moves of the past few days, reminded him of Adolf Hitler's hatred for the Czechs and counseled him to stay home. But no one told him. "I had no suspicion of what they were going to do to me," he said afterward.

He was a foolish old man. Only thirteen months earlier the Austrian Chancellor, Schuschnigg, had gone to see Hitler to ask for advice and help, Hácha might have remembered what had happened to him and to Austria, or at least Chvalkovský might have reminded him that Austria was now a part of Germany and that Chancellor Schuschnigg was cleaning latrines in a German concentration camp.

"Look," said President Hácha to his daughter, "they are doing us proud."

It was eleven o'clock on the night of March 14. Because of the weather the special train had arrived an hour late, but the German government was evidently determined to observe all the amenities. The Czechoslovak flag flew beside the swastika from the flagpoles,

---

[4] Elite SS regiment, which had originally been formed for the sole purpose of protecting the Führer's life.

and an SS guard of honor (ironically enough, from the same regiment which was at that moment operating inside Czechoslovakia) was drawn up on the platform of the Anhalter Station. Accompanied by Cabinet Minister Dr. Otto Meissner, Chief of the Presidential Chancellery, Dr. and Mrs. Voytech Mastny, Chvalkovský and the commanding SS general, the old man solemnly marched with his daughter along the serried rows, and peering through the frigid gloom, tried to pretend that he was inspecting the burnished troops drawn up before him. A high wind was blowing and scurries of snow whipped through the drafty station.

Eventually it must have occurred even to the Germans that the proceedings were a farce. A huge bouquet of flowers intended for Hácha's daughter, to be presented by a buxom German maiden, was waved away and the old man and his party were whisked off to the Adlon Hotel. There, while the old man retired to the bedroom, the flowers and a box of chocolate were duly presented to Mrs. Radlova. It seemed a good augury to her, as it did to her father when she popped a candy into his mouth just before midnight, as he prepared to leave for the Reich Chancellery.

"In the Reich Chancellery, to which I was accompanied by Minister Meissner and Chvalkovský," Hácha reported later to his government, "I was met in the courtyard by a guard of honor and then immediately by the Reich Chancellor, Adolf Hitler, who came to meet me and to whom I said how much I appreciated this personal meeting with the most powerful statesman of our time. The Reich Chancellor then invited me to be seated at his right hand among a circle of the foremost personalities of the Reich, among whom were General Field Marshal Göring, Minister von Ribbentrop, General Keitel and also Meissner."

The journey, the cold, the fatigue and worry had all had their effect upon the old man; by now his voice was almost gone and he spoke in a croak. His accent was peculiar, and this, combined with his hoarseness, made him sound like a wounded frog. The Nazi hierarchy present had some difficulty in keeping their faces straight as they listened to him, and at one point Hitler whispered to Keitel that "the old gentleman sounds like a drunken sot."

Of course, Hácha still had no inkling that his country was going to be invaded by Germany in a few hours' time. He had come to ask not for mercy but for help against the forces of disintegration in his own state. He began with a long, humble and groveling dissertation of his career in the Austrian civil service. Hitler interrupted him and said that as the hour was late, they should discuss the political reasons why Hácha had asked to be received by him. He signaled to all the others to withdraw save Chvalkovský, Ribbentrop and the interpreter, Dr. Walter Hewel. But twice Keitel returned. The first time it was to report that the Leibstandarte Adolf Hitler had successfully and without opposition occupied Vítkovice and its steel works in Moravská Ostrava. This news was given to the Führer in writing, and of course Hitler, nodding satisfaction, did not communicate it to the Czechs. The second occasion was to warn Hitler of the lateness of the hour; "the army was asking for a final decision on whether they were to march or not," Keitel wrote later. But he was dismissed abruptly by the Führer with the muttered reply that it was now only two o'clock in the morning, that the troops were not due to march until six, and that the order would be issued before four o'clock.

By this time Hácha was beginning to realize that the lifeguard whom he had come to summon to the rescue of Czechoslovakia was showing signs of turning into a shark, and he launched into an appeal for his country.

"Now I come to the thought which moves me most." His voice was not much more than a throaty whisper. "I have already given my opinion of the Slovaks in seizing their independence. I am not shedding tears over them. But the fate of my own people, the Czechs: I believe that you, your Excellency, are one of the few people who will understand me if I say that Czechoslovakia has the right to a national life. The geographical location of Czechoslovakia requires her to have the best possible relations with Germany. This is and will be the basis of her existence as an independent nation, and it is one approved by the great majority of the Czech people. Czechoslovakia is being reproached for still harboring many adherents of the Beneš system, but there really aren't all that many now. It is only the journalists who are giving them publicity, and the government will soon silence them for good. . . ." His voice trailed away, and then he added pathetically, "That is all I have to say, really . . . I'm an old man . . ."

Hitler had been listening to the Czechoslovak President with obvious signs of impatience. Now he began to speak, and Ribbentrop and Hewel prepared themselves for the inevitable monologue. It went on for a long time, for the Führer, now that the opportunity was there, had a great deal of venom to dispense. All his rancor against the Czechs welled up as he contemplated the two little men standing humbly in front of him (for he had risen from his seat, and they had automatically jumped to their feet too). He went back as far as 1936 to list examples of Czech hostility to Germany; his grating voice rising as his passion spilled over, he came down the years, incident by incident, to indict the country for daring to stand up to him.

As the hatred gushed forth, the two Czechs kept glancing stealthily at each other, and Hácha furtively wiped away tears with a trembling finger. Every so often Chvalkovský, who had an arthritic knee, would surreptitiously raise his leg and bend it slightly to ease the ache.[5]

Now Hitler reached his peroration. "If Czechia had drawn closer to Germany after Munich," he said, "I would have felt an obligation to protect her in times of unrest. I no longer have that obligation . . . I have always made it clear that I would ruthlessly smash her if the old, pro-Beneš tendencies were not revised. Chvalkovský understood this and asked me to have patience. I understood his point of view, but then the months went by without change. This new regime failed to eliminate the old one psychologically. I knew this from what appeared in your press, from word of mouth, from the dismissal of German civil servants, and many other things indicative of the general attitude. . . . The consequences were plain to see—in a few years, Czechia would be back where it was six months ago [before Munich]. Why didn't Czechia immediately reduce her army to a reasonable size? It was a tremendous burden for such a small state, and it only made sense if it was there to back a foreign policy. And that is meaningless, because Czechia doesn't have a foreign policy! No foreign policy! No mission, except to face the facts of her situation! No future unless she does so!"

His voice dropped as he turned toward the two Czechs, as if remembering suddenly that they were there. Unfortunately, he said,

[5] Dr. Paul Schmidt, Hitler's official interpreter, says that at this point the visitors "sat as if turned to stone. Only their eyes showed they were alive." But Dr. Schmidt was not at this meeting. The above account comes from the remarks later made by Dr. Hewel to his Foreign Ministry colleagues, and by Dr. Josef Klement, a member of Hácha's staff who afterward talked about the meeting with him.

the Czech people had refused to understand the facts of their situation. "Thus it was that the die was cast last Sunday. I sent for the Hungarian minister and I told him that I am washing my hands of this country. And now we face the new situation. I have given the order to the soldiers of the German army. At six o'clock this morning they will march into Czechia and incorporate it in the German Reich."

He paused to let the news sink into the minds of the two men standing before him. Then he continued, quietly now, "I want to give Czechia the fullest autonomy and a life of her own to a much larger extent than she was ever allowed during Austrian rule. But Germany's attitude toward Czechia will be determined by her behavior tomorrow and the day after tomorrow, and it depends on the attitude of the Czech people and the Czech army toward the German troops." His voice took on a new tone of grievance. "I no longer trust your government. I believe in your honesty, Herr President, and your straightforwardness, Herr Minister, but I have fears that your government cannot assert itself over the people."

Hácha was now weeping openly and Chvalkovský was looking at the map-covered table.

"All I can say is, they had better! The German army has already crossed the frontier today, and one barracks where resistance was offered was ruthlessly destroyed. Another barracks gave in at the deployment of heavy artillery. At six this morning the German army will invade from all sides and the German air force will occupy Czech airfields. There are two possibilities, Herr President. The first is that there will be resistance and the invasion of the German troops will lead to a battle. In that case, this resistance will be broken up by all and every means of physical force. The other possibility is that the invasion of the German troops occurs in a bearable form. In that case, I will be generous and give Czechia a generous life of her own, her autonomy, a certain national liberty. . . . But if fighting breaks out today or tomorrow, the pressure will result in counterpressure. The annihilation will begin and it will no longer be possible for me to alleviate the lot of the Czech people. Within two days the Czech army will be wiped out. . . . The world will look on and not move a muscle."

It was now nearly three o'clock. Hácha looked for a chair and sank into it. "You have made the situation quite clear, your Excellency," he said. "In any case, resistance is quite useless. But how am I to go about it? How can I tell the Czech army not to resist, with only four hours left before the invasion?"

As if at a signal, Göring and Keitel had come back into the room. Keitel said, "You could telephone Prague and have the orders issued to the army at once."

"But that is not possible," Chvalkovský exclaimed. "All the lines to Prague have been cut."

"All the civilian lines," said Keitel. "But there is one line open. You can speak to Prague at once."[6]

"If you will go with these gentlemen," Hitler said, indicating Göring and Ribbentrop, "they will be able to help you make arrangements."

As the Führer signaled for Keitel to remain, the other four sidled out of the room, Göring's hand helpfully holding up the tottering figure of the Czech President as they passed through the door.

But the hand which supported President Hácha as he went through the door was being brandished before him in fury a few minutes later. Despite Adolf Hitler's lackadaisical manner, the time when the German forces were due to move was dangerously near, and no one was more apprehensive about the operation than Göring. He was even more nervous than General Keitel, for though bad weather would make the advance hazardous for the troops, at least they could move. The Luftwaffe could not. All evening he had been receiving reports from his three assistants, Generals Milch, Udet and Bodenschatz, telling him that the air force was grounded.[7] The situation was extremely risky. What if the Czechs decided to resist? Their army was tough and well directed, and in this weather they would have all the advantages.

At this point President Hácha began to recover his nerve, and this sudden access of resistance could not have been more dismaying for the Reich ministers. Göring, who was against the whole operation anyway, grew agitated when Hácha suddenly began to speak rapidly in Czech to Chvalkovský. He was telling his Foreign Minister

---

[6] A German army intelligence group, aided by Sudeten Germans operating on both sides of the Czech frontier, had protected the line expressly for this purpose.
[7] It was still grounded twenty-four hours later, and had to cancel a projected victory flight over Prague.

that it was really too much, that he realized Czechoslovakia was helpless in face of this ultimatum but that he could not bring himself to give in.

"What is it?" asked Göring nervously.

"It is several things. But principally, for the moment, it is this." Chvalkovský indicated a draft agreement which Ribbentrop had unceremoniously thrust under the old man's nose. With Chvalkovský's help, the President had fingered and muttered his way through it. It was a proclamation to be signed by Adolf Hitler, Ribbentrop, Hácha and Chvalkovský, announcing the acquisition of Czechoslovakia by Germany, with Czechoslovakian consent.

> Ribbentrop: *What's wrong with it? Hasn't he already agreed that there is no use resisting?*
> Hácha: *You don't understand, Herr Minister. It says here that I should sign this proclamation in my own name and in the name of my government. [With a sudden straightening of his shoulders] That I could never do. It is not fitting. According to the Constitution of the Czechoslovak state, I am not empowered to make a statement in the name of the government.*
> Ribbentrop: *All right. Simply sign for yourself.*
> Göring: *No. It must be legal. He must sign for the government as well as for himself.*
> Ribbentrop: *But it is nearly three o'clock! We haven't much time.*
> Göring: *Leave it to me.*

The Field Marshal advanced upon President Hácha and said in a wheedling voice, "Excellency, why don't you sign? It's only a formality. It will save so much trouble."

Neither he nor Ribbentrop seemed to acknowledge the fact that the old man had already conceded defeat and that this was only a spasm of geriatric stubbornness—a last, desperate clutch at the letter of Czechoslovakian law by a sick and frightened man. With typical Teutonic respect for form they insisted on the letter of the law, when all they needed to do was lead Hácha to the telephone and tell him to speak to Prague.

"Excellency, please sign," Göring prodded him. "I hate to say it, but my job is not the easiest one. Prague, your capital—I should be terribly sorry if I were compelled to destroy this beautiful city. But I would have to do it, to make the English and French understand that my air force can do all it claims to do. Because they still don't want to believe that this is so, and I should like an opportunity of giving them proof."[8]

It took some time for the significance of Göring's statement to sink in. Hácha had no means of knowing that the Luftwaffe was grounded and that Keitel was concerned about the obstacles facing his troops. All he could think of was the prospect of Prague being bombed.

"Sign," said Ribbentrop.

Almost by reflex action Hácha continued to resist. Like a lady in a Victorian melodrama, he even pretended to faint. Ribbentrop did not turn a hair; he was prepared for everything. In scuttled Adolf Hitler's personal physician, Dr. Theodor Morell, who felt the old man's pulse, which was fluttering weakly, and prescribed a stimulant. Hácha protested; his aim seemed to be to gain time. But at the sight of Göring and Ribbentrop glowering over him, the Field Marshal shouting "Think of Prague!," he allowed himself to be given an injection of dextrose and vitamins.

After coffee and a ham sandwich, the old man nodded his head. "Bring me the telephone," he said. Later he wrote: "I telephoned Army General Syrový about the situation and gave him precise orders to direct all garrisons not to resist the German troops. Afterward I informed the Premier by telephone, and a short while later I received his reply to the effect that the government, which had meanwhile assembled, takes heed of my procedure and agrees with it."

Hácha was led in to see Adolf Hitler once more, and then signed the document which proclaimed the Protectorate of Bohemia and Moravia:

Berlin, March 15, 1939

At their request, the Führer today received the Czechoslovak President, Dr. Hácha, and the Czechoslovak Foreign Minister, Dr. Chvalkovský, in Berlin in the presence of Foreign Minister von Ribbentrop. At the meeting the serious situation created by events in recent weeks in the present Czechoslovak territory was examined with complete frankness.

The conviction was unanimously expressed on both sides that the aim

---

[8] *"Ich habe ein schweres Amt. Es würde mir ungemein leid tun, wenn ich diese schöne Stadt vernichten müsste. Aber ich müsste es tun, damit die Engländer und Franzosen wissen dass meine Luftwaffe eine hundertprozentige Arbeit zu leisten vermag. Denn sie wollen es noch immer nicht glauben und ich möchte den Beweis hierüber bringen."*

of all efforts must be the safeguarding of calm, order and peace in this part of Central Europe. The Czechoslovak President declared that in order to serve this object, and to achieve ultimate pacification, he confidently placed the fate of the Czech people in the hands of the Führer of the German Reich. The Führer accepted this declaration and expressed his intention of taking the Czech people under the protection of the German Reich and of guaranteeing them an autonomous development of their ethnic life as suited to their character.

At last the old man was led off and taken back to the Adlon Hotel, where his daughter was waiting for him. Adolf Hitler came out into the hall, great gusts of laughter braying from his throat, his hands outstretched to grasp and shake those of anyone in his path.

General Keitel approached the Führer and asked him to issue forthwith an order for the invasion to the General Staff, "but with a clear instruction not to open fire, in similar vein to the instructions issued to the Czech army. . . . This order was passed to the [German] army at three o'clock, which left three clear hours for its distribution." He added, "It was a great weight off the minds of us soldiers; Brauchitsch and I admitted to each other how relieved we were at this outcome."

In the Anhalter Station, on the chill morning of March 15, President Hácha could not understand why the train which was to take him back to Prague was so late in starting. Nor why, once it got on its way, it stopped and dawdled at so many small stations.

For Adolf Hitler's special train, there were no such delays. It delivered him as fast as it could carry him through Dresden to the Czechoslovak border, where the party switched to automobiles.

"From the frontier onward, we drove in a long convoy of motorcars along the broad road to Prague," wrote General Keitel. "Very shortly we came across the marching columns of our army. It was cold and wintry, there were snow drifts and black ice, and the mobile columns with their trucks and guns had to overcome the most formidable obstacles to their progress, particularly whenever our convoy wanted to overtake them."

It was dusk when the motorcade reached the outskirts of Prague. Here they paused, and Hitler got out to look at the valley of the Vltava with the misted shapes of Prague below him. The first German units had already driven into the city, and the news came back that there had been no resistance at all and that the few people in the streets had simply stood and stared in a state of shock.

The convoy started off again and soon was making its way swiftly through the darkening streets across the river to the diplomatic quarter, and then through the narrow streets of the Old City to the majestic cliffs of Hradčany Castle. A guard of Leibstandarte Adolf Hitler was waiting at the entrance. There were no Czechs in sight, and the city was freezingly cold and still. Even Hitler, staring down into the gloom, shivered a little. But not for long. After he had retired to wash and change, Ribbentrop led him to the magnificent banquet hall of the old castle. Candles were burning, and lights glowed on the paintings, sculptures and armor of ancient German kings. From the window, Hitler could look down and see the glow of lights among the statues of the saints on the Charles Bridge. On the table in the banquet hall was an impressive cold buffet of Prague ham, pâtés, cold meats, game, cheese, fruit and beer.

Turning from the window, the Führer beat his fists on his chest, as if he were a victorious gorilla in the jungle. Suddenly, in a gesture quite out of character, he picked up a small stein of Pilsner, and putting it to his lips, drained it dry. He grimaced, and then laughed. It was the only time anyone had ever seen him take an alcoholic drink. But it measured his mood. This was the great moment of his career; now he was not only Führer of the German Reich and Austria, but of Bohemia and Moravia too. "Czechoslovakia has ceased to exist!" he cried exultantly.

Would anyone dare to stop him now? Was anything beyond his grasp?

President Hácha's train arrived in Prague at eleven o'clock that evening, six hours after the Germans had established themselves. He was driven at once to Hradčany Castle, but began to protest when his chauffeur skirted the main entrance and took him to the servants' quarter in the back.

"Don't worry, Father," said his daughter. "Just let us get home."

It was not until Hácha was tucked in bed that Chvalkovský came to tell him that the main part of the castle was now in German hands, and that henceforth he and the Czechs must use the servants' entrance in their own land.

Roger Parkinson

THE GUARANTEE

An ex-military correspondent for the Scotsman, *Roger Parkinson has written books on Clausewitz and the American Revolution. His* Peace in Our Time *(1971), from which this selection has been excerpted, was one of the first studies that drew on 'the hitherto secret minutes of the British cabinet meetings. It reveals the hesitations, the confusion, the doubts and indecision that plagued those who were charged with formulating British foreign policy, and provides an insight into the way an historic policy decision was made by the Chamberlain cabinet.*

News of the invasion reached the Foreign Office at 7:25 a.m., when Newton telephoned from Prague. The *Wehrmacht* forced forward against minimum resistance. The proclamation announcing the transfer of the country into a German protectorate was declared from the windows of the historic Hradshin Palace. The first comment from Henderson on these dramatic events, came at 9:50 a.m. "HMG will doubtless consider advisability of postponing the visit of the President of the Board of Trade to Germany." Sir Nevile wrote in his memoirs: "There was some question of my sitting up on the night of 14 March. . . . But I could do nothing more, and preferred to go unhappily to bed." His first glance at the morning newspapers was sufficient to confirm his worst fears. "It was the final shipwreck of my mission to Berlin. Hitler had crossed the Rubicon."

"Do you wonder that I regard Berlin as a soul-scarifying job?" he wrote to Halifax. "Hitler has gone straight off the deep end again." Then: "What distresses me more than anything else is the handle which it will give to the critics of Munich." British Ministers hurriedly assembled to discuss policy; and the Minutes of the meeting seemed to indicate that those critics of Munich would be justified, that appeasement was by no means finished, and the change at the beginning of February merely temporary. And yet the attitude displayed was a legacy of appeasement, not appeasement itself; Chamberlain's excuses for not assisting the Czechs may have been shameful, but he believed he could do nothing else.

From *Peace in Our Time: Munich to Dunkirk—The Inside Story,* by Roger Parkinson (New York, 1971), pp. 112–128. Copyright © 1972 by Roger Parkinson. Reprinted with permission of David McKay Company, Inc., and Granada Publishing Ltd. Footnotes omitted.

The meeting opened with Halifax's report; the French Government, he said, "took much the same view of the matter as we do, and held that there is no possibility of effectively opposing what is taking place, or of influencing the position." Phipps had seen Bonnet and Beranger, who both felt that "the less we interfered in this crisis the better. They had both remarked that this renewed rift between the Czechs and the Slovaks showed that we nearly went to war last autumn on behalf of a state which was not 'viable.' " Almost immediately, Chamberlain put forward his reasons for British nonintervention, based on these remarks: "I think the fundamental fact is that the State whose frontiers we undertook to guarantee against unprovoked aggression has now completely broken up." He conveniently ignored the fact that German aggression, direct or indirect, was partly responsible. Halifax put forward another suggestion. "We . . . regarded the terms of our guarantee as morally binding before the guarantee had technically come into force, because we intended our action to be a means of steadying the position during what was thought to be a purely transitional situation. We had, however, never intended permanently to assume responsibility for a monopoly of obligation in this matter."

But this excuse clashed with Chamberlain's who therefore declared: "If it is agreed that the argument which I have suggested is valid, it will perhaps be undesirable to supplement it with the argument put forward by the Foreign Secretary. I also think that it would be wise to take an early opportunity of saying that, in the circumstances which have arisen, our guarantee has come to an end." Then, sensing no doubt the obvious criticism of his excuse for nonaction, Chamberlain added: "It might be true that the disruption of Czechoslovakia has been largely engineered by Germany, but our guarantee was not a guarantee against the exercise of moral pressure." The German actions had all been taken under the guise of agreement with the Czech Government, and the Germans could, therefore, plead innocence.

The Cabinet agreed Stanley's visit should be postponed, though he warned: "The German Government's reaction is likely to be to break off the existing trade talks." Halifax wondered whether Henderson should be recalled: "On the whole I am against this step, although it is easy to recall an Ambassador, it is not so easy to find reasons to justify his return. . . . The same argument, however, does not apply if we recall our Ambassador to report, in which case he could return to Berlin after a week or so. While I do not feel strongly on the matter, I think there is something to be said for adopting this course. I am reluctant to allow public opinion in America or in South-eastern Europe to think that we are inert." But the general view of the Cabinet was that "the step suggested was premature. The post-ponement of the visit of the British Minister to Berlin will be a signal mark of our disapproval."

The Prime Minister's statement to the House was discussed. The Opposition was pressing for a debate, in which Chamberlain would have to make a full speech. Chamberlain proposed to start by "ex-pressing HMG's regret," and to end with an announcement of the cancellation of Stanley's visit. Halifax evidently wanted something stronger. "It is significant that this is the first occasion on which Germany has applied her shock tactics to the domination of non-Germans. I think it is important to find language which will imply that Germany is now being led on to a dangerous path." Chamber-lain and Halifax would prepare a draft.

Of the loan to Czechoslovakia, Simon disclosed that £3 million had so far been drawn; he had sent a message that further payment should be suspended.

Chamberlain defended his Government's policy in the Commons debate that afternoon. "The position has altered since the Slovak Diet declared the independence of Slovakia. The effect of this dec-laration put an end by internal disruption to the State whose frontiers we had proposed to guarantee, and HMG cannot accordingly hold themselves bound by this obligation." Chamberlain added: "It is nat-ural that I should bitterly regret what has now occurred, but do not let us on that account be deflected from our course. Let us remember that the desire of all the peoples of the world still remains concen-trated on the hopes of peace."

But despite the apparent unity at the morning Cabinet meeting, some Ministers were uneasy. Hoare, an ardent supporter of appease-ment, "felt that my part in the Government was finished, and that I had better retire from public life." Halifax seemed to want to take a vigorous line, but to feel that such an attitude would be useless. He told the German Ambassador that afternoon: "I can well understand Herr Hitler's taste for bloodless victories, but one of these days he will find himself up against something that will not be bloodless."

But he told the French Ambassador later he wanted to avoid either of the two countries taking a position which might lead to conflict.

Within hours, though, Chamberlain was to display—publicly now—his radical change of attitude. He took this drastic step for three reasons: first, he had simply had more time to think, and second—adeptly—he now realized that public opinion had changed. *The Times* and the *Daily Mail,* both strong supporters of appeasement, both now hardened their attitudes. More startling was the reaction to Simon's speech in the Commons, when he tried to explain away Germany's invasion. Members erupted "in a pitch of anger rarely seen." By contrast Duff Cooper labeled Hitler "thrice-perjured traitor and breaker of oaths," and was massively applauded.

The third reason was a sudden alarm over Rumania, on Thursday, 16 March. The Rumanian Ambassador, V. F. Tilea, asked for an urgent interview at the Foreign Office, and told Sir Orme Sargent that his Government, from secret sources, had good reason to believe the Germans would reduce Hungary to vassalage within the next few months, and would then proceed to disintegrate Rumania as they had Czechoslovakia. In the turmoil of Foreign Office activity, Tilea's warning attracted minimum notice; concentration was still fixed on Prague—the first German mechanized units had squealed through the cobbled streets of the Czech capital at 9:30 a.m., and during the day Hitler strutted into Hradschin Castle to announce the Protectorate of Bohemia and Moravia.

Meanwhile Henderson, like Chamberlain, had had time to think: in a telephone call to Halifax on 16 March, he strongly condemned Hitler's action as "entirely contrary to right of self-determination and utterly immoral. It constitutes a wrong which will soon call for redress." Opinion in Britain and especially in Parliamentary circles was strengthening so fast that Chamberlain's position would be untenable unless he acted soon. "The feeling in the lobbies is that Chamberlain will either have to go or completely reverse his policy," wrote Nicolson next day. And, contrary to the Cabinet decision of 15 March, Chamberlain and Halifax now decided temporarily to recall Henderson, who, on 18 March, "left Berlin feeling that I might well never return."

Also on 17 March, Tilea came again to the Foreign Office, and this time saw Halifax. During the last few days, he said, the Rumanian Government had received a "request" from the Germans to grant them a monopoly of Rumanian exports, and "to adopt certain measures of restriction of Rumanian industrial production in German interests." Tilea added: "If these conditions were accepted, Germany would guarantee the Rumanian frontiers." It seemed to his Government "something very much like an ultimatum." He stressed an invasion might follow in a matter of days; pointing out that "Germany had more troops in Czechoslovakia than were needed in that country."

A terrifying account of Hitler's warlike preparations was now given by a correspondent newly returned from Berlin. Rumors reaching the Foreign Office indicated that Mussolini might emulate Hitler and make exorbitant claims in North Africa, or occupy Albania; other reports said Hitler might launch a surprise attack on the British Fleet; a note arrived from Phipps in Paris, the typing full of mistakes because he had done it himself. "Hitler's personal wish . . . is to make war on Great Britain before June or July. . . ." Together with these other alarms, Tilea's warning now had dramatic effect. Chamberlain had urgent talks with Halifax; they studied the draft text of the speech which Chamberlain was to make in the evening in Birmingham, mainly on domestic affairs and social security—and they began to make alterations.

Soon afterwards Halifax told Joseph Kennedy that "the speech that the Prime Minister was making . . . would be generally regarded as an indication of how deeply British opinion was moved and what might be the reactions from this emotion in the fields of policy." He added that a great many people were reexamining past attitudes. Next, he telegraphed Henderson a last task before leaving Berlin. "Please inform German Government that HMG desire to make it plain to them that they cannot but regard the events of the past few days as a complete repudiation of the Munich Agreement. . . . HMG must also take this occasion to protest against the changes in Czechoslovakia by German military action, which are in their view devoid of any basis of legality." As this telegram was dispatched, the Prime Minister was delivering his speech in Birmingham's ornate Town Hall. Chamberlain, man of peace, small and insignificant in the huge chamber, issued a solemn public warning to Hitler.

"Public opinion in the world has received a sharper shock than has every yet been administered to it, even by the present regime in Germany. . . . I am sure that it must be far-reaching in its results upon the future. . . . It has been suggested that this occupation of Czechoslovakia was the direct consequence of the visit which I paid to Germany last autumn . . . really, I have no need to defend my visits to Germany last autumn, for what was the alternative? Nothing that we could have done, nothing that France could have done, or Russia could have done, could possibly have saved Czechoslovakia." Another reason for Munich, he added, had been the belief that by "mutual goodwill and understanding of what were the limits of the desires of others, it should be possible to resolve all differences by discussion." But now had come the "disappointment, the indignation, that those hopes have been so wantonly shattered. . . . What has become of this declaration of 'No further territorial ambition'? What has become of the assurance 'We don't want Czechs in the Reich'? What regard has been paid here to that principle of self-determination on which Herr Hitler argued so vehemently with me?" The invasion marked a new turn in German policy. "The events which have taken place this week in complete disregard of the principles laid down by the German Government itself seem to fall into a different category, and they must cause us all to be asking ourselves: 'Is this the end of an old adventure, or is it the beginning of a new?' 'Is this the last attack upon a small State, or is it to be followed by others? Is this, in fact, a step in the direction of an attempt to dominate the world by force?'" And he warned: "No greater mistake could be made than to suppose that, because it believes war to be a senseless and cruel thing, this nation has so lost its fiber that it will not take part to the utmost of its power in resisting such a challenge if it ever were made." The small figure sat down; Birmingham Town Hall echoed with acclaim; appeasement had been publicly ended.

Meanwhile, Halifax worked late at the Foreign Office over Tilea's warning: he was anxious to sound out other countries who might be affected, and at 10 p.m. cables were sent to the British Ambassadors at Warsaw, Ankara, Athens and Belgrade, with instructions to report the opinions of the respective Governments. Similar instructions were dispatched to Phipps, and Seeds was asked to discover whether the Soviet Government would actively help Rumania if requested. But at lunchtime next day, an urgent message arrived from Bucharest: the British Ambassador, Hoare, asked Halifax to cancel the telegrams. The Foreign Secretary had to wait another three hours to learn why and meanwhile disturbing news reached him from Riga. Arms were apparently being brought into Memel from Germany, and German troops were being moved by sea to East Prussia.

Hoare telephoned from Bucharest at 3:40 p.m. "It appeared to be so utterly improbable that the Minister for Foreign Affairs would not have informed me that an *immediate* threatening situation had developed here that I called on him as soon as your telegram had been decyphered. . . . He told me that there was not a word of truth in it."

A special Cabinet meeting had been called for 5 p.m. The Prime Minister, celebrating his 70th birthday, opened with regrets for having asked his colleagues to meet at the weekend, "but it seems we are entering upon another rather troubled period." Halifax reported: "Although it seems that Rumania is not faced with the immediately threatening situation which was thought to exist, I think that it will be an advantage if the Cabinet took this opportunity of considering what our position would be if a situation such as was envisaged were to arise in the future." Gone were the times when Britain's position would remain undecided, in the hope that entanglements would thereby be avoided. It made no difference that the threat to Rumania was nonexistent; and the subsequent Cabinet discussions, stemming from the false ultimatum report, were to have consequences which led Britain to war.

"Looking at the matter on political grounds," said Halifax, "my view is that, if Germany committed an act of naked aggression on Rumania, it would be very difficult for this country not to take all the action in her power to rally resistance . . . and to take part in that resistance herself." Lord Chatfield gave the military view. The Chiefs of Staff believed Britain alone could not stop an invasion of Rumania without the support of Poland and Russia.

Chamberlain gave the reasoning behind his speech the night before. "Last Wednesday, the German action in Czechoslovakia had only just been taken, and the information available was so imperfect, that neither I nor any of you had had time to give the matter proper consideration, or to decide how far the situation had changed. It was unfortunate that, owing to the Opposition's demands, it was necessary to have a debate in the House of Commons immediately on the heel of these events." Since then, he had "come definitely to the conclusion that Herr Hitler's attitude makes it impossible to continue to negotiate on the old basis with the Nazi regime. . . . No reliance can be placed on any of the assurances given by the Nazi leaders." The Cabinet expressed full agreement.

"The real point," said Stanley, "is not whether we can prevent Rumania from being overrun, but whether, if we went to war with Germany, we could defeat her. If this happened, the fact that Rumania might be temporarily overrun would not affect the final issue." A danger existed of speaking in terms of military attacks on this or that country, warned Hore-Belisha. "We are now faced with a new technique, which brought about collapse from inside." He was "in favor of reconsidering our policy and contracting frank and open alliances with countries such as Poland and Russia. I also think it will be necessary to take steps vastly to increase our military strength." The Prime Minister declared: "I think Poland is very likely the key to the situation." The Cabinet agreed. And the decision had been taken which would lead Britain direct to conflict. At this crucial meeting, Chamberlain wanted to move even faster than his colleagues, to raise the issue of compulsory conscription, or the establishment of a Supply Ministry—but the Cabinet decided to defer further consideration of these points.

The next step must be to approach Poland. But that evening Phipps cabled from Paris that the Secretary-General of the Foreign Ministry, Léger, "strongly suspected that M. Beck had betrayed Rumania or was in the process of doing so." Léger had declared: "M. Beck was entirely cynical and false." His theory must have caused considerable embarrassment in London—he wondered "whether HMG knew what was the real object of M. Beck's journey to London. He [Léger] knew from a source very secret, but absolutely sure and highly authoritative, that the plan of the Polish Foreign Minister was to ask HMG to make an alliance with Poland, so that there would be a triple Anglo-Franco-Polish alliance under which Great Britain should undertake to come to Poland's help if attacked. . . . [Beck] knew that HMG could not undertake a definite commitment of the sort. . . . He would then return to Poland and report his request and its rejection . . . and that now it was clear Poland must lean on Germany."

"It would be wrong," the German Ambassador at London cabled to Berlin, "to cherish any illusions that a fundamental change has not taken place in Britain's attitude towards Germany." The Bulgarian Ambassador reported back that "energetic diplomatic activity" by the British was imminent in the Balkans; this report was intercepted by German intelligence. Russia's reaction to latest events was revealed to Halifax in a message from Seeds on Sunday morning. "The Soviet Government proposed that delegates appointed by Britain, the Soviet Union, France, Poland and Rumania should meet to discuss possibilities of common action." Maisky followed this up with Halifax on Sunday afternoon: he urged Britain to answer Litvinov's call for a conference, but Halifax in his reply said Britain was against the idea for two reasons; first, "we could hardly in present circumstances manage to send a responsible Minister to take part in the conference," and second, "to hold such a conference as M. Litvinov suggested without any certainty that it would be successful was dangerous." Instead, Britain preferred a less drastic step. Chamberlain told the Cabinet next morning, Monday, 20 March, that at a meeting the previous day, Halifax, Simon, Stanley and himself, had concluded that an announcement by France, Russia, Poland and Britain should be made as soon as possible. The Cabinet agreed to this draft declaration: "We, the undersigned, hereby declare that inasmuch as peace and security in Europe are matters of common interest and concern, and since European peace and security may be affected by any action which constitutes a threat to the political independence of any European state, we have pledged ourselves immediately to consult together if it appears that any such action is taken." This declaration, with its reference to "any European state," widened the area of commitment from the Cabinet conclusion, which had specified "Southeast Europe." Now Chamberlain claimed: "The precise form which the *casus belli* might take is perhaps not very material. The real issue is that if Germany showed signs that she intended to proceed with her search for world domination, we must take steps to stop her by attacking her on two fronts. We should attack Germany, not in order to save a particular victim, but in order to pull down the bully." His statement, in its no-nonsense determination, was worthy of Churchill. Only for a brief moment did Munich seem to echo in the Cabinet Room: the Prime Minister considered "writing to Mussolini, expressing my unease at Herr Hitler's attitude," out he added immediately that the letter must not convey "the impression that the Democracies were alarmed at the position, and wanted the Duce to get them out of a difficulty." This had been precisely the motive for the Munich appeal to Mussolini. The Cabinet agreed to Chamberlain's proposal.

The letter was sent later on Monday. Meanwhile Mussolini's distress was even more acute than that in London or Paris. The Duce had always believed Munich his personal triumph; now, as Ciano noted, the Czechoslovakia of Munich had been shattered. The day before Chamberlain sent his letter, Mussolini had agreed with Ciano that the alliance with Germany must be broken—if it were continued, "the very stones would cry out." With Mussolini in this state of mind, action by Chamberlain might well have persuaded him to move away from Hitler, though Mussolini rather believed that even if Italy and all other nations worked together, Germany would still be victorious. But the shadow of appeasement still lingered, and the message did have the effect Chamberlain feared it might. "Mussolini will answer after striking at Albania," wrote Ciano. "This letter strengthens his decision to act, because in it he finds another proof of the inertia of the Democracies." And the Führer had also decided to write to the Duce; when this message arrived it would drench the weak Italian leader in praise.

Hitler was about to demonstrate his strength once more, this time over Memel. Lithuania's Foreign Minister, Juozas Urbays, was in Berlin on his way back from Rome, and at noon on Monday was summarily informed by Ribbentrop that the question of a Memelland cession could be postponed no longer. Urbays was told to telephone President Smetona of Lithuania "at once," or "the Führer will act with lightning speed"; frightened, he hurriedly flew back to Kovno to convey the message in person.

Even if Memel could not be helped, a British initiative to deter further aggression seemed all the more imperative. "It seems to HMG to be desirable to proceed without delay to the organization of mutual support," cabled Halifax to the Ambassadors at Paris, Moscow and Warsaw just before Monday midnight. He revealed the declaration agreed by the Cabinet, and instructed the Ambassadors to sound out the respective Governments. "HMG would be prepared to sign Declaration immediately the three other Governments indicate their readiness." Events of the last few days had made Beck's visit "even more opportune than before," Halifax told the Polish Ambassador, Count Raczynski, next morning, 21 March. He told the Ambassador "that I would put the question to him quite bluntly . . .

if Rumania was threatened by Germany, would Poland come in?"
The Pole replied "there was a 99 percent chance." When the Count
was told of Britain's proposal for a joint declaration, he "warmly
applauded the idea."

As Halifax was seeing Raczynski in London, von Ribbentrop had
"invited" Ambassador Lipski to see him at the German Foreign
Ministry, and for the first time displayed a hostile attitude. The
Führer was becoming "increasingly amazed at Poland's behavior. . . .
Poland must realize that she could not take a middle course between
Russia and Germany." She must have a "reasonable relationship"
with Germany, which must include a joint "anti-Soviet policy." Beck
should visit Berlin for talks with Hitler, soon, "lest the Chancellor
should come to the conclusion that Poland was rejecting all his
offers." And as this meeting took place, Urbays arrived back at
Kovno, to be told that Hitler demanded Lithuanian representatives
before him in Berlin—the following day. These delegates should have
authority to sign over Memelland. The Lithuanian Cabinet hurriedly
assembled; five hours later they agreed to dispatch representatives.
Hitler, on hearing the news, decided to make a triumphant sea
voyage to Memel on the pocket battleship *Deutschland*; plans were
made for the warship to leave early next day. A week had passed
since his victorious entry into Prague.

There were serious difficulties in the way of the joint declaration
by Britain, France, Russia and Poland, despite Raczynski's enthusiasm. "It is clear that our invitation faces Polish Government
and particularly M. Beck with the necessity for a crucial decision,"
cabled Kennard. Acceptance would almost certainly entail an immediate German reaction, and Poland disliked the idea of strengthening
ties with Russia, especially after Ribbentrop's threats to Lipski. The
possibility increased of the British Cabinet having to choose between
Poland and Russia—but, Halifax pointed out: "It would be unfortunate
if we were now so to act as to give the Soviet Government the idea
we were pushing her to one side." With these considerations in
mind, the Cabinet met on 22 March. Halifax reported that the general
French reaction was favorable. As far as Russia was concerned,
"M. Litvinov seems to be somewhat perturbed that we have not been
more enthusiastic over his proposals for a conference." He added:
"It is probably true that an *Anschluss* of Memel with Germany is to
be expected," and that the reports in the morning newspapers were

based upon fact. "There is, of course, more justification for this course than for certain recent events." The takeover could be explained away under the list of Versailles grievances.

Chamberlain told the Cabinet that he had had talks with Chatfield and the Service Ministers on defense preparations. "From the point of view of a sudden air attack without warning, the position is very disturbing, and we are totally devoid of ground defenses against such an air attack." Some way had to be found of bringing stations into action sooner. Conscription would be one answer, to enable stations to be continually manned; but he stressed: "Unless there is a very marked change in their opinion, the Labour Party will continue to oppose conscription strongly." Hore-Belisha would have to wait longer for conscription—but Chamberlain was wavering.

On Wednesday the Lithuanian delegation arrived in Berlin, to be confronted by Ribbentrop. Hitler had already sailed for Memelland. But the Nazi Foreign Minister was to find the Lithuanians more stubborn than expected, and by the time night fell the talks were still continuing. In London, Anglo-French discussions began. Attending, apart from Chamberlain and Halifax, were Cadogan, and Phipps who had just flown from Paris; on the French side were only Bonnet and Corbin. Bonnet suggested Britain and France should ask Poland this question: supposing Germany attacked Rumania and Britain and France rendered assistance, what would Poland do? "If the question were to be put in this form, it would be difficult for Poland to give a negative answer." It would be an advantage if Soviet help could be obtained, but "the important thing, however, was not to give Poland a pretext for running out on account of Russia." Halifax stressed that Russia should not feel ignored.

Chamberlain then apologized for raising a "rather delicate point." In Paris in November 1938, Daladier had told him French aircraft production would reach 400 machines a month by the end of spring, 1939. "Present information seems to confirm the doubts I expressed." Bonnet admitted "he had his doubts about the figures given by M. Daladier"; the previous month 100 aircraft had been produced. Chamberlain displayed great satisfaction at the British record. "Our own difficulties have been successfully overcome, and our production is now nearly 600 aircraft a month." Could Britain help France build up her output?

Discussions ended at 6:45 p.m. with a firm assurance from France that she would join Britain in the declaration, and shortly a cable arrived from Warsaw with the Polish answer. "M. Beck said today that he is instructing the Polish Ambassador to propose that HMG and the Polish Government should immediately enter into a secret agreement of consultation." By keeping the agreement secret, Beck believed, the Poles would not be compelled openly to insist on the exclusion of the Soviets. But now the situation suddenly became still more complicated. As Halifax was considering this Polish suggestion, Litvinov told Seeds: "We are in agreement with the British proposal and accept the text of the declaration." But he then insisted on informing the Press the following day. Seeds, unable to dissuade him, hurried off to cable London.

Meanwhile Hitler, seasick on the tossing warship, waited anxiously for news from Berlin. During the evening he had twice sent to Ribbentrop for information on the talks with the Lithuanian delegation. At 1:30 a.m. on Thursday, 23 March, the good news was radioed to the *Deutschland*: Memel belonged to the Reich. This latest news reached London early on Thursday morning. Chamberlain, like Léger, believed the seizure did not call for Anglo-French action; it did not affect the European balance; occupation of the port did not materially increase Germany's strength or her capacity to wage war against France or Britain. And Memel was a residual problem of Versailles. Rumania was a different matter, because she possessed vital war materials which would boost Germany's military potential. The takeover of Memel might even be an advantage to Britain and France—the Poles might now be more willing to cooperate. Chamberlain made a statement on Memel in the Commons on Thursday: Britain would not intervene, but Germany would meet determined opposition if she went further. Bonnet, in resumed talks with Halifax during the afternoon, again raised the question of conscription; once more he met British hesitation. In fact, earlier in the day Chamberlain and Chatfield had seen representatives of the TUC, to discuss this, and possible methods of accelerating rearmament. The response had been "most unsympathetic."

Thursday was therefore Hitler's day of triumph. Final signatures were put to the German "Treaty of Protection" with the Czechs; and the Führer strutted ashore at Memel, his latest conquest. "You have returned to a mighty new Germany," he declared. Back in Berlin, Poland became a major preoccupation for Hitler—as she still was for the British Government. On Friday, 24 March, Halifax received the Polish Ambassador with Poland's proposal for a secret agreement. He had also to bear in mind the contents of a report received during the day from Seeds: Stalin was vigorous in his condemnation of the "so-called Democracies," and especially of the British. His criticisms were more violent than those he made of the Fascists, "for whose tactics he seems to nourish a certain admiration. . . . Those innocents at home who believe that Soviet Russia is only waiting an invitation to join the Western democracies should be advised to ponder M. Stalin's advice to his Party: 'To be cautious and not allow Soviet Russia to be drawn into conflicts by warmongers who are accustomed to have others pull chestnuts out of the fire.' "

And in Poland, fears were multiplying. The German treaties with Memel and the Czechs were followed by a trade agreement with Rumania on 24 March. "Signature in rapid succession by Germany of one-sided treaties . . . has made Polish public opinion indignant, alarmed, and at the same time defiant," reported Kennard. According to the Military Attaché, about 10,000 Polish reservists had been called up. On Sunday, 26 March, Lipski was scheduled to return to Berlin, after consultations following the heated interview with Ribbentrop. Lipski would bring with him a reply to Germany's demands for Danzig. Hitler reacted almost nervously to the possibility of a Polish refusal: he left Berlin on Saturday night, 25 March, leaving negotiations to Ribbentrop. Before his departure, he conferred with General von Brauchitsch, C-in-C of the German Army, who wrote: "The Führer does not wish to solve the Danzig question by the use of force. He would not like to drive Poland into the arms of Great Britain by doing so." Hitler was prepared to wait, but not for too long. So Lipski was received by Ribbentrop; as expected, Poland refused Germany's demands, and Ribbentrop reacted with routine bluster—Polish mobilization measures "reminded him of certain risky steps taken by another State."

It seemed a race between Hitler's reaction to Poland's defiance and the conclusion of a protection arrangement by Warsaw; yet Poland still feared that Russian inclusion in any declaration would bring dangers both from the Soviet Union, whom Poland suspected, and from Germany. Nor did Chamberlain believe the Soviets valuable allies. "I must confess to the most profound distrust of Russia," he wrote that Sunday. "I have no belief whatever in her ability to maintain an effective offensive, even if she wanted to. And I distrust her motives." And later: "I can't believe that she has the same aims and objectives as we have, or any sympathy with democracy as such. She is afraid of Germany and Japan, and would be delighted to see other people fight them." Chamberlain displayed his attitude at an FPC meeting on 27 March. In view of Poland's reluctance to be linked with Russia in a Four-Power declaration, he proposed a public declaration, plus a secret-bilateral understanding. Britain, France and Russia should join in the first, Britain and Poland in the second. Existing Franco-Polish obligations would be merged into this framework. Efforts to build a front against Germany would be frustrated if Russia were too closely involved. "In these circumstances . . . we must abandon the policy of the Four-Power Declaration and concentrate on the country likely to be the next victim of aggression—Rumania." Rumania had to be protected both for her oil and because "control of that country by Germany would go far to neutralize an effective naval blockade" by Britain. Rumania, moreover, shielded Poland's flank. "Poland is vital to the scheme, because the weak point of Germany is her present inability to conduct war on two fronts." Chamberlain added: "It will be observed that this plan leaves Soviet Russia out of the picture. . . . We should have to explain to her that the objections to her open inclusion come not from ourselves but from other quarters." Chamberlain emphasized the necessity for urgent and immediate action, but "did not think it expedient to summon an emergency meeting of the Cabinet . . . this might cause undue publicity." Halifax prepared to take the necessary steps.

Lipski had been summoned to the German Foreign Ministry for a further meeting during the day. He was given no opportunity to talk; Ribbentrop harangued him over Polish outrages against the German minority in Poland—an ominous tactic. At the War Office in London, Britain and France attempted talks on closer military cooperation. The French were horrified by details of the size and condition of the troops Britain hoped to use in France, and the British equally perturbed at French reluctance to disclose plans.

Just before midnight on the 27th, Halifax cabled to the Ambassadors at Warsaw and Bucharest: "It will not be possible to proceed without modification to the proposed Four-Power Declaration. . . .

In any scheme, the inclusion of Poland is vital as the one strong Power bordering on Germany in the East, and the inclusion of Rumania is also of the first importance, since Rumania may be the State primarily menaced by Germany's plans for Eastern expansion." Although the Cabinet had not been consulted, Halifax claimed the Government had decided on a new idea. Poland and Rumania were to be asked if they were prepared actively to resist if their independence were threatened by Germany; if so, Britain and France would be prepared to come to the help of the threatened State. The assurance to Poland would be dependent upon Poland agreeing to help Rumania, and vice-versa. The Ambassadors were instructed to be ready to discover the views of the Polish and Rumanian Governments.

A Nazi press campaign against the Poles opened next day. German women and children were being molested in the Polish streets, claimed *Die Zeitung,* Göring's newspaper; German houses and shops had been smeared with tar, German farmsteads attacked at night. Ciano noted in his diary that the campaign was a disagreeable reminder of the previous press attacks on Austria and Czechoslovakia. Beck summoned the German Ambassador and gave a strong warning against aggressive attempts to change the Danzig *status quo.* A veiled warning to Hitler came also from Chamberlain, who told the Commons that contacts with European countries went a good deal further than mere consultations. Meanwhile, work hurriedly continued both to complete the work on Britain's new commitment in East Europe and to further improve Britain's ground forces. Both were fully discussed at the Cabinet meeting on 29 March, but even now, Ministers were not informed of the initiative considered in their name; Chamberlain and Halifax merely described the differences encountered with the joint declaration proposal, and hinted that Russia might have to be left out. Germany must be faced with war on two fronts simultaneously, so Poland was "the key to the situation." Halifax would, however, "take what steps are possible to keep in with Russia."

"I wish at this point to deal with a matter of great urgency and importance, which is not on the agenda," said Chamberlain. "Although we are not actually at war, the state of affairs in which we now live could not be described as peacetime in the ordinary sense of the word." But compulsory conscription could have a "disastrous effect" on relations with the Labour Party and the Trade Union movement; organized, open opposition would mean decreases in industrial output, and a deplorable psychological effect. So for the moment he still ruled this out; instead, he had asked the War Secretary if he could find any alternatives, and if he could design a scheme which would secure a large increase in the territorial force. Hore-Belisha said the peace strength of the territorial Field Divisions amounted to 130,000 men: he now proposed to raise these divisions to war strength, 170,000 men, and then to double the Field Army to 340,000. Every Territorial Army (TA) unit would be over-recruited, to form in due course two duplicate units. For maximum effect abroad, Chamberlain himself would announce these measures to the Commons. And when he did so, his critics immediately condemned them as grossly insufficient: Eden's group combined with Churchill's in tabling a resolution demanding immediate conscription and a National Government. Thirty-six signed the resolution; a few days later, 180 Tory loyalists countered with a resolution pledging full support for Chamberlain. Both were eclipsed by events.

Meanwhile, recruits poured into the TA headquarters throughout Britain; drill halls were crammed; severe shortages arose of instructors, equipment, and uniforms. But training began at weekends, in the evenings, and even in lunch-hours. Time was short.

Britain would have declared war almost immediately, if Mason-MacFarlane had had his way. Ogilvie-Forbes reported: "The Military Attaché here is in a very warlike mood, and is anxious that we should declare war on Germany within the next three weeks!" He believed: "If we delay I believe that from the military point of view we shall be taking an unwarrantable risk, and an indefinitely greater one than war in the immediate future ought to represent if we play our cards properly and swiftly."

Fears of a German attack upon Poland suddenly increased late on Wednesday night and early on Thursday, 29–30 March. British Ministers hastily assembled at 11 a.m. for a special meeting. Halifax apologized for summoning them at such short notice: "My reason for doing so is that information received yesterday appeared to disclose a possible German intention to execute a *coup de main* against Poland." The US Ambassador, Mr. Kennedy, had received a message from his colleague in Warsaw, which reported Hitler's plan to act against Poland while Britain and France were still discussing action they should take. This information had been reinforced by a report brought to London by the Berlin Correspondent of the *News Chronicle*—contacts in Germany had told him Poland was the next item on Germany's program. Halifax continued: "This thesis was supported by a good deal of detailed information, including the statement of a local industrialist that he had been given orders to accumulate rations opposite Bromberg by 28 March." The journalist had also brought Mason-MacFarlane's dispatch. Halifax feared Hitler might make some immediate move. "We should make a clear declaration of our intention to support Poland, if Poland is attacked by Germany."

Halifax admitted this drastic idea had a number of drawbacks. "First, we should be giving Colonel Beck what he wanted without obtaining any reciprocal understanding from him. Second, there is some risk of upsetting the prospects of direct agreement between Germany and Poland. Third, such a declaration would be very provocative to Germany. Fourth, it has the appearance of leaving Rumania out of the picture." And he added: "The draft statement is a rather heroic action to take, on the meager information available to us." A draft should therefore be made ready for use at a moment's notice. And Chamberlain declared: "The action now proposed is a serious step, and is the actual crossing of the stream."

"We would be exposed to great humiliation," said Halifax, "and would suffer a serious setback, if Germany took any action against Poland before we are prepared." To speed matters, Chatfield suggested it might be better to issue a more general statement at an earlier date, "which would give more timely warning." Ministers agreed the Prime Minister should make this preliminary announcement to Parliament next day. First, telegrams would have to be sent to Warsaw and Paris; Chamberlain now revealed that the Opposition leaders had already given their general consent. The Cabinet approved a draft statement, with this critical paragraph: "I wish to say on behalf of HMG in the United Kingdom, that, in the event of resort by the German Government to any action which the Polish Government feels obliged to regard as a threat to their independence and accordingly to resist, His Majesty's Government will at once lend the Polish Government all support in their power."

Replies from Warsaw and Paris arrived that evening. "M. Beck agreed without hesitation," said Kennard, who then hinted that he himself disagreed with the move; "Your Lordship doubtless possesses much information not available to me," but while Poland was unlikely deliberately to provoke Germany, the "possibility of some impulsive action cannot altogether be excluded." Britain would then be involved in war, even though Germany might not have made the first move. "I venture to suggest insertion of word 'unprovoked.' . . . I might add for what it is worth that both the German Ambassador and M. Beck have assured me today that German Government have not made any demands in the nature of an ultimatum, and that there is no indication that they intend to take more menacing action in the immediate future." Phipps's message was short: "French Government agree. They do not apprehend any imminent *coup* against Poland."

Coup or not, Chamberlain intended to go ahead. But on 31 March came a last-minute delay. On the afternoon of 30 March, Arthur Greenwood, acting Labour leader, and Sir Archibald Sinclair, Liberal leader, both warned of trouble "in certain quarters" if Russia were to be excluded; Chamberlain replied "the present arrangement is only intended to cover the interim period, and that the position in regard to Russia would no doubt be cleared up during Colonel Beck's visit." Pressed to include in his statement that Russia had been consulted, he answered that Halifax intended to see Maisky next morning. He had to agree to delay the statement until the Friday afternoon, to give Halifax more time. Chamberlain also told Cabinet Ministers the draft statement had been modified to read: "As the House is aware, certain consultations are now proceeding with other Governments. In order to make perfectly clear the position of HMG in the meantime before those consultations are concluded, I now have to inform the House that during that period, in the event of any action which clearly threatened Polish independence, and which the Polish Government accordingly considered it vital to resist with their national forces, HMG would feel themselves bound at once to lend the Polish Government all support in their power." He pointed out that two conditions were embodied in the new draft. First, the action must clearly threaten Polish independence, and in the new version "it would, of course, be for us to determine what action threatened Polish independence, and this left us some freedom of maneuver." Second, the Poles must themselves resist with their national forces. "This will prevent us becoming embroiled as the result of a mere frontier incident." Halifax had been unable to see Maisky that morning, but would try to do so before 3:00 p.m. Chamberlain commented that the

Labour Party seemed to feel the Government "were prejudiced against Russia and were neglecting a possible source of help."

"Chamberlain comes into the House looking gaunt and ill," wrote Harold Nicolson in his diary. "The skin above his high cheekbones is parchment yellow. He drops wearily into his place." A few moments later, he rose to make his announcement. He read his statement very slowly, his grey head bent down as if he were having difficulty in seeing the words; and the cheers and shouts from MPs contrasted with his quiet voice. He had not had such an enthusiastic reception from the House since he announced his invitation to Munich.

Britain's continuing at peace now depended on Hitler's not attacking Poland, and despite the final changes in the statement, also on Poland—until recently an active scavenger for scraps dropped by Hitler, and an unreliable ally. Chamberlain, after years of caution, had run to the other extreme; he had jumped into committing Britain following false reports of a German invasion, and without a pledge of support from Russia. Halifax finally saw Maisky on Saturday morning, and later admitted: "I was not surprised that M. Maisky took the opportunity of saying that, as he had not been consulted yesterday, it was obviously impossible for him to say at a moment's notice what the position of his Government would be." Soviet trust in Britain, already low, plummeted to new depths.

But, at last, Britain was committed. And united. "This was no time for recriminations about the past," wrote Churchill. "The guarantee to Poland was supported by the leaders of all parties and groups in the House. 'God helping, we can do no other,' was what I said. . . . But no one who understood the situation could doubt that it meant in all human probability a major war, in which we should be involved." Britain now blocked Hitler's path. "I'll cook them a stew they'll choke on," raged the Führer when he heard the news.

Adam B. Ulam

THE RUSSIAN CONNECTION

The biographer of Joseph Stalin, Adam B. Ulam, director of the Russian Research Center at Harvard University, is a specialist in the history of Soviet Russia. His work from which this selection is taken, Expansion and Coexistence *(1968), is a study of Soviet foreign relations since the Russian Revolution. Ulam shows that Russian foreign policy was not aimed at lead ing a crusade against fascism but at keeping the Soviet Union out of war. Nowhere was this more obvious than in the Nazi-Soviet Pact of 1939.*

The Soviet government had little sympathy for the Polish regime or indeed for Poland as it emerged after World War I. Poland had been first part of France's *cordon sanitaire* around the Soviet Union. Later on Poland appeared to flirt with Hitler's Germany. Throughout, the country had been an obstacle and threat to Russia's aims. The Soviet leaders, however, knew Poland and the Polish mentality. Unlike some people in the West, they probably never made the mistake of considering the Polish government as a simple accomplice of Hitler's or as likely to offer Poland as a passageway for German armies. But in 1939 the prospect of Poland becoming a German satellite or being conquered by Germany had to be viewed as a mortal danger to the Soviet Union. Were Poland to agree to Hitler's "moderate" proposals, she would enter on the fatal path Czechoslovakia had taken. Were she to resist and fight Germany, she would be conquered. Either way, Germany would effectively become a neighbor to the Soviet Union. Such neighborhood, devoutly wished for by the Soviet leaders in the years following the Revolution, was now thought of in a quite different light. In view of what was to happen within a few months, it may seem paradoxical but is nevertheless true that it became a vital objective for Soviet foreign policy that Poland should resist the German demands and, if attacked, should find allies in the West. The joint Polish-Soviet communiqué was a small but significant contribution in that direction.

From *Expansion and Coexistence: The History of Soviet Foreign Policy, 1917–1973,* by Adam Ulam, pp. 261–277. Copyright © 1968, 1974 by Praeger Publishers, Inc., New York. Reprinted by permission of Praeger Publishers, Inc., and Martin Seckeι & Warburg Ltd.

The Polish government had additional reasons for second thoughts after the Czechoslovak drama. What remained of Czechoslovakia was in an obvious state of dissolution, and all its parts were within a few weeks of Munich satellites of Germany. The central government felt compelled to grant substantial autonomy to Slovakia, and part of the irredentist movement there, financed by Berlin, was clamoring for full "independence," i.e., a direct rather than indirect status as Germany's satellite. The prospect of German troops along a still longer stretch of Poland's frontier was already bad enough. But what was even worse was the emergence within post-Munich Czechoslovakia of an autonomous Carpatho-Ukraine also clamoring to be "independent." When further surgery was performed by Germany on the rump of Czechoslovakia in November, most of this backward area, inhabited by a few hundred thousand Ukrainians, remained an autonomous part of the decomposing Czechoslovak state. Needless to say, with discreet German encouragement, the miniscule state became the center of nationalist Ukrainian propaganda directed to brethren in eastern Poland and in the Soviet Ukraine.

Indeed, the backward mountainous region became for a few months the focal point of East European politics. Poland's pleas in Berlin for a joint Polish-Hungarian frontier were being answered playfully by the question as to why such a frontier was thought to be necessary, and the Hungarians were sternly warned that a violation of the territorial integrity of Czechoslovakia and the right of self-determination of the Carpatho-Ukrainians could not be tolerated by the Führer. The Soviet Union did not choose to confess its nervousness over the Carpatho-Ukraine. In a speech to the Eighteenth Congress of the CPSU on March 10, 1939, Stalin, while ridiculing the whole notion that a country of 30 million (the Soviet Ukraine) could be annexed by a region of 700,000 (Carpatho-Ukraine), still devoted an unusually lengthy passage to this apparently ridiculous proposition of a "merger of an elephant with a gnat." Litvinov, in conversation with Western diplomats, likewise ridiculed the notion. His information was that Hitler would turn next against Poland, if not indeed the West. And, indeed, the whole winter was spent by the Western cabinets waiting nervously to see where Hitler would strike next. At one time, London became almost convinced that Germany was about to invade the Netherlands or Switzerland, and even the possibility of an aerial strike against London was mentioned. No one has ever traced satis-factorily the source of those rumors.

It is against this background that Stalin addressed the Eighteenth Party Congress. The survivors of the great purge were treated to a confident assessment of the international situation. Only a "lunatic" would dream of detaching the Ukraine from the Soviet Union. In fact, Stalin accused the Western press of spreading such rumors "in order to poison the atmosphere and provoke a conflict with Germany for which there are no visible reasons." Stalin insinuated further that "one might think that they gave the Germans regions of Czechoslo-vakia for a pledge to begin war against the Soviet Union and the Germans now refuse to honor their pledge." The tone was distinctly unfriendly toward the West: taunts, insinuations, and, against this, a reassertion of Soviet indifference since the Soviet Union was strong and confident of its ability to take on all aggressors.

Stalin himself and his colleagues obviously could not believe this confident assessment. The stories of German designs on the Ukraine, far from being invented by the Western press, had been publicly stated in the great purge trials, and on charges of treasonous collu-sion with Germany the highest Party, diplomatic, and military officials had been sentenced and sent before a firing squad within the past three years. In fact, Stalin's main and equally transparent purpose was to undo the fatal impression created abroad by the purges. What are all those lies, he asked, about the "weakness of the Soviet army," the "decomposition of the Soviet air force," the "unrest in the Soviet Union"? Wasn't the purpose of all those lies to suggest to the Ger-mans: "You just start a war with the Bolsheviks, everything will go easy"? . . .

Stalin's performance at the Congress was later on interpreted as a clear-cut indication that the Soviet Union was already seeking a bargain with Germany. His words that the Soviet Union would not be involved in a conflict "to pull somebody else's chestnuts out of the fire" have been quoted to that effect time and time again since September 1939. Yet in fact his statement was in line with every aspect of Soviet policy after Munich: through taunts, expressions of self-confidence, and insinuations of an as yet nonexistent *rapproche-ment* with Germany, it was intended to draw out the Western Powers. "We don't need you, but you may need us; if so, better hurry up" is the most sensible translation of what Stalin was saying.

On March 10 nothing indicated that a bargain with Hitler was a real possibility. Stalin had nothing to sell. For all his dark hints, it was obvious that he did not believe in any stories of Hitler's forthcoming attack in the West. In fact the Soviet leaders had a flattering opinion of Western strength. "Peaceful, democratic states," said Stalin, lapsing into very strange language for a Communist, "are without doubt stronger than the fascist ones both militarily and economically." Soviet military intelligence must have been in a deplorable state (not surprising, considering the wholesale liquidation of its personnel), for Voroshilov gave comparative figures for the air strength of various states in 1938 which indicated that the French air force was not much inferior to Germany's and which credited Poland with more than 1,000 combat planes. Under these circumstances the prospects of Germany attacking in the West and requiring Soviet neutrality were not very great.

The Eighteenth Party Congress was still sitting when the international situation underwent a drastic change. What was left of Czechoslovakia was swallowed up. Bohemia and Moravia became a Reich Protectorate, Slovakia got its "independence" and was immediately occupied by German troops. After some hesitation, Berlin allowed the Hungarians to annex the Carpatho-Ukraine and thus liquidate the focal point of Ukrainian irredentism. That this was done as a gesture toward the Russians, as *the Germans* were to claim when negotiating toward the Molotov-Ribbentrop pact, is unlikely. The main reason appeared to be Hitler's conviction that after such a magnificent gesture by Germany, the Poles would surely not hedge over trifles like Danzig. The Poles were likely to be unhappy over the German troops in Slovakia, which Polish diplomacy with its megalomania had begun to imagine to be in the Polish sphere of influence. Let them have their Polish-Hungarian frontier!

The latest aggression by Hitler was met by a Soviet note to Germany which denounced in the strongest terms the rape of Czechoslovakia and refused to acknowledge its legality. For all the "disappearance" of the Carpatho-Ukraine, the fact was that Hitler was moving eastward closer to the U.S.S.R. . . .

On March 17, Chamberlain gave vent in a public speech to the indignation that seized him, along with the British public, at this most flagrant breach of faith yet on the part of Germany. From then on, just as diligently as he had pursued appeasement in the past—but, alas, equally unintelligently—the Prime Minister was to pursue the policy of mounting a united front against further German aggression. The immediate threat in those hectic March days appeared to be directed against Rumania. To give an effective guarantee to Rumania, it was necessary to obtain the concurrence of her neighbors: the U.S.S.R. and Poland. Drawing in Poland at this stage was believed to be one way of assuring Soviet concurrence: the Polish clash with the Russians at the time of Munich was vividly remembered; and the British ministers thought that by bringing in Poland, still believed to be close to Germany, they would increase the chances of Russia's associating herself with the rebuilding of collective security in Eastern Europe.

The Russians "played it cool." On March 22 an official communiqué denied rumors that "the Soviet Government recently offered its aid to Poland and Rumania in the event of their becoming victims of aggression." The Soviet government, in answer to a British inquiry as to its intentions in the case of an aggression against Rumania, once again proposed the holding of a conference, this time of Britain, France, Rumania, Poland, Turkey, and the U.S.S.R., to investigate the situation.

Linking Poland with Rumania as threatened nations was an improvisation on the Russians' part. There were indeed rumors that Poland was being threatened, but officially the Poles kept denying, though more and more feebly, to the British and French that any German threat had been issued over Danzig or anything else. In any event, the Soviet proposal for consultation was vetoed by Poland and Rumania. Foreign Minister Beck was striving for guarantees from Britain and France and tried still to keep them in the dark as to the seriousness of the situation. He thought that bringing in Russia would incense Hitler still further. And Rumania too feared Russian guarantees almost as much as German aggression—a fact of which the Russians were aware and by which they were not too displeased!

The pace of the crisis quickened. On March 23 Hitler exacted the region of Memel from Lithuania. Some conservative elements in Germany, fearful of Hitler's next move, decided to inform the British government as to what was going on between Poland and Germany and thus to press it to take a firm stand to avoid Hitler's sudden move in that direction. A British newspaperman was briefed, and he brought the news to London on March 29. Though the British ministers still were being lulled by Polish reassurances, they decided now to issue a *unilateral* guarantee to Poland. Beck, needless to say, jumped at the proposal. Without the British guarantee, the eventually inevitable revelation of the menacing German pressure would have meant his being hounded out of office once his country realized the ominous turn of events.

The British formula, drafted by Chamberlain himself, pledged the British and French governments to "lend . . . all support in their power" if the Polish government felt compelled to resist aggression. Before Chamberlain's historic declaration to that effect in the House of Commons on March 31, Lord Halifax invited Ambassador Maisky to acquaint him with it.

Halifax's minute on the conversation reflects considerable obtuseness on the part of the noble lord. The Soviet ambassador did not bat an eye at a declaration that meant a historic and fateful reversal of British foreign policy. "His first comment was that the phrase 'lend the Polish government all support in their power' might be a phrase greatly minimized by those who . . . would profess doubts as to the genuine character of British intentions." Halifax asked Maisky whether the Soviet government would agree to the Prime Minister saying that the Soviet government approved of the declaration. Maisky was noncommittal, but not too much so. He, of course, could not speak without consulting his government, but, as Stalin had said, the U.S.S.R. was ready to help all "those who fought for their independence." The Poles, the ambassador thought, might not be very happy about too strong a Soviet endorsement. "Although they thought it groundless, they understood the fear of the Poles, which was that if Russian troops come into Poland, Polish conditions were such that the contacts that would be made would probably produce disturbing effects on Polish society." But Maisky believed that the Prime Minister might say *on his own authority* (!) that the Soviet government understood and appreciated the principles on which the British government acted. And so it was stated the same afternoon in the House of Commons by Mr. Chamberlain.

With incredible blindness Halifax did not observe Maisky's concern that the declaration be made as strong as possible. (It was already much stronger than any declaration made by the British during the Czechoslovak crisis.) Nor did he notice Maisky's concern that the pledge to Poland should not be jeopardized by a refusal to permit Chamberlain to speak of the Soviet government's understanding and sympathizing with it. On issues much smaller than this, the Soviet ambassador had previously asked for an opportunity to consult with his government. To a man more perceptive than Lord Halifax, it would have been clear that Maisky must have been briefed for precisely such an occasion and that beneath his nonchalant and amiable behavior there was an obvious anxiety that the declaration be made and that it not be delayed by one day, one hour.

It is not too much to say that the British declaration of March 31 made possible the whole train of events leading to the Molotov-Ribbentrop pact of August 23, 1939, and thus was indirectly responsible for the most momentous development of Soviet foreign policy since Brest Litovsk. On its face, the British government's pledge guaranteed Poland; in fact, *its timing and circumstances* provided a guarantee to the U.S.S.R. and doomed the Polish state.

Prior to the declaration, the power most vitally interested in the preservation of Polish independence was the Soviet Union. Were Germany to attack Poland and were the Western Powers to stand aside, it would have been a staggering blow to their prestige and an incitement to Hitler to proceed elsewhere, but to the U.S.S.R., it would have been a mortal danger. Without allies the U.S.S.R. would now stand face to face with German power. In eastern Poland, Germany could create "independent" Ukrainian and Byelorussian states exerting strong attraction on the contiguous Soviet areas. Following the Polish conquest, Hitler might still decide to turn westward, but in view of his anticommunism and the universal conviction of Russia's internal and military weakness, the U.S.S.R. would most likely be next on his timetable of aggression. The British-French guarantee completely changed this dismal perspective: even were Hitler to conquer Poland, he would now be embroiled in a war with Britain and France. They in turn would *need* the U.S.S.R. as an ally, and for all his contempt for Soviet power Hitler might wish to avoid fighting on two fronts. A few words spoken by Mr. Chamberlain transformed the U.S.S.R. from being in a hopeless diplomatic situation to being the arbiter of Europe's fate. . . .

. . . It became a vital necessity for the Soviets to have the British commit themselves as unequivocally as possible to the defense of Poland and to extend their guarantees to other areas of importance for the U.S.S.R. On April 6 the British pledge, now accompanied by a reciprocal pledge by Poland, was announced in London. On April 13 Chamberlain gave unilateral guarantees against aggression to Rumania and Greece. At each step the Russians probed for the exact nature and extent of the British commitment. Were Polish-British military talks in prospect? asked Maisky of Halifax on April 6. And Litvinov in effect demanded of the British ambassador, "How do we know that Great Britain will declare war in case of aggression?"

There must remain a strong conjecture that following Chamberlain's declaration on Poland on March 31 and its reaffirmation on April 6, the Soviet government expected to be approached by Germany. No such step took place. The reason may be found in a dispatch to his ministry by the German counsellor in Moscow, who wrote with an insight subsequently missing among German policymakers: "The Soviets wish to join the Concert of Europe and desire also a development which would preferably bring about war between Germany, France, and Britain, while they can, to begin with, preserve freedom of action and further their own interests." The Germans were not biting, and the British for the moment appeared to have acquiesced in Litvinov's statement to them of April 1: they could pursue their own policy; "the Soviet government would stand aside." Hence, in an apparent reversal of the last sentiment, Maisky called on Halifax on April 14 to inform him: "On instructions from his Government that in view of the interest shown by His Majesty's Government in the fate of Greece and Rumania the Soviet Government were prepared to take part in giving assistance to Rumania." Thus within two weeks the Russians seemingly changed their position: from a complete aloofness they now wanted to be engaged in negotiations with the West and, as we shall see, as publicly as possible and on as wide a variety of issues as possible, as the means of erecting a barrier to German aggression.

The British government responded: it was under attack from the Opposition and Mr. Churchill for ignoring the Soviet Union in its plans. Such attacks were readily reproduced in the Soviet press and quoted in Litvinov's and Maisky's conversations with the English diplomats. Hence, Halifax invited the Russians to elucidate their position. On April 18 Litvinov handed the British ambassador the Soviet proposals: the three powers were to guarantee militarily all the "Eastern European states situated between the Baltic and Black Seas and bordering on the U.S.S.R." They were to hold military conversations as to the details of such help. They would pledge themselves not to conclude any separate peace following the outbreak of war. The English were "to explain that assistance recently promised to Poland concerns exclusively aggression on the part of Germany." Britain could not readily comply with these conditions. Under them, Britain and France would be compelled to come to Russia's aid in the case she fought Germany over Latvia, but Russia would not be equally bound in case of an attack on Holland or Belgium. Knowing the British mentality, it was clear that the negotiations would be long and drawn-out and that at the same time, given the political pressure at home, the British and French governments would not break them off. Once a political agreement was reached, military conversations would have to take place, and the Russian pledge would not be given until and unless a military convention was agreed on down to the last detail.

The subsequent charge of bad faith against the Russians is inaccurate or, rather, irrelevant. For the U.S.S.R., the negotiations with the Western Powers were meant both as a bait to Germany and as reassurance. This is the probable sequence of priorities in the Soviets' mind. If war came, the first priority was that it not be fought on Soviet territory. The Western Powers could not guarantee that. Over and above the Polish objections, which the Soviets anticipated, to having Soviet troops on Polish soil, the experience of World War I clearly taught that even with the best intentions the West would be unable to prevent a considerable penetration of Soviet territory and the consequent political catastrophe to the Soviet regime. Were the capitalists of the West eager to save the Soviet system, something which Stalin was unlikely to be convinced of, to put it mildly, they still could not dictate German military strategy. And in view of the Maginot Line and the reputed strength and *defensive* intentions of the French army.

Germany's logical first blow would be eastward. This had to be the prime consideration in Stalin's mind, or, for that matter, the mind of any other Russian statesman in his place. It is unlikely that even the prospect of a long and exhausting war between the capitalist states (except insofar as it would prevent or long delay Hitler's eventual move against Russia) or of the territorial loot to be gathered by Russia under an agreement with Hitler approached the importance or urgency of this first consideration.

About the same time that the negotiations with the British were begun, an approach was made to Germany. On April 17, the Russian ambassador in Berlin, Alexei Merekalov, called upon Secretary of State Weizsäcker. This was his first call on an important German official since he had assumed his post one year before. "The Russian asked me frankly what I thought of German-Russian relations. . . . There exists for Russia no reason why she should not live with us on a normal footing. And from normal the relations might become better and better." Having dropped this hint Merekalov vanishes from the scene. Future contacts in Berlin were made by officials of a lower rank, the Soviet counsellor Astakhov and members of the Soviet trade mission. These negotiations went on in some secrecy, in contrast to the ones with Britain and France which, of course, were accorded full publicity.

In the diplomatic game that went on well into August 1939, each of the three parties had its own primary and secondary objectives. The British hoped to exact solid Russian guarantees that would dissuade Hitler from attacking Poland and, if he did attack, to make the U.S.S.R. an ally in war. Hitler hoped until the very last that signing a treaty with Russia would persuade the Western Powers to leave Poland to her fate. Or rather to himself. If he could not have that, then he needed Russian benevolent neutrality: Goering and his generals balked at a war with the West, and the generals might rebel at the prospect of fighting both the West and the U.S.S.R. Stalin wanted most of all a situation where Russia would have a free hand while Germany would be locked in a war with the West. Barring that, he needed military help from Britain and France. Of all the parties concerned, only Stalin got his first wish, but already in September 1939, he was to realize that he had bought considerably more than he bargained for. Hitler got his second wish, the Western Powers neither.

Merekalov's interview was not followed, as the Soviets had probably hoped it would be, by German inquiries and approaches. The situation grew more ominous. On April 28 Hitler renounced the Polish-German nonaggression treaty and the Anglo-German naval treaty. On May 3 Litvinov was replaced as Foreign Commissar by Molotov. The official statement that Soviet foreign policies would remain unaffected by the change was only too true. But for some time the Soviets had built up the legend that Litvinov was a proponent of collective security and had half-insinuated that Stalin, a "realist," did not quite see eye to eye with him. Thus the change was a "come on" both to the Western Powers and to Germany.

It worked. The Western Powers were shocked into speeding up the hitherto agonizingly slow negotiations with the Russians. The Germans, though still wary, were yet pleased that a Jew was no longer directing Soviet foreign policy. On May 5, Astakhov, in a conversation with a German trade official, casually mentioned Litvinov's dismissal "and tried without asking direct questions to learn whether this event would cause a change in [the Germans'] position toward the Soviet Union." But a serious approach to the Soviet Union did not take place until May 30. On that date Weizsäcker wired the German embassy in Moscow. "Contrary to the policy previously planned we have now decided to undertake definite negotiations with the Soviet Union." The German State Secretary invited Astakhov for a comprehensive conversation.

This decision on the part of Germany was clearly influenced by two factors. The negotiations between the U.S.S.R. and the West were picking up; and on May 23, following the signing of a military alliance with Italy, Hitler instructed his generals that he intended to smash Poland even if it involved war with Britain and France. Hitler on that occasion raved and ranted in a wilder fashion than usual: if need be he would smash Britain in a few lightning strokes; the war might last fifteen years. On Russia he was quite incoherent. The U.S.S.R. might intervene in the war, or, he implied as he had one year before, Japanese pressure might keep the Russians fully occupied. (In fact, fighting between the Russians and the Japanese started once more in the Far East.) But to the military mind it was inconceivable to begin a war on the basis of such "ifs." Hence Hitler had to mollify the generals with prospects of an agreement with Russia. He himself abhorred the necessity of such a step, and several times in the next few weeks when the conversations were to take a decisive turn they were interrupted on express orders of the Führer. It is only because Ribbentrop virtually convinced him that a pact with the Russians would make the West abandon Poland, and that he would thus be able in effect to doublecross Stalin, that Hitler gave in.

The bait was finally swallowed on July 27, 1939, when Julius Schnurre, in charge of commercial negotiations with the Russians, invited Astakhov and the Russian trade delegate Babarin for dinner

in a Berlin restaurant. Here he laid down the German suggestions,
which bore Ribbentrop's unmistakable imprint—there was some nonsense about the similarity of the Bolshevik and Nazi *Weltanschauung,*
which must have made Stalin smile when it was reported to him.
But hints were clearly formulated as to the future points of agreement and the definition of spheres of interest of the two powers.
Astakhov kept questioning closely on the Ukraine. Schnurre was en-
couraging on this point as well as on the Baltic countries and Rumania. The Soviet diplomat "would report it to Moscow, and he
hoped it would have visible results in subsequent developments
there."

The "visible results" were that "Molotov abandoned his usual reserve," in Schulenburg's words, but also that the Russians *now*
appeared in no hurry to come to an agreement. There were preliminary problems to be solved between the two countries. The legacy
of the past distrusts was so great, the Russians kept explaining, that
it might be best first to sign a commercial agreement, then *gradually*
to arrive at a political one. Ribbentrop was burning with impatience,
which he thought he was concealing from the Russians. It was August
now. The British-French military mission was about to arrive in Moscow. Most of all, autumn rains would soon turn the Polish roads into
quagmires and military operations against Poland could not be postponed much longer.

What were the Russians waiting for? Even Ribbentrop perceived
dimly that they were waiting to be absolutely sure that a war would
break out following the signature of the Russo-German agreement.
They saw through Ribbentrop's game. If another Munich were to take
place, the German-Soviet treaty would immediately become a meaningless piece of paper—or worse. Germany in one way or another
would become a neighbor of the U.S.S.R. and the Western Powers,
having been deceived, would not be likely to interfere if Hitler's next
venture were in the Ukraine or the Baltic area. Quite possibly the
Russians would have liked to have the war break out while they were
still negotiating with both sides.

Now driven to distraction, Ribbentrop wired to his ambassador on
August 18 that he must immediately be invited to Moscow to con-
clude the treaty, that otherwise the whole deal might be off: "The
Führer considers it necessary that we be not taken by surprise by

the outbreak of a German-Polish conflict. . . . He therefore considers a previous clarification necessary if only to be able to consider Russian interests in case of such a conflict, *which would of course be difficult without such a clarification.*"

Molotov at first would not budge. Ribbentrop's trip would be welcome, but it would require preparation; "it was not possible even approximately to fix the time of the journey," he said on August 19 to Schulenburg. But half an hour later Molotov recalled the ambassador to the Kremlin: the Soviet government were ready to receive Ribbentrop on August 26 or 27. He also handed Schulenburg the proposed draft of the nonaggression treaty. In that half hour Stalin evidently decided not to push the game with Hitler too far.

The latter was frantic to use some August weather for the destruction of Poland. There came the first test of nerves between the two dictators. Hitler's personal message to Stalin reached Moscow on the night of August 21. Ribbentrop *must* be received in Moscow on August 23 *at the latest.* He would not be able to stay more than two days. This could mean only one thing: Germany planned to start hostilities on the 26th, and such indeed was the case.

The two hours that Stalin took to agree to what was virtually an ultimatum must have been occupied by one agonizing problem: was the West to be trusted to declare war on behalf of Poland? In a message to Hitler, Stalin agreed that Ribbentrop should arrive in Moscow on August 23.

The story of the Western negotiations with the Russians between April 18 and August 21 has often been told and needs no repetition in detail. The Western statesmen have been blamed, and justly, for the dilatory and half-hearted character of the negotiations. Indeed, Messrs. Daladier and Chamberlain appeared almost determined to provide future Soviet historians and propagandists with abundant material to justify the charge of the West's bad faith. They took their time; they dispatched a second-echelon Foreign Office man to Moscow instead of a cabinet member; when their joint military mission finally departed in August, it traveled to Moscow by a slow boat instead of a plane. But it can be said that none of those facts vitally influenced the final outcome of the negotiations, i.e., their failure. The Russians, it is true, always answered promptly, but at each crucial turn of the talks they raised new demands which were guaranteed at least to lead to long deliberations in the West and to the kind of commitments they knew the Western Powers could not immediately agree to.

The final issue on which the negotiations allegedly broke down was the Soviet demand that the Red Army be allowed to operate on and through Polish territory against Germany. This was something, as Maisky had told Halifax on March 31, the Soviets knew the Poles would not agree to. Had the Poles by any chance been willing to concede to it under Western pressure, the Soviets would undoubtedly have demanded that Russian troops be allowed to enter Poland in peacetime. Had *that* by any stretch of the imagination been agreed on, the Russians had another condition that clearly belonged in the realm of political and military fantasy: the British and French fleets were to enter the Baltic and to occupy Finnish, Latvian, and Estonian ports. Even in World War I, the Baltic had remained a German lake, and to demand that the British fleet operate in that narrow sea in the airplane age "with the object of defending the independence of the Baltic states" could not have been meant seriously. The Baltic states would not have agreed and at least one of them, Finland, would have fought.

There was one and only one argument that could have swayed Stalin to accept an alliance with Britain and France. This would have been a declaration that the West would *not* defend Poland *unless* the U.S.S.R. joined in her defense. But both morally and intellectually Chamberlain and Halifax were incapable of such Machiavellian diplomacy, and even had they been capable of it, public opinion in Britain would have forced their resignation when news of such an agreement had been leaked.

Were the negotiations with the West then conducted entirely for the purpose of deception? No. The Russians were not sure until August 21 that they would sign with Germany. Hence they wanted to have the most precise information of what the West would and could do for them in case the German gambit failed and they found themselves in war. Some of the information they got was clearly mendacious. Thus the French stated that the Maginot Line extended *all the way to the sea.* But this lie probably had the opposite effect to that intended: it implied that the French army in case of war would sit snugly behind its fortifications. Hence Russia made *numerical* demands which, unlike the demands about passage through Poland

and in the Baltic, were serious and intended to become operative in case of war: the British and French should pledge that 70 percent of their forces would be committed to an offensive against Germany if the latter struck in the East; the Soviets would pledge a similar proportion of their army if the blow were delivered in the West. (Incidentally, the conversations reveal what was to become apparent in 1940 and 1941: neither the French nor the Russian army was ready for modern war. The Russians were to learn from the Polish and French campaigns, but in 1939 they still thought that cavalry was an important offensive weapon. The Soviet military confrontation with Germany in 1941 was to be disastrous enough; in 1939 it would have been a catastrophe.)

On August 21 Voroshilov adjourned the military conversations. He did not break them off even now, when Stalin was wiring Hitler to send Ribbentrop, but asked a longer postponement because the Soviet participants were needed at the Red Army's fall maneuvers(!). Not until August 25, when the Nazi-Soviet Pact had been announced and Britain reiterated her determination to stand by Poland if attacked, did Voroshilov break off the negotiations and send the Anglo-French mission home.

The Nonaggression Pact entered into by Germany and the Soviet Union on the night of August 23 was indeed very much like any other pact of this kind except for one detail: the usual provision allowing one of the signatories to opt out if the other one commits aggression against a third party was missing. A Secret Additional Protocol provided that in case of a "territorial and political rearrangement" taking place in Poland the two signatories' "spheres of interest" would run roughly through the middle of the country. Russia would thus receive the Ukrainian and Byelorussian territories *but also a sizable portion of ethnic Poland* in the province of Lublin and part of Warsaw province. The possibility of preserving some rump of the Polish state was to be decided by Germany and Russia after the "rearrangement" took place. A similar "rearrangement" was envisaged in the Baltic area, and here Russia was to have a free hand in Estonia, Latvia, and Finland, Germany in Lithuania. The U.S.S.R. declared its "interest" in Rumania's Bessarabia.

On almost every point Ribbentrop conceded to Soviet demands. He was burning with eagerness to produce the great coup. The social hour that followed the signing was amiable. Stalin drank to

Hitler's health; he knew, he said, that the German nation "loves its Führer." Ribbentrop drank to Stalin's. But there were already dissonances. The Foreign Minister vented his hatred and contempt of the British and implied they would never fight. Stalin gave his opinion: England "would wage war craftily and stubbornly." He could not enjoy Ribbentrop's attempted injection of humor: a joke was making the rounds in Berlin that Stalin would yet join the Anti-Comintern Pact. But he had a joke of his own: "the Germans desired peace." Ribbentrop bit, and reassured Stalin that for all their love of peace the German people *would* fight Poland. Stalin gave his "word of honor" that the Soviet Union would not betray Germany.

On August 25, Hitler and his "Bismarck," as he now dubbed Ribbentrop, had their first shock. Far from capitulating at the news of the Nonaggression Pact, Britain reaffirmed her obligations to Poland and signed a formal alliance. Momentarily, Hitler faltered. The marching orders to the German army for August 26 were canceled. The Nazi-Soviet Pact had not worked the way the Germans had thought it would. But even when the German armies did cross into Poland on September 1 and for two days afterward, the Germans half-believed that the Western Powers would dishonor their pledge. Stalin's estimate of the British mentality and his gamble on it proved more correct than Ribbentrop's. . . .

V   A VERDICT

Alan Bullock
HITLER RECONSIDERED

Since 1945, thanks to the publication of new documentary materials and books on the origins of World War II, the responsibility for the outbreak of the war in 1939 seems to have shifted to other powers: the British, American isolationists, Stalin, the Third Republic, and the obstinate Poles. In this essay, originally presented as a lecture, Alan Bullock examines the belief, widely held before 1945, that Hitler and the Nazis were chiefly responsible for World War II. Bullock, author of the classic biography Hitler: A Study in Tyranny, *is master of St. Catherine's College and vice-chancellor of Oxford University.*

There are two contrasted versions of Hitler's foreign policy which for convenience's sake I will call the fanatic and the opportunist.

The first fastens upon Hitler's racist views and his insistence that the future of the German people could be secured, neither by economic development nor by overseas colonization, not even by the restoration of Germany's 1914 frontiers, but only by the conquest of living space (*Lebensraum*) in Eastern Europe. Here the scattered populations of Germans living outside the Reich could be concentrated, together with the surplus population of the homeland, and a Germanic empire established, racially homogeneous, economically self-sufficient, and militarily impregnable. Such *Lebensraum* could only be obtained at the expense of Russia and the states bordering on her and could only be won and cleared of its existing population by force, a view which coincided with Hitler's belief in struggle as the law of life, and war as the test of a people's racial superiority.

. . . Not only did he consistently hold and express these views over twenty years, but in 1941 he set to work to put them into practice in the most literal way, by attacking Russia and by giving full rein to his plans, which the S.S. had already begun to carry out in Poland, for the resettlement of huge areas of Eastern Europe.

The alternative version treats Hitler's talk of *Lebensraum* and racist empire in the East as an expression of the fantasy side of his personality and fastens on the opportunism of Hitler's actual conduct of foreign policy. In practice—so this version runs—Hitler

From *Proceedings of the British Academy* 53 (1967): 260–282. Footnotes omitted.

was an astute and cynical politician who took advantage of the mistakes and illusions of others to extend German power along lines entirely familiar from the previous century of German history. So little did he take his own professions seriously that he actually concluded a pact with the Bolsheviks whom he had denounced, and when Hitler belatedly began to put his so-called program into practice, it marked the point at which he lost the capacity to distinguish between fantasy and reality and, with it, the opportunist's touch which had been responsible for his long run of successes. Thereafter he suffered nothing but one disaster after another. . . .

It is a mistake, however, I believe, to treat these two contrasting views as alternatives, for if that is done, then, whichever alternative is adopted, a great deal of evidence has to be ignored. The truth is, I submit, that they have to be combined and that Hitler can only be understood if it is realized that he was at once both fanatical *and* cynical; unyielding in his assertion of will-power *and* cunning in calculation; convinced of his role as a man of destiny *and* prepared to use all the actor's arts in playing it. To leave out either side, the irrational or the calculating, is to fail to grasp the combination which marks Hitler out from all his imitators.

The same argument, I believe, applies to Hitler's foreign policy which combined consistency of aim with complete opportunism in method and tactics. This is, after all, a classical receipt for success in foreign affairs. It was precisely because he knew where he wanted to go that Hitler could afford to be opportunistic and saw how to take advantage of the mistakes and fears of others. Consistency of aim on Hitler's part has been confused with a timetable, blueprint, or plan of action fixed in advance, as if it were pinned up on the wall of the General Staff offices and ticked off as one item succeeded another. Nothing of the sort. Hitler frequently improvised, kept his options open to the last possible moment, and was never sure until he got there which of several courses of action he would choose. But this does not alter the fact that his moves followed a logical (though not a predetermined) course—in contrast to Mussolini, an opportunist who snatched eagerly at any chance that was going but never succeeded in combining even his successes into a coherent policy. . . .

Shortly after he became Chancellor, on 3 February 1933, Hitler had met the leaders of the armed forces privately and told them that, once his political power was secure, his most important task would be to rearm Germany and then move from the revision of the Versailles Treaty to the conquest of *Lebensraum* in the East.

Just over a year later, on 28 February 1934, Hitler repeated this at a conference of Army and S.A. leaders, declaring that here was a decisive reason for rejecting Roehm's plan for a national militia and for rebuilding the German Army. The Western Powers would never allow Germany to conquer *Lebensraum* in the East. "Therefore, short decisive blows to the West and then to the East could be necessary," tasks which could only be carried out by an army rigorously trained and equipped with the most modern weapons.

Nonetheless, in the first two years, 1933 and 1934, Hitler's foreign policy was cautious. Politically, he had still to establish his own supremacy at home. Diplomatically, Germany was isolated and watched with suspicion by all her neighbors. Militarily, she was weak and unable to offer much resistance if the French or the Poles should take preventive action against the new regime. . . .

Although Nazi propaganda made the most of them, none of Hitler's foreign policy moves in his first two years did much to improve Germany's position. Leaving the Disarmament Conference and the League was a gesture; the Pact with Poland clever but unconvincing, and more than counter-balanced by Russia's agreement to join the League and start negotiations for an alliance with France. The hurried repudiation of the Austrian Nazis in 1934 was humiliating, and the Saar plebiscite in January 1935 was largely a foregone conclusion. When Hitler announced the reintroduction of conscription in March 1935, Germany's action was condemned by the British, French, and Italian governments meeting at Stresa, as well as by the League Council, and was answered by the conclusion of pacts between Russia and France, and Russia and France's most reliable ally Czechoslovakia.

Between 1935 and 1937, however, the situation changed to Hitler's advantage, and he was able not only to remove the limitations of the Versailles Treaty on Germany's freedom of action but to break out of Germany's diplomatic isolation.

It is true that the opportunities for this were provided by the other Powers: for example, by Mussolini's Abyssinian adventure and the quarrel to which this led between Italy and the Western Powers. But Hitler showed skill in using the opportunities which others provided, for example, in Spain where he reduced the policy of nonintervention to a farce and exploited the civil war for his own purposes with only a minimum commitment to Franco. He also provided his own opportunities: for example, the offer of a naval treaty to Britain in 1935 and the military reoccupation of the Rhineland in 1936. This was a bold and risky stroke of bluff, taken against the advice of his generals, without anything like sufficient forces to resist the French if they had marched, and accompanied by a brilliantly contrived diversion in the form of the new peace pacts which he offered simultaneously to the other Locarno Powers.

Of course, there were failures—above all, Ribbentrop's failure to get an alliance with Britain. But between April 1935, when the Powers, meeting at Stresa, had unanimously condemned German rearmament, and Mussolini's state visit to Germany as a prospective ally in September 1937, Hitler could claim with some justification to have transformed Germany's diplomatic position and ended her isolation. . . .

The Nazis' claims about German rearmament were widely believed. Phrases like "Guns before butter"—"total war"—"a war economy in peacetime" made a deep impression. When Goering was appointed Plenipotentiary for the Four Year Plan in October 1936, this was taken to mean the speeding up of rearmament, and Hitler's secret memorandum to Goering found among Speer's papers after the war confirms this view. Irritated by Schacht's opposition to his demands, he declared that the shortage of raw materials was "not an economic problem, but solely a question of will." A clash with Bolshevik Russia was unavoidable: "No State will be able to withdraw or even remain at a distance from this historical conflict. . . . We cannot escape this destiny."

Hitler concluded his memorandum to Goering with the words:

I thus set the following task:
1. The German Army must be operational (einsatzfähig) *within 4 years.*
2. The German economy must be fit for war (kriegsfähig) *within 4 years.*

Yet the evidence now available does not bear out the widespread belief in Germany's all-out rearmament before 1939. The figures show that the rearmament program took a long time to get under way and did not really begin to produce the results Hitler wanted until 1939. Even then Germany's military superiority was not as great as both public opinion and the Allies' intelligence services assumed.

The really surprising fact, however, is the scale of German rearmament in relation to Germany's economic resources. At no time before September 1939 was anything like the full capacity of the German economy devoted to war production. The figures are well below what German industry could have achieved if fully mobilized, below what German industry had achieved in 1914–18, and below what was achieved by the British when they set about rearmament in earnest.

The immediate conclusion which one might well draw from these facts is that they provide powerful support for the argument that Hitler was not deliberately preparing for war but was thinking in terms of an armed diplomacy in which he relied on bluff and the *threat* of war to blackmail or frighten the other Powers into giving way to his demands. . . .

. . . Hitler was persuaded to commit the full resources of the German economy to an all-out effort.

This puts the facts I have mentioned in a different light. For, if Hitler believed that he could defeat the Western Powers, subdue the Balkans, and conquer Russia without demanding more than a partial mobilization from the German people, then the fact that German rearmament before the war had limited rather than total objectives is no proof that his plans at that time did not include war.

The truth is that, both before and after September 1939, Hitler was thinking in terms of a very different sort of war from that which Germany had lost in 1914–18 or was to lose again between 1942 and 1945. With a shrewder judgment than many of his military critics, Hitler realized that Germany, with limited resources of her own and subject to a blockade, was always going to be at a disadvantage in a long-drawn-out general war. The sort of war she could win was a series of short campaigns in which surprise and the overwhelming force of the initial blow would settle the issue before the victim had time to mobilize his full resources or the other Powers to intervene. This was the sort of war the German Army was trained as well as equipped to fight, and all the German campaigns between 1939 and 1941 conformed to this pattern—Poland, four weeks; Norway, two months; Holland, five days; Belgium, seventeen; France, six weeks;

Yugoslavia, eleven days; Greece, three weeks. The most interesting case of all is that of Russia. The explanation of why the German Army was allowed to invade Russia without winter clothing or equipment is Hitler's belief that even Russia could be knocked out by a blitzkrieg in four to five months, before the winter set in. And so convinced was Hitler that he had actually achieved this that in his directive of 14 July 1941 he spoke confidently of reducing the size of the Army, the Navy, and the armaments program in the near future.

This pattern of warfare, very well adapted both to Germany's economic position and the advantages of secrecy and surprise enjoyed by a dictatorship, fits perfectly the pattern of German rearmament. What was required was not armament in depth, the long-term conversion of the whole economy to a war footing which (as in Britain) would only begin to produce results in two to three years, but a war economy of a different sort geared (like German strategy) to the concept of the blitzkrieg. It was an economy which concentrated on a short-term superiority and the weapons which could give a quick victory, even when this meant neglecting the proper balance of a long-term armament program. What mattered, as Hitler said in his 1936 memorandum, was not stocks of raw materials or building up productive capacity, but armaments ready for use, plus the will to use them. How near the gamble came to success is shown by the history of the years 1939–41 when Hitler's limited rearmament program produced an army capable of overrunning the greater part of Europe, and very nearly defeating the Russians as well as the French.

But we must not run ahead of the argument. The fact that Germany was better prepared for war, and when it began proceeded to win a remarkable series of victories, does not prove that Hitler intended to start the war which actually broke out in September 1939. We have still to relate Hitler's long-term plans for expansion in the East and his rearmament program to the actual course of events in 1938 and 1939.

A starting-point is Colonel Hossbach's record of Hitler's conference with his three Commanders-in-Chief, War Minister, and Foreign Minister on 5 November 1937. It was an unusual occasion, since Hitler rarely talked to more than one Commander-in-Chief or minister at a time, and he came nearer to laying down a program than he ever had before. . . .

To speak of this November meeting as a turning-point in Hitler's foreign policy at which Hitler made an irreversible decision in favor of war seems to me as wide of the target as talking about timetables and blueprints of aggression. Hitler was far too skillful a politician to make irreversible decisions in advance of events: no decisions were taken or called for.

But to brush the Hossbach meeting aside and say that this was just Hitler talking for effect and not to be taken seriously seems to me equally wide of the mark. The hypotheses Hitler outlined—civil strife in France, a Mediterranean war—did not materialize, but when Hitler spoke of his determination to overthrow Czechoslovakia and Austria, as early as 1938 if an opportunity offered, and when both countries *were* overthrown within less than eighteen months, it is stretching incredulity rather far to ignore the fact that he had stated this as his immediate program in November 1937.

The next stage was left open, but Hitler foresaw quite correctly that everything would depend upon the extent to which Britain and France were prepared to intervene by force to prevent Germany's continental expansion and he clearly contemplated war if they did. Only when the obstacle which they represented had been removed would it be possible for Germany to carry out her eastward expansion.

This was a better forecast of the direction of events in 1938–41 than any other European leader including Stalin made at the end of 1937—for the very good reason that Hitler, however opportunist in his tactics, knew where he wanted to go, was almost alone among European leaders in knowing this, and so kept the initiative in his hands.

The importance of the Hossbach conference, I repeat, is not in recording a decision, but in reflecting the change in Hitler's attitude. If the interpretation offered of his policy in 1933–37 is correct, it was not a sudden but a gradual change, and a change not in the objectives of foreign policy but in Hitler's estimate of the risks he could afford to take in moving more rapidly and openly towards them. . . .

I find nothing at all inconsistent with what I have just said in the fact that the timing for the first of Hitler's moves, the annexation of Austria, should have been fortuitous and the preparations for it improvised on the spur of the moment in a matter of days, almost of hours. On the contrary, the *Anschluss* seems to me to provide, almost in caricature, a striking example of that extraordinary combination of consistency in aim, calculation, and patience in preparation with opportunism, impulse, and improvisation in execution which I regard as characteristic of Hitler's policy.

The aim in this case was never in doubt: the demand for the incorporation of Austria in the Reich appears on the first page of *Mein Kampf*. After the Austrian Nazis' unsuccessful *Putsch* of 1934, Hitler showed both patience and skill in his relations with Austria: he gradually disengaged Mussolini from his commitment to maintain Austrian independence and at the same time steadily undermined that independence from within. By the beginning of 1938 he was ready to put on the pressure, but the invitation to Schuschnigg to come to Berchtesgaden was made on the spur of the moment as the result of a suggestion by an anxious Papen trying hard to find some pretext to defer his own recall from Vienna. When Schuschnigg appeared on 12 February, Hitler put on an elaborate act to frighten him into maximum concessions with the threat of invasion, but there is no reason to believe that either Hitler or the generals he summoned to act as "stage extras" regarded these threats as anything other than bluff. Hitler was confident that he would secure Austria, without moving a man, simply by the appointment of his nominee Seyss-Inquart as Minister of the Interior and the legalization of the Austrian Nazis—to both of which Schuschnigg agreed.

When the Austrian Chancellor, in desperation, announced a plebiscite on 9 March, Hitler was taken completely by surprise. Furious at being crossed, he decided at once to intervene before the plebiscite could be held. But no plans for action had been prepared: they had to be improvised in the course of a single day, and everything done in such a hurry and confusion that 70 percent of the tanks and lorries, according to General Jodl, broke down on the road to Vienna. The confusion was even greater in the Reich Chancellery: when Schuschnigg called off the plebiscite, Hitler hesitated, then was persuaded by Goering to let the march in continue, but without any clear idea of what was to follow. Only when he reached Linz, did Hitler, by then in a state of self-intoxication, suddenly decide to annex Austria instead of making it a satellite state, and his effusive messages of relief to Mussolini show how unsure he was of the consequences of his action.

No doubt the *Anschluss* is an exceptional case. On later occasions the plans were ready: dates by which both the Czech and the Polish crises must be brought to a solution were fixed well in advance, and nothing like the same degree of improvisation was necessary. But in all the major crises of Hitler's career there is the same strong impression of confusion at the top, springing directly (as his generals and aides complained) from his own hesitations and indecision. It is to be found in his handling of domestic as well as foreign crises—as witness his long hesitation before the Roehm purge of 1934—and in war as well as peacetime.

The paradox is that out of all this confusion and hesitation there should emerge a series of remarkably bold decisions, just as, out of Hitler's opportunism in action, there emerges a pattern which conforms to objectives stated years before.

The next crisis, directed against Czechoslovakia, was more deliberately staged. This time Hitler gave preliminary instructions to his staff on 21 April 1938 and issued a revised directive on 30 May. Its first sentence read: "It is my unalterable decision to smash Czechoslovakia by military action in the near future." It was essential, Hitler declared, to create a situation within the first two or three days which would make intervention by other powers hopeless: the Army and the Air Force were to concentrate all their strength for a knock-out blow and leave only minimum forces to hold Germany's other frontiers.

It is perfectly true that for a long time in the summer Hitler kept out of the way and left the other Powers to make the running, but this was only part of the game. Through Henlein and the Sudeten Party, who played the same role of fifth column as the Austrian Nazis, Hitler was able to manipulate the dispute between the Sudeten Germans and the Czech Government, which was the ostensible cause of the crisis, from within. At a secret meeting with Hitler on 28 March, Henlein summarized his policy in the words: "We must always demand so much that we can never be satisfied." The Führer, says the official minute, approved this view.

At the same time through a variety of devices—full scale press and radio campaigns, the manufacture of incidents, troop movements, carefully circulated rumors, and diplomatic leaks, a steadily mounting pressure was built up, timed to culminate in Hitler's long-awaited speech at the Nuremberg Party Congress. Those who study only the diplomatic documents get a very meager impression of the war of nerves which was maintained throughout the summer and which was skillfully directed to play on the fear of war in Britain and France and to heighten the Czechs' sense of isolation. It was under the pressure of this political warfare, something very different from diplomacy as it had been traditionally practiced, that the British and French governments felt themselves impelled to act.

What was Hitler's objective? The answer has been much confused by the ambiguous use of the word "war."

Western opinion made a clear-cut distinction between peace and war: Hitler did not, he blurred the distinction. Reversing Clausewitz, he treated politics as a continuation of war by other means, at one stage of which (formally still called peace) he employed methods of political warfare—subversion, propaganda, diplomatic and economic pressure, the war of nerves—at the next, the threat of war, and so on to localized war and up the scale to general war—a continuum of force in which the different stages ran into each other. Familiar enough now since the time of the Cold War, this strategy (which was all of a piece with Hitler's radical new style in foreign policy) was as confusing in its novelty as the tactics of the Trojan horse, the fifth column, and the "volunteers" to those who still thought in terms of a traditionally decisive break between a state of peace and a state of war.

So far as the events of 1938 go, there seem to be two possible answers to the question, What was in Hitler's mind?

The first is that his object was to destroy the Czech State by the sort of blitzkrieg for which he had rearmed Germany and which he was to carry out a year later against Poland. This was to come at the end of a six-months' political, diplomatic, and propaganda campaign designed to isolate and undermine the Czechs, and to maneuver the Western Powers into abandoning them to their fate rather than risk a European war. The evidence for this view consists in the series of secret directives and the military preparations to which they led, plus Hitler's declaration on several occasions to the generals and his other collaborators that he meant to settle the matter by force, with 1 October as D-day. On this view, he was only prevented from carrying out his attack by the intervention of Chamberlain which, however great the cost to the Czechs, prevented war or at least postponed it for a year.

The other view is that Hitler never intended to go to war, that his objective was from the beginning a political settlement such as was offered to him at Munich, that his military preparations were not intended seriously but were designed as threats to increase the pressure.

The choice between these two alternatives, however—*either* the one *or* the other—seems to me unreal. The obvious course for Hitler to pursue was to keep both possibilities open to the very last possible moment, the more so since they did not conflict. The more seriously the military preparations were carried out, the more effective was the pressure in favor of a political settlement if at the last moment he decided not to take the risks involved in a military operation. If we adopt this view, then we remove all the difficulties in interpreting the evidence which are created either by attempting to pin Hitler down on any particular declaration and say *now,* at this point, he had decided on war—or by the dogmatic assumption that Hitler *never* seriously contemplated the use of force, with the consequent need to dismiss his military directives as bluff.

Neither in 1938 nor in 1939 did Hitler deliberately plan to start a general European war. But this was a risk which could not be ignored, and in 1938 it was decisive. The generals were unanimous that Germany's rearmament had not yet reached the point where she could face a war with France and Britain. The Czech frontier defenses were formidable. Their army on mobilization was hardly inferior at all, either in numbers or training, to the thirty-seven divisions which the Germans could deploy and it was backed by a first-class armaments industry. To overcome these would require a concentration of force which left the German commander in the West with totally inadequate strength to hold back the French Army.

While the generals, however, added up divisions and struck an unfavorable balance in terms of material forces, Hitler was convinced that the decisive question was a matter of will, the balance between his determination to take the *risk* of a general war and the determination of the Western Powers, if pushed far enough, to take the *actual decision* of starting one. For, however much the responsibility for such a war might be Hitler's, by isolating the issue and limiting his demands to the Sudetenland, he placed the onus of actually start-ing a general war on the British and the French. How far was Hitler prepared to drive such an argument? The answer is, I believe, that while he had set a date by which he knew he must decide, until the very last moment he had not made up his mind and that it is this alternation between screwing up his demands, as he did at his second meeting with Chamberlain in Godesberg, and still evading an irre-vocable decision, which accounts both for the zigzag course of German diplomacy and for the strain on Hitler.

In the end he decided, or was persuaded, to stop short of military operations against Czechoslovakia and "cash" his military prepara-tions for the maximum of political concessions.

No sooner had he agreed to this, however, than Hitler started to regret that he had not held on, marched his army in, then and there, and broken up the Czechoslovak State, not just annexed the Sude-tenland. His regret sprang from the belief, confirmed by his meeting with the Western leaders at Munich, that he could have got away with a localized war carried out in a matter of days, and then con-fronted the British and French with a *fait accompli* while they were still hesitating whether to attack in the West—exactly as happened a year later over Poland.

Almost immediately after Munich, therefore, Hitler began to think about ways in which he could complete his original purpose. Every sort of excuse, however transparent, was found for delaying the international guarantee which had been an essential part of the Munich agreement. At the same time, the ground was carefully pre-pared with the Hungarians, who were eager to recover Ruthenia and at least part of Slovakia, and with the Slovaks themselves who were cast for the same role the Sudeten Germans had played the year before. The actual moment at which the crisis broke was not deter-mined by Hitler and took him by surprise, but that was all. The Slovaks were at once prodded into declaring their independence and putting themselves in Hitler's hands. The Czech Government, after Hitler had threatened President Hacha in Berlin, did the same. The "legality" of German intervention was unimpeachable: Hitler had been invited to intervene by both the rebels and the government. War had been avoided, no shots exchanged, peace preserved—yet the independent state of Czechoslovakia had been wiped off the map.

Within less than eighteen months, then, Hitler had successfully achieved both the immediate objectives, Austria and Czechoslovakia, which he had laid down in the Hossbach meeting. He had not foreseen the way in which this would happen, in fact he had been wrong about it, but this had not stopped him from getting both.

This had been true at every stage of Hitler's career. He had no fixed idea in 1930, even in 1932, about how he would become Chancellor, only that he would; no fixed idea in 1934–35 how he would break out of Germany's diplomatic isolation, again only that he would. So the same now. Fixity of aim by itself, or opportunism by itself, would have produced nothing like the same results.

It is entirely in keeping with this view of Hitler that, after Czechoslovakia, he should not have made up his mind what to do next. Various possibilities were in the air. Another move was likely in 1939, if only because the rearmament program was now beginning to reach the period when it would give Germany a maximum advantage and Hitler had never believed that time was on his side. This advantage, he said in November 1937, would only last, at the most until 1943–45; then the other Powers with greater resources would begin to catch up. He had therefore to act quickly if he wanted to achieve his objectives.

Objectives, yes; a sense of urgency in carrying them out, and growing means to do so in German rearmament, but no timetable or precise plan of action for the next stage.

Ribbentrop had already raised with the Poles, immediately after Munich, the question of Danzig and the Corridor. But there is no evidence that Hitler had committed himself to war to obtain these, or to the dismemberment of Poland. If the Poles had been willing to give him what he wanted, Hitler might well have treated them, for a time at any rate, as a satellite—in much the same way as he treated Hungary—and there were strong hints from Ribbentrop that the Germans and the Poles could find a common objective in action against Russia. Another possibility, if Danzig and the Corridor could be settled by agreement, was to turn west and remove the principal obstacle to German expansion, the British and French claim to intervene in Eastern Europe.

After Prague, the German-Polish exchanges became a good deal sharper and, given the Poles' determination not to be put in the same position as the Czechs, but to say "No" and refuse to compromise, it is likely that a breach between Warsaw and Berlin would have come soon in any case. But what precipitated it was the British offer, and Polish acceptance, of a guarantee of Poland's independence. In this sense the British offer is a turning-point in the history of 1939. But here comes the crux of the matter. If Mr. Taylor is right in believing that Hitler was simply an opportunist who reacted to the initiative of others, then he is justified in calling the British offer to Poland a revolutionary event. But if the view I have suggested is right, namely, that Hitler, although an opportunist in his tactics, was an opportunist who had from the beginning a clear objective in view, then it is very much less than that: an event which certainly helped—if you like, forced—Hitler to make up his mind between the various possibilities he had been revolving, but which certainly did not provoke him into an expansionist program he would not otherwise have entertained, or generate the force behind it which the Nazis had been building up ever since they came to power. On this view it was Hitler who still held the initiative, as he had since the *Anschluss,* and the British who were reacting to it, not the other way around: the most the British guarantee did was to give Hitler the answer to the question he had been asking since Munich, Where next?

The answer, then, was Poland, the most probable in any event in view of the demands the Nazis had already tabled, and now a certainty. But this did not necessarily mean war—yet.

Hitler expressed his anger by denouncing Germany's Non-Aggression Pact with Poland and the Anglo-German Naval Treaty, and went on to sign a secret directive ordering the Army to be ready to attack Poland by 1 September. The military preparations were not bluff: they were designed to give Hitler the option of a military solution if he finally decided this way, or to strengthen the pressures for a political solution—either direct with Warsaw, or by the intervention of the other powers in a Polish Munich. Just as in 1938 so in 1939, Hitler kept the options open literally to the last, and until the troops actually crossed the Polish frontier on 1 September none of his generals was certain that the orders might not be changed. Both options, however: there is no more reason to say dogmatically that Hitler was aiming all the time at a political solution than there is to say that he ruled it out and had made up his mind in favor of war.

Hitler's inclination, I believe, was always towards a solution by force, the sort of localized blitzkrieg with which in the end he did destroy Poland. What he had to weigh was the risk of a war which could not be localized. There were several reasons why he was more ready to take this risk than the year before.

The first was the progress of German rearmament—which was coming to a peak in the autumn of 1939. By then it represented an eighteen-fold expansion of the German armed forces since 1933. In economists' terms this was not the maximum of which Germany was capable, at least in the long run, but in military terms it was more than adequate, as 1940 showed, not just to defeat the Poles but to deal with the Western Powers as well. The new German Army had been designed to achieve the maximum effect at the outset of a campaign and Hitler calculated—quite rightly—that, even if the British formally maintained their guarantee to Poland, the war would be over and Poland crushed before they could do anything about it.

A second reason was Hitler's increased confidence, his conviction that his opponents were simply not his equal either in daring or in skill. The very fact that he had drawn back at Munich and then regretted it made it all the more likely that a man with his gambler's temperament would be powerfully drawn to stake all next time.

Finally, Hitler believed that he could remove the danger of Western intervention, or at least render the British guarantee meaningless, by outbidding the Western Powers in Moscow.

In moments of exaltation, e.g. in his talks to his generals after the signature of the Pact with Italy (23 May) and at the conference of 22 August which followed the news that Stalin would sign, Hitler spoke as if the matter were settled, war with Poland inevitable, and all possibility of a political settlement—on his terms—excluded. I believe that this was, as I have said, his real inclination, but I do not believe that he finally made up his mind until the last minute. Why should he? Just as in 1938, Hitler refused to make in advance the choice to which historians have tried to pin him down, the either/or of war or a settlement dictated under the threat of war. He fixed the date by which the choice would have to be made but pursued a course which would leave him with the maximum of maneuver to the last possible moment. And again one may well ask, Why not—since the preparations to be made for either eventuality—war or a political settlement under the threat of war—were the same?

Much has been made of the fact that for the greater part of the summer Hitler retired to Berchtesgaden and made no public pronouncement. But this is misleading. The initiative remained in

Hitler's hands. The propaganda campaign went ahead exactly as planned, building up to a crisis by late August and hammering on the question, Is Danzig worth a war? So did the military preparations which were complete by the date fixed, 26 August. German diplomacy was mobilized to isolate Poland and, if the pact with Italy proved to be of very little value in the event, and the Japanese failed to come up to scratch, the pact with Stalin was a major coup. For a summer of "inactivity" it was not a bad result.

Hitler's reaction when the Nazi-Soviet Pact was signed shows clearly enough where his first choice lay. Convinced that the Western Powers would now give up any idea of intervention in defense of Poland, he ordered the German Army to attack at dawn on 26 August: i.e. a solution by force, but localized and without risk of a general European war, the sort of operation for which German rearmament had been designed from the beginning.

The unexpected British reaction, the confirmation instead of the abandonment of the guarantee to Poland—this, plus Mussolini's defection (and Mussolini at any rate had no doubt that Hitler was bent on a solution by force) upset Hitler's plans and forced him to think again. What was he to do? Keep up the pressure and hope that the Poles would crack and accept his terms? Keep up the pressure and hope that, if not the Poles, then the British would crack and either press the Poles to come to terms (another Munich) or abandon them? Or go ahead and take the risk of a general war, calculating that Western intervention, if it ever took place, would come too late to affect the outcome?

It is conceivable that if Hitler had been offered a Polish Munich, on terms that would by now have amounted to capitulation, he would still have accepted it. But I find it hard to believe that any of the moves he made, or sanctioned, between 25 August and 1 September were seriously directed to starting negotiations. A far more obvious and simple explanation is to say that, having failed to remove the threat of British intervention by the Nazi-Soviet Pact, as he had expected, Hitler postponed the order to march and allowed a few extra days to see, not if war could be avoided, but whether under the strain a split might not develop between the Western Powers and Poland and so leave the Poles isolated after all.

Now the crisis had come, Hitler himself did little to resolve or control it. Characteristically, he left it to others to make proposals, seeing the situation, not in terms of diplomacy and negotiation, but as a contest of wills. If his opponents' will cracked first, then the way was open for him to do what he wanted and march into Poland without fear that the Western Powers would intervene. To achieve this he was prepared to hold on and bluff up to the very last minute, but if the bluff did not come off within the time he had set, then this time he steeled his will to go through with the attack on Poland even if it meant running the risk of war with Britain and France as well. All the accounts agree on the strain which Hitler showed and which found expression in his haggard appearance and temperamental outbursts. But his will held. This was no stumbling into war. It was neither misunderstanding nor miscalculation which sent the German Army over the frontier into Poland, but a calculated risk, the gambler's bid—the only bid, Hitler once told Goering, he ever made, *va banque,* the bid he made when he reoccupied the Rhineland in 1936 and when he marched into Austria, the bid he had failed to make when he agreed to the Munich conference, only to regret it immediately afterwards.

Suggestions for Additional Reading

No attempt will be made in this bibliographical essay to list all of the many books that deal with the background to World War II. Instead, suggestions will be made only of the more important works that students should find useful and interesting.

There is as yet no satisfactory full-scale study of the interwar diplomacy. Students could well begin with two brief surveys of the pre-World War II diplomacy, Laurence Lafore, *The End of Glory: An Interpretation of the Origins of World War II* (Philadelphia, 1970), and Keith Eubank, *The Origins of World War II,* from which a selection has been taken for this book. Raymond Sontag, *A Broken World, 1919–1939* (New York, 1971) is a masterful survey of the history and culture of the era between the wars. Two collections of interesting articles on prewar diplomacy are *European Diplomacy between Two Wars, 1919–1939,* edited by Hans W. Gatzke (Chicago, 1972), which includes a very helpful bibliographical essay, and *The Origins of the Second World War,* edited by Esmonde M. Robertson (New York, 1971). A useful collection of documents can be found in *The Road to World War II: A Documentary History,* edited by Keith Eubank (New York, 1973).

The best study of the origins of appeasement is Martin Gilbert, *The Roots of Appeasement* (London, 1966). Martin Gilbert and Richard Gott, *The Appeasers* (rev. ed., Boston, 1963), is a more critical study of appeasement. Neville Thompson, *The Anti-Appeasers: Conservative Opposition to Appeasement in the 1930s* (Oxford, 1971) is a scholarly work on the story of those who tried to halt appeasement. The relation of British military and technological development to foreign policy can be found in the brilliant study of Derek Wood and Derek Dempster, *The Narrow Margin* (New York, 1961).

There are some important books covering the 1920s, although most of them are dated. Jon Jacobson, *Locarno Diplomacy: Germany and the West, 1925–1929* (Princeton, 1972) is an excellent study based on extensive research in the German archives. The standard work on the League of Nations is still F. P. Walters, *A History of the League of Nations* (2 vols.; New York, 1952). The Paris Peace Conference and the Treaty of Versailles have been treated in monographic works; there is no recent study that examines the entire question of the controversial treaty and its influence on European history. Arno J. Mayer, *Politics and Diplomacy of Peacemaking: Containment and Counterrevolution at Versailles, 1918–1919* (New York, 1967) is a massive study of the forces and ideologies that influenced the peacemakers.

There is a greater wealth of works dealing with the period 1933–1939. The Franco-Soviet Pact can be studied in William E. Scott, *Alliance against Hitler: The Origins of the Franco-Soviet Pact* (Durham, 1962). For the question of Austria and the *Anschluss* there are Gordon Brook-Shepherd, *The Anschluss* (Philadelphia, 1963), and Jurgen Gehl, *Austria, Germany, and the Anschluss, 1931–1938* (London, 1963).

The crisis over the Sudetenland and the fate of Czechoslovakia produced a number of solid studies. Dagmar Perman, *The Shaping of the Czechoslovak State* (Leyden, 1962) is a thorough examination of the diplomacy that founded Czechoslovakia. On the Munich crisis, in addition to the works that have been excerpted in this book, there are J. W. Breugel, *Czechoslovakia before Munich: The German Minority Problem and British Appeasement Policy* (Cambridge, 1973); Keith Robbins, *Munich, 1938* (London, 1968). John W. Wheeler-Bennett, *Munich: Prologue to Tragedy* (New York, 1948) is a brilliantly written work. Keith Middlemas, *Diplomacy of Illusion: The British Government and Germany, 1937–1939* (London, 1972) is concerned chiefly with the Czechoslovak crisis and makes use of unpublished materials from the Foreign Office.

One of the best studies of the Polish crisis is Anna M. Cienciala, *Poland and the Western Powers, 1938–1939* (Toronto, 1968). A vivid account of the events from March 15, 1939 to the outbreak of war can be found in Sidney Aster, *1939: The Making of the Second World War* (New York, 1973). For a detailed analysis of the Nazi-Soviet Pact, which sealed the fate of Poland, the best work is Gerhard Weinberg, *Germany and the Soviet Union, 1939–1941* (Leyden, 1954).

John W. Wheeler-Bennett, *The Nemesis of Power: The German Army in Politics, 1918–1945* (New York, 1964), and Telford Taylor, *Sword and Swastika: Generals and Nazis in the Third Reich* (New York, 1952), both are excellent studies of the role the German armed forces played in bringing on the crisis that produced the war.

Alan S. Milward, *The German Economy at War* (London, 1965), and Bernice A. Carroll, *Design for Total War: Arms and Economics in the Third Reich* (The Hague, 1968) deal with German economic plans for war. Gordon Craig and Felix Gilbert, in *The Diplomats* (Princeton, 1953), offer fascinating studies of a variety of diplomats and their activities during the 1920s and 1930s.

Other crises contributed to the mounting diplomatic crisis that culminated in the war. These are examined by Hugh Thomas, *The Spanish Civil War* (New York, 1961), a classic work, and by George W. Baer, *The Coming of the Italo-Ethiopian War* (Cambridge, 1967), a masterful study; K. W. Watkins, *Britain Divided: The Effect of the Spanish Civil War on British Political Opinion* (London, 1963); and David T. Cattell, *Soviet Diplomacy and the Spanish Civil War* (Berkeley, 1957).

There are many memoirs that provide personal views of the causes of this great conflict. Of course many of them are nothing more than apologia; nevertheless, they ought not to be overlooked. Among the more interesting are Winston S. Churchill, *The Gathering Storm* (Boston, 1948), which is useful but not infallible. An illuminating memoir, based on letters and diaries, is Anthony Eden, *Facing the Dictators* (Boston, 1962), which sheds light on British policy. Appeasement is defended by Sir Samuel Hoare, Viscount Templewood, in *Nine Troubled Years* (London, 1954). Thomas Jones, *A Diary with Letters* (London, 1954) discloses a great deal about appeasement and appeasers—he was very close to Baldwin. Two opponents of appeasement tell their stories, in Lord Vansittart, *The Mist Procession* (London, 1958), and in Alfred Duff Cooper, *Old Men Forget* (London, 1953). Cooper was the only cabinet member to resign in disgust over the Munich agreement. *The Diaries of Sir Alexander Cadogan* (London, 1971) reveal much about the implementation of British foreign policy. The condition of British defenses, which restricted British policy toward Hitler's aggressions, can be studied in *Time Unguarded: The Ironside Diaries, 1937–1940* (New York, 1962); and Sir John Slessor, *The Central Blue: Recollections and Reflections* (London, 1956). *The Liddell Hart Memoirs* (2 vols.; New York, 1956–66) offer a military expert's view of the prewar years. For the British view from Berlin there are Neville Henderson, *Failure of a Mission* (London, 1940), and Ivone Kirkpatrick, *The Inner Circle* (London, 1959). A little-known book by Neville Henderson, *Water under the Bridge* (New York, 1945) is a personal defense of appeasement.

On the French side the memoirs available in English have little to offer. André François-Poncet, *The Fateful Years: Memoirs of a French*

Ambassador in Berlin, 1931–1939 (New York, 1949) are not as useful as his dispatches, which are now being published in the French documents. Paul Reynaud, *In the Thick of the Fight, 1930–1945* (New York, 1955) is a revealing account by a French opponent of appeasement.

Probably no top official from any government has been as revealing in the record he left behind as Count Galeazzo Ciano, Mussolini's foreign minister and son-in-law. Ciano's diaries were smuggled out of Italy into Switzerland by Edda Ciano, his wife. They are frank and very revealing as to the day-to-day determination of Italian foreign policy. *The Ciano Diaries, 1939–1943* (New York, 1946), *Ciano's Hidden Diary, 1937–1938* (New York, 1953), and *Ciano's Diplomatic Papers* (London, 1948) indict the Fascist leaders for their irresponsibility and superficiality.

Chief among the German memoirs is of course *Mein Kampf* (Boston, 1943), which is an important historical document containing Hitler's ideas and program before he came to power. Other sources for Hitler's ideas are *Hitler's Secret Conversations, 1941–1944* (New York, 1953), chiefly after-dinner conversations. *The Speeches of Adolf Hitler, April 1922–August 1939* (2 vols.; Oxford, 1942) are important as examples of Nazi propaganda. A selection has been published in this collection from *Hitler's Secret Book* (New York, 1961), which was published only posthumously.

Memoirs of those who served Hitler must be used with caution because too often the authors are concerned with justifying their past conduct. Ernst von Weizsäcker, *Memoirs* (Chicago, 1960), chief of the German Foreign Ministry, are informative but not always reliable. A better source is Paul Schmidt, *Hitler's Interpreter* (New York, 1951). *The Von Hassell Diaries, 1938–1944* (London, 1948) tell the story of a member of the Hitler opposition who was executed after the attempt on Hitler's life failed. A fascinating source of information on the personality and life-style of Hitler can be found in Albert Speer, *Inside the Third Reich* (New York, 1970). Insights into relations between Nazi Germany and Soviet Russia can be found in Gustav Hilger and A. G. Meyer, *The Incompatible Allies: A Memoir-History of German-Soviet Relations, 1918–1941* (New York, 1953).

There are some American memoirs from this period that are helpful. George F. Kennan, *From Prague after Munich* (Princeton, 1968) is, as always, interesting to read. Cordell Hull, *The Memoirs of Cor-*

dell Hull (New York, 1948) is important for the view from Washington, as is *The Moffat Papers: Selections from the Diplomatic Journals of Jay Pierrepont Moffat* (Cambridge, 1956). For an American ambassador in Berlin see Martha Dodd and William Dodd, Jr., eds., *Ambassador Dodd's Diary* (New York, 1941).

There are a few memoirs by diplomats and politicians from among the smaller European powers worth reading. Joseph Beck, the suave Polish foreign minister, does not tell all that he should in his *Final Report* (New York, 1957). There is much of value in books by two Polish ambassadors: *Papers and Memoirs of Jozef Lipski, Ambassador of Poland: Diplomat in Berlin, 1933–1939* (New York, 1968); and *Diplomat in Paris, 1936–1939: Papers and Memoirs of Juliusz Lukasiewicz, Ambassador of Poland* (New York, 1970). Kurt von Schuschnigg tells his story of the *Anschluss* in *Austrian Requiem* (New York, 1946). Two accounts by journalists are valuable: G. E. R. Gedye, *Fallen Bastions* (London, 1939); and William L. Shirer, *Berlin Diary* (New York, 1941).

Among the biographies that can be read with profit, Alan Bullock, *Hitler: A Study in Tyranny* (New York, 1964) is still the best account of Hitler's life. Joachim Fest, *Hitler* (New York, 1973) is the most recent study, though it does not replace Bullock's book. A new biography is needed on Neville Chamberlain to replace both Keith Feiling's *The Life of Neville Chamberlain* (New York, 1946) and Ian Macleod's *Neville Chamberlain* (London, 1961), both of which were too kind to their subject; both volumes, however, contain excerpts from Chamberlain's diaries and letters. For Baldwin there is Keith Middlemas and John Barnes, *Baldwin: A Biography* (London, 1969). Ivone Kirkpatrick, *Mussolini: A Study in Power* (New York, 1964) is the best biography of Hitler's ally.

Documentary source materials from government archives have been published in multivolume series. The German Foreign Ministry archives were captured almost intact by the Allied armies at the end of World War II. The documents relating to the Nazi period have been published in *Documents on German Foreign Policy, 1918–1945*, series C and D (Washington, 1949–). The years prior to 1933 are covered in *Akten zur deutschen auswärtigen Politik, 1918–1945* (Göttingen, 1966–). These documents from the German Foreign Ministry archives do not tell the entire story because official dispatches were supplemented by telephone conversations, unofficial contacts, and private correspondence that did not find its way into the files. Some of the missing material can be found in the collections dealing with the trials of German war criminals at Nuremberg, 1945–1946. Among these collections are *Trials of the Major War Criminals before the International Military Tribunal, Proceedings and Documents* (42 vols.; Nuremberg, 1947–49); *Nazi Conspiracy and Aggression* (10 vols.; Washington, 1946–48), which are documents presented in evidence by the prosecution; *Trials of the War Criminals before the Nuremberg Military Tribunals under Control Council Law No. 10* (15 vols.; Washington, n.d.).

British documentary materials can be found in *Documents on British Foreign Policy, 1919–1939* (London, 1917–). The collection is still in the process of being published; only series III from the *Anschluss* to the outbreak of World War II is complete. The records of the British government are now open up to 30 years from the current year with certain exceptions. On the other side of the Channel, the French government has begun to publish documents from the files of the Foreign Ministry for the years 1932–1939 in the collection *Documents diplomatiques français, 1932–1939* (Paris, 1964–). The delay in publishing the French documents is a result of the need to reconstruct the archives since many of the Foreign Ministry files were destroyed by fire when the French government left Paris in 1940. The Italian documents will ultimately cover the period 1869–1943 in the collection *I Documenti Diplomatici Italiani* (Rome, 1952); series VI–VIII deal with the years 1918–1939. The Soviet government has begun to publish archive materials in *Dokumenty vneshnei Politiki SSSR* [Documents on the Foreign Policy of the USSR] (Moscow, 1957–). A selection of documents from the archives of the Belgian Ministry of Foreign Affairs is available in *Documents diplomatiques belges, 1920–1940* (Brussels, 1964–).

The only published collection of official documents available for the period 1919–1939 is *Foreign Relations of the United States: Diplomatic Papers,* published annually. The reports of American diplomats are an important source of information regarding the prewar negotiations and events. State Department files in the National Archives are open to 30 years from the current year. However, access to documents beyond that date is restricted to the years covered in the published volumes of *Foreign Relations of the United States.*

For additional information on the documentary collections, students should consult Mario Toscano, *The History of Treaties and International Politics: Part I, The Documentary and Memoir Sources* (Baltimore, 1966).

The Royal Institute for International Affairs has published two collections whose annual volumes are helpful. *Documents on International Affairs* (London and New York, 1923–) contains a useful selection of documents. *Survey of International Affairs* (London and New York, 1923–) offers a valuable annual account of developments in international affairs since 1920. The volumes on 1938 and 1939 are outstanding.

For the current materials being published on this subject, students should consult the current issues of *Journal of Contemporary History; Journal of Modern History; International Affairs; Revue de l'Histoire de le deuxieme guerre mondiale; Vierteljahrshefte für Zeitgeschichte; The American Historical Review; Central European History;* and *Foreign Affairs.*